The Good Polity

To the memory of
Stanley Benn

The Good Polity

Normative Analysis of the State

Edited by
Alan Hamlin and
Philip Pettit

Basil Blackwell

First published 1989

Basil Blackwell Ltd
108 Cowley Road, Oxford, OX4 1JF, UK

Basil Blackwell Inc.
432 Park Avenue South, Suite 1503
New York, NY 10016, USA

British Library Cataloguing in Publication Data

The Good polity : normative analysis of the state.
1. States
I. Hamlin, Alan II. Pettit, Philip
320.1

ISBN 0-631-15804-9

Library of Congress Cataloging in Publication Data

The Good polity: normative analysis of the state/edited by
Alan Hamlin and Philip Pettit.
p. cm.
Bibliography: p.
Includes index.
ISBN 0-631-15804-9: $60.00 (U.S.: est.)
1. State, The. 2. Political ethics. 3. Democracy.
I. Hamlin, Alan P., 1951– . II. Pettit, Philip,
1945– .
JC325. G59 1989
320. 1—dc19   88-23366
                                                          CIP

Typeset in 10 on 12 pt Plantin
by Colset Private Limited, Singapore
Printed in Great Britain by
Bookcraft Ltd., Bath, Avon

Contents

Preface

The rediscovery of normative political analysis is one of the intellectual events of the last quarter-century. There is now a growing interdisciplinary concern with fundamental questions of social organization: questions of rights and liberty, democracy and decision rules, institutions and conventions, and above all questions concerning the nature of the good polity. This concern is not uniquely modern, since it is also a hallmark of many of the great works of eighteenth- and nineteenth-century moral science. However, interest in the central questions of normative political analysis all but disappeared in the first half of the twentieth century, driven out by a variety of intellectual and institutional pressures. The rediscovery of the enterprise is associated particularly with John Rawls but also with others such as Kenneth Arrow, Brian Barry, James Buchanan, Ronald Dworkin, John Harsanyi, Herbert Hart, Robert Nozick and Amartya Sen.

Like those figures, the contributors to this volume come from the three disciplines of economics, philosophy and political science. Although they differ in their normative commitments, they represent a second wave in the contemporary development of normative political analysis. Their concerns range widely, but the essays presented here focus on the state in particular. The essays are united by a common style of analysis as well as by a common focus. We say something of this style, and of the commitments it entails, in a preliminary essay.

The pattern of connections among the remaining essays is not simple. We have chosen to present them in three parts, identifying each part with a major theme of contemporary normative analysis of the state: democracy, contract and compliance, and the responsibility of the state. Democracy is frequently held to be the ideal structure of political organization, and the essays in part I analyse the status of democracy as a normative ideal from a variety of perspectives. In part II attention shifts to the fundamental justification of the state and the implications of a contractual or mutual advantage theory for such questions as compliance and political obligation. Finally, in part III, devoted to the responsibility of the state, questions concerning the goals which the state is expected to further are addressed. Other themes link the essays in a variety of ways; we leave these to be discovered by the reader.

The idea for a collection of this type first arose whilst Hamlin was visiting the Australian National University, and was partly the result of a series of seminars on the state organized by Pettit. The idea developed when Pettit was an Overseas Fellow at Churchill College, Cambridge, and it has come to fruition via other, shorter meetings in Canberra and Southampton. We thank all the institutions involved for their support. We dedicate the book to the memory of Stanley Benn. The coverage of these essays reflects some of his life-long interests and he participated actively in the seminars where the idea for the book emerged. He would have applauded our efforts, not least because of our affiliations: the early part of his career was spent in Southampton, the later in Canberra.

Alan Hamlin and Philip Pettit
Southampton and Canberra

1

The Normative Analysis of the State: Some Preliminaries

Alan Hamlin and Philip Pettit

The journals of economics, philosophy and political science have recently begun to house a literature which is the common property of all three disciplines, and indeed a literature in which many lawyers would also claim a stake. The literature is analytic in character and is devoted to the variety of issues involved in the assessment of social and political institutions, in particular the state. It is characterized by an emphasis on rationality, bargaining and contract, combined with the more traditional concerns with liberty, equality, rights and the like. It is informed by the concepts of decision theory, game theory, public-choice and social-choice analysis, while staying in touch with standard questions of political evaluation. We think of it as the literature of normative political analysis.

Although normative political analysis is in the ascendant, it also attracts a good deal of criticism. Three lines of assault are particularly common. First, it is claimed that the analysis is uncritical concerning its own assumptions about the nature of the state and the relations between the state and individuals. Secondly, it is claimed that the framework of analysis involves a commitment to an extreme and unsustainable individualism. And, thirdly, it is claimed that this individualism almost guarantees liberal or libertarian conclusions, so that, whilst the analysis may provide an appropriate method for explicating liberalism, it cannot provide a more general method of inquiry.

We believe these criticisms to be mistaken, and in this essay we try to say something in rebuttal. We address three themes, corresponding to the different lines of criticism. In the first section we consider questions to do with the definition of the state. In the second and third we inquire how far this definition entails a commitment to individualism. And in the last section we offer an overview of the ways in which the normative analysis of the state can give rise to widely differing theories.

I The state

In order to motivate a definition of the state, in particular a definition of the state of the kind associated with normative political analysis, we go back to something that the state presupposes. This is the system of rules whereby mutual expectations are established between people. Such a system of rules characterizes a society, as distinct from a collection of individuals, and it is only in societies that states can exist. The rules serve individuals by indicating what they may each do or not do without exposing themselves to complaint.

Where we have a system of rules we also have a system of rights. We can distinguish, roughly, four sorts of rule-based rights (following Hohfeld 1923). First, liberty rights: if there is no rule enjoining someone in position α to do A, then that person has a liberty right to do not-A. Second, claim rights: if it is a rule that someone in position β is expected to do B to anyone in position γ, then the person in γ has a claim right to B against the person in β. Third, power rights: if it is a rule that someone in position δ can alter the allocation of certain rights over certain other individuals, then that person has a power right over those rights and individuals. And, finally, immunity rights: if it is a rule that someone in position ϵ cannot have certain of her rights altered by another, so that no one holds a power right over her in respect of those rights, then that person has an immunity right.

The system of rights embedded within a society will vary with the richness of the underlying system of rules. It will give rise to a state if and only if it is rich enough to include certain power rights. Specifically, it must include the power rights associated, in common parlance, with legislative, executive and judicial authority (see Hart 1961).

The legislative power right entitles its holder to pronounce on what the rules of the society are or will be, and to pronounce therefore on the sort of rights allocated within the society. The executive power right entitles its holder to ensure that the rules legislated to exist, and those legislated into existence, are complied with. The executive will usually be required to ensure compliance according to rules that are themselves part of the overall system. Finally, the judicial power right entitles its holder or holders to adjudicate in cases of dispute concerning rules and to pass judgement on those who are found to have violated rules. Again the judicial power right holder is constrained in the exercise of this power right by rules that are a part of the overall system.

Wherever there are power rights of these three types, there is a state. Under one aspect, what that state will be is the apparatus of rules which define and distribute the power rights, identifying who is entitled to what kind and degree of power.[1] We have the state in mind under this aspect when we speak of it as the socio-political system or the constitutional structure.

But, wherever there are power rights of these three types, the state will also display a second aspect: that of a corporate agent rather than an apparatus of rules. Anything done in accordance with the rules will be done by individual people, but, if we wish to abstract from the particular identities of those people, then we will naturally say that what they do is done by the state. Thus we will give life to the state in the role of an agent.

That the state calls to be regarded as an agent and not just as an apparatus is suggested in particular by the following consideration. The system of rules that constitutes the state is not of a closed and fixed sort. It authorizes suitable officials to alter the rules, specifying the process by which they may do so. Thus, although the state is just an apparatus of rules, it is itself a major influence on the form that these rules take. Under the one aspect the state is passive; under the other it is active and self-directing.

In summary, then, the state is constituted, both in the guise of an apparatus and in the guise of an agent, by the set of legislative, executive and judicial power rights which put some individuals, the agents of the state, in positions of authority over others. There are many issues raised by this account and we shall comment on three. They concern the notions, respectively, of legitimacy, sovereignty and territorialism.

Legitimacy

The definition requires that the agents of the state claim a certain legitimacy for the actions they take in the state's name. The alleged legitimacy is simply that what is done is done in accordance with the system of rules and rights that characterizes the society. This remark provides a connection with the tradition that defines the state as a body exercising an effective monopoly of force in a certain territory and claiming to do so legitimately.[2]

However, the legitimacy that agents of the state claim under our definition is so minimal that we can recognize as states regimes which are free of any moral status. The reason is that, for all our account says, a group of agents who usurp power, perhaps for the basest of reasons, may be able to alter the rules so as to legitimate their assumption and exercise of power rights. Our definition requires that the state operates according to a system of effective social rules, but does not require these rules to be commonly endorsed.

Sovereignty

The definition emphasizes the vertical relationship between the state, the society and the individual members of society. The notion of sovereignty can be introduced if we consider the horizontal relationships that a state may have with other institutional bodies, including other states. We may say that a state is a sovereign state to the extent that it retains the unilateral and effective right to withdraw from any contractual or quasi-contractual relationship that it may have with such other bodies. This usage connects with the traditional distinction between a federation such as the United States and a confederation such as the European Economic Community. A confederation is an alliance of sovereign states, each of which retains full rights of self-determination; a federation is a partial merger of states in which each irrevocably gives up certain rights to an external authority.

The distinction between sovereign and non-sovereign states operates within the definition we have offered, for, while each is equally a state according to that definition, there is a further and important fact distinguishing them. A sovereign state is simply a state that reigns supreme over some jurisdiction, ascribing no irrevocable power rights to external agents. A non-sovereign state is one for which this is not true.

Territorialism

The notion of a jurisdiction points us to a further indeterminacy in our definition of the state. One apparent distinction between our definition and other approaches lies in the role of territory. Our definition makes no reference to any geographic aspect of the state, whilst other views emphasize the spatial. The indeterminacy concerning the jurisdiction of the state is whether this jurisdiction is defined over a specified territory, whoever it contains, or over specified individuals, wherever they may be. Is the state held to have power rights over all those who reside in this or that area, or over a certain set of people wherever they may reside?

It seems clear that an entirely nomadic society may embody a state, even if other nomadic societies (which may themselves embody states) range over the same territory. In this way it is perfectly possible for more than one state to exist in any given geographic territory. On the other hand, it seems difficult to imagine two or more settled societies that could sustain separate states whilst their members were intermingled arbitrarily within the same geographic boundaries. The upshot is that, while it is probably a mistake to build a territorial reference into the definition of a state, there is good reason to expect that states will generally be associated with determinate territories.

II Methodological individualism

Does this account of the state, and the normative analysis in which it is invoked, imply an individualistic view of the relationship between the state and its people? The question is important, since the type of definition we offer, and normative political analysis in general, is often associated with a rigorously individualistic stance.

Individualism must be distinguished into at least two strands: methodological and moral. Here our concern is with the methodological strand; we shall have something to say about moral individualism in the next section. But even methodological individualism comes in a variety of forms.[3] At its most severe it holds that no non-individual social entities are real. A less virulent strain maintains that, even if social entities are real, they are reducible to non-social correlates. And the mildest form says that, even if social entities are real and irreducible, still they do not compromise individual autonomy: they do not undermine or pre-empt individual agency.

Our definition of the state may appear to be individualistic because it depicts the state as secondary to the individuals who actually act in its name. Nevertheless, we wish to argue that it does not involve any serious commitment to individualistic doctrine. It is an advantage in our definition that it does not beg the substantive and important questions raised in the debate about the relationship between individuals and their institutions.

The definition certainly does not entail the strongest variety of methodological individualism which would require the state to be unreal – which would require, in Ayer's words, that 'the English state, for example, is a logical construction out of individual people' (Ayer 1946, p. 85). The only sense to the idea that the state is unreal can be captured by analogy. Peter Geach once introduced a sort of entity which he named a 'surman'. Surmen are men – and no doubt women – who share the same surname; two men called Jones may be different and unrelated men, but they are the same surman (Geach 1972, pp. 222–3). It is clear that surmen are unreal, and it is also clear why. The concept of a surman plays no part in explicating the experiential or explanatory order of the world (Bealer 1982).

Does our definition of the state put the state in the same category as Geach's surmen? Obviously not, since our definition allows us to acknowledge that our experience of the social world and our explanations of at least some of its patterns make considerable use of the concept of the state. We can recognize that the state is no artifice created for entirely theoretical purposes, but a reality that looms salient in the world we all inhabit. The question of the reality of the state is not begged by our definition, so there is no commitment to the strongest form of methodological individualism.

But what of the reducibility of the state and the second sort of methodological individualism? A state, according to our definition, is a certain sort of system of rules and rights. In one sense that makes the state reducible; it means that we can define the property of being a state in other terms. But the sense of reducibility in question is not relevant to methodological individualism, since the terms in which the property of being a state is defined are not themselves individualistic. We do not define the property in terms of properties of individuals that they would exhibit even outside of society; rather we define it in terms of social properties – those involved in the recognition of certain rules and rights – that already presuppose communal existence.

The question of reducibility turns, then, on whether we can define the property of being a state strictly in terms of non-social properties. And it should be clear, we hope, that nothing said in our account of the state implies that the individualistic answer is the correct one. For the record, our own inclination is to go for a non-individualistic response.

What is true, given our definition of the state, is that the property of being a state is supervenient on the non-social properties realized in the world. If we are given any two possible worlds, or at least any two possible worlds conforming to the same basic laws as ours, then the fact that they are identical in respect of all non-social properties seems to ensure that they will be identical in respect of the rights and rules recognized by people, and identical therefore in respect of the states that exist in the two worlds.[4] But this individualistic supervenience of the property of being a state does not involve its individualistic reducibility.

If a property P is to be defined by certain properties $q_1, q_2 \ldots q_n$, then we must not only be able to assert the supervenience claim that given that a particular configuration of the q properties obtains then P also obtains; we must be able to assert in addition that whenever P obtains then one of a determinable set of configurations of the q properties must obtain. Otherwise we cannot claim to be in a position to define the P property in q terms.

The supervenience of the property of being a state means, we may suppose, that any full configuration of the individualistic properties of the world fixes what states there are in that world. But, for all that this supervenience tells us, the fact of what states there are in the world does not put any determinable limits on the individualistic properties that may obtain there. An effectively open-ended variety of individualistic configurations would seem to be consistent with any such fact about states. And so the property of being a state would not appear to be definable in individualistic terms. Thus our definition of the state does not entail its reducibility.

The final question is whether our definition imposes methodological individualism of the third and weakest type identified above. Does it rule out the view that the state has an intrinsic power that undermines or pre-empts individual autonomy?

Even here, the answer is less than a full yes. Our definition certainly rules out the wholesale undermining of individual autonomy, for it assumes that individuals act in a proper intentional manner when they act in the name of the state. But this is scarcely a burdensome exclusion. The sort of view prohibited is one which would present people as pawns in the hands of non-personal entities such as the state: agents who are likely to come under the control of psychologically inscrutable forces as institutional exigencies require them to do this or that.[5]

But, if our definition rules out such undermining of individual autonomy, it does not rule out its pre-emption. The following possibility is left open, for example, although we do not find it particularly plausible. It may be that there has been evolutionary selection at the level of societies, and that this has selected societies for the presence of the sorts of states we know. If this is so, then societies with people having characters that militate against the emergence of states will have been selected against. The ultimate explanation of states will not then be based on the character, psychology and agency of individual people. It will be the structural explanation referring us to institutional features important in the evolutionary selection of societies.

Given that this sort of possibility is left open by our definition, it may be that states pre-empt individual agency. It may be that the existence of the states we know is to be explained, not by the dispositions in people which actually support them, but by the fact that such states display certain institutional features: as our example has it, those features that are selected for in an evolutionary process. We do not think that states actually pre-empt individuals in this way, but it is important to point out that our definition does not beg the question.

It turns out then that our definition does not entail methodological individualism in any of the three forms identified. To be sure, the definition does involve commitments to the thesis that states are supervenient on individuals, and to the thesis that individual agency is not entirely eroded by the existence of states, but these commitments should be acceptable to many who reject methodological individualism.

III Moral individualism

In the last section we discussed the question of how far our definition of the state entailed a methodological individualism. We turn now to the related question of how far it inclines us, when we ask after what makes a state good or bad, towards an individualism of a moral kind.

According to our definition the state is constituted by a system of power rights which are held by some people over others. This suggests that how good a state is ought to be determined by how the system of rights affects the people involved: the people who exercise the rights, the people over whom the rights are exercised, and perhaps further parties too. The principle that states ought to be judged by how they affect individuals is a sort of moral individualism. We shall refer to it as the principle of individual relevance; it is related to, though strictly weaker than, what have elsewhere been described as the principle of personal good and the humanistic principle.[6] This principle is motivated, if not strictly implied, by our definition of the state and we do ourselves subscribe to it. More generally, the principle is endorsed by the tradition of assessing the state that is associated with normative political analysis.

Thus, although our definition of the state is not tied up with a methodological individualism, it is tightly bound to one sort of moral individualism. But only to one sort. In the remainder of this section we would like to emphasize that the moral individualism involved in the principle of individual relevance is an extremely mild and indeed attractive doctrine. It does not entail individualism in any potentially objectionable sense. This point can be made quickly and positively or slowly and negatively. We shall try both tacks.

The quick way of making the point is to consider the sort of possibility that the principle of individual relevance disallows, and, equivalently, the sort of possibilities that it rules in. What it disallows is any appeal to aspects of the state that do not have an impact on individuals, so that, if two sorts of states differ only in ways that do not affect individual people, those states must be held to be equally good. What it allows is that any difference between states in respect of the impact of the state on individuals is capable, at least in the abstract, of providing a reason for different evaluations of the states under comparison. The principle says, in other words, that the value that a given state has must supervene on how people fare when that system is realized. This is surely an innocuous and compelling claim.

The slow way of making the point that the principle of individual relevance does not entail an objectionable individualism is to distinguish it from some more controversial doctrines with which it is liable to be mistakenly associated. The principle says that what makes a state good is that it constitutes or brings about something that affects people appropriately: something, we may suppose, that is good *for* people. We wish to distinguish this from three parallel doctrines. These say, respectively, that what makes a state good is that it constitutes or brings about something that is a good *in* people, or something that is a good *by* people, or something that is a good *of* people.

The doctrine that what makes a state good is that it constitutes or brings about a good *in* people asserts an extreme moral individualism. It says that states are to be assessed by effects within people of a wholly individualistic kind: effects such that those people could logically have each enjoyed them in isolation from one another. An example of such individualism is the utilitarian doctrine that what matters is just the pleasure, or the subjective preference satisfaction, enjoyed by people taken separately; other examples are offered by the Paretian relatives of that doctrine.[7]

It should be clear that the principle of individual relevance does not entail any such atomistic morality. Being a good *for* individuals does not entail being a good *in* individuals. For all that the principle of individual relevance says, the good brought about by the state may logically require social relations between individuals. It would do so, for example, if it were a good like that of a person's actual equality in some regards with this fellows.[8]

The second doctrine from which we wish to distinguish the principle of individual relevance says that what makes a state good is that it constitutes or brings about something that is good *by* individuals: that is, something that individuals explicitly judge to be good. This doctrine will be found plausible by many, particularly those who insist that the state should be responsive to people's actual perceptions and preferences. Still, the appeal of the doctrine is not overwhelming. After all, it rules out any political philosophy that praises the state for satisfying rights, needs or other claims that individuals themselves do not recognize at the time, or for failing to respond to claims that are grounded on individuals' misperceptions (see Goodin 1986; Hamlin 1986b).

Again, we hope that it is clear that the principle of individual relevance does not entail this doctrine. Being a good *for* individuals does not entail being a good *by* individuals. It may be that something's being a good for individuals entails that it would be a good by those people if they were fully reflective concerning their preferences. But the proposition entailed falls far short of the approach embodied in the *by* doctrine.

The third doctrine from which we should distinguish the principle of individual relevance says that what makes a state good is that it constitutes or brings about a good *of* individuals. This doctrine involves a less strict form of moral individualism than the previous two but it is still more restrictive than the principle of individual relevance. The *of* doctrine prescribes that the only goods in virtue of which a state can be praised are items that belong to individual people: items such as their liberty, their happiness, their equality or whatever. It rules out the approval of a state for the production of goods which belong in the first place to aggregate-level entities, even if their realization affects people. Examples of such aggregate goods might be the solidarity of a community, the continuity of a culture, or the harmony of relations between racial groups. It is typical of such goods that, while their realization affects individuals, there is no one way in which it affects them all: the goods relate in a one-many fashion to individual goods.

It should be clear that the principle of individual relevance does not entail even this relatively mild version of moral individualism. A good that is not a good of individuals can still be argued to be a good for individuals. Community solidarity may be judged good according to the extent that it furnishes good for the individuals involved even though those individual goods may differ from person to person; thus being a good *for* individuals does not entail being a good *of* individuals.[9]

We conclude that the for-individuals principle which we defend is distinct from the in-individuals, by-individuals and of-individuals doctrines discussed. The principle of individual relevance is an extremely weak form of moral individualism and, as such, it ought to commend itself widely. But one further thing needs to be said to make this principle seem as persuasive, even as platitudinous, as we take it to be. This is that the class of individuals by reference to whom a state is to be assessed under the principle is left open in our formulation. For example, it need not be restricted to the citizens of the state in question, nor even to human beings. Those who would wish to judge states in part on their treatment of the members of other societies, or those who would wish to take animals into account at the political level, can do so simply by defining the constituency of individuals appropriately. We find it hard to see how the for-individuals principle can fail to commend itself; it is moral individualism of the most ecumenical kind.

IV A taxonomy of theories

So much for the definition of the state that goes naturally with normative analysis, and its allegedly individualistic character. We turn in this section to review briefly the different approaches that can be and are taken to the normative analysis of the state. Any particular normative theory offers a criterion for distinguishing between better and worse states. The criterion offered may be motivated by considerations of feasibility, eligibility or desirability; and, if by the latter, by considerations of different kinds depending on what is thought desirable and on how it is thought that the state ought to respond to what which is desirable.

Considerations of feasibility are foremost in such a theory as Hayek's, which may be summarized as follows. Any state that aims at the satisfaction of individuals requires information concerning those individuals, and yet the production and transmission of such information depends crucially on the set of social institutions that obtain. Thus, Hayek argues, a decentralized market system of exchange is a crucial element of a good state's activity, not because it produces demonstrably better results but because it is the only feasible way of utilizing reliable information regarding individuals (see, for example, Hayek 1937, 1945). A further example of a feasibility argument is provided by Riker (1982). He argues that any state which relies on democratic procedures of decision-making must avoid problems of arbitrary outcomes, and that this requires a liberal regime under which areas of particular concern must be constitutionally protected against majority choice.

Considerations of eligibility are dominant in theories which argue that what is important about a state is whether it would have been collectively chosen in certain circumstances, or would have come about as a result of what would have been individually chosen there. Such considerations are marshalled in contractarian theories such as those of Rawls (1971), Buchanan (1975) or Gauthier (1986), but also in the invisible-hand theory of the minimal state advanced by Nozick (1974). Contractarianism in one form or another is perhaps the dominant contemporary approach to normative political theory.[10] Sometimes it is put forward as a useful but inessential strategy of argument, at other times as the uniquely appropriate way of explicating the notion of the right (Scanlon 1982).[11] However it is understood, the strategy varies depending on different conceptions of the circumstances of contract, and of the means whereby contract ought to be pursued.

The feasibility and eligibility approaches are of great importance in political theory, for they can shed new light on old political issues. This accounts for their great popularity amongst current theorists of the state. Still, these approaches remain secondary to the high road of the discipline: the exploration of what is politically desirable and of how the politically desirable ought to be reflected in the organization and behaviour of the state. They remain secondary because they each require independent judgements as to what it desirable, no matter how foundational they are made to appear. Considerations of feasibility will normally leave some alternatives open and only considerations of desirability can select between them. Again, considerations of eligibility are bound to presuppose a judgement as to what are the appropriate circumstances for contract, or what is the appropriate starting point for an invisible-hand process, and only considerations of desirability can determine these matters.

Turning then to the desirability strategy in the normative analysis of the state, there are two different ways in which that strategy can generate a variety of theories.[12] First of all, the strategy can generate distinct theories by identifying different sorts of value as the relevant concern of the state. And secondly it can generate distinct theories by going in either of two directions on the issue of how the state should respond to the relevant value. A theory may recommend that the state promote the value by whatever behaviour is required, or that the state should exemplify respect for the relevant value in its own actions. In other words, the theory may represent the value as a maximand or as a constraint.

Taking this last distinction first, the divide in question corresponds to the traditional dichotomy between teleological or consequentialist and deontological strategies. The teleologist sees the realization of any value he invokes as a target at which the state ought to aim. The deontologist sees it as a constraint that the state ought to honour in its own behaviour at least in respect of those who have not themselves offended against the constraint.

Suppose that the value in question is the realization of certain liberties. The teleologist will think that the state ought to do whatever is necessary to maximize the realization of those liberties overall. Thus, he will say even that the state ought to invade the liberties of a particular, unfortunate individual if this is required to maximize the realization of such liberties overall; it ought to frame and punish the innocent individual if this makes for greater freedom in the land. The deontologist, by contrast, will think that the duty imposed on the state by the consideration of liberty is that of respecting the freedom of every innocent person, even if this respect implies that there is less freedom overall. Thus, he will say that it is never right to frame and punish the innocent, whatever the gain in overall liberty that this would achieve.

If a normative theory of the state goes the deontological way, then it will almost certainly invoke the notion of individual rights in a foundational role. It will identify certain privileged claims – such as claims to liberty – and will denounce any neglect of these claims by the state, or at least any neglect under certain circumstances or beyond certain limits (Pettit 1987a; Hamlin forthcoming). If a normative theory of the state goes the teleological way, then a question arises as to whether it can give any place to substantial rights. This is a hotly debated topic and divides even the present authors (Pettit 1988; Hamlin forthcoming). Its importance should be obvious, for the teleological stance must look decidedly shaky if it implies that the state should not take individual rights seriously.

The other distinction which means that the desirability approach to normative analysis can generate a variety of theories is the distinction between the different types of value or good that may be invoked under the approach. There are many possible ways of dividing up these types and here we shall mention two.

The first way distinguishes between three sorts of goods: those values which depict individual people primarily as centres of agency, those values which depict individuals as centres of welfare in a more or less broad interpretaton of welfare (see Sen 1979a, 1985b, 1987; Griffin 1986), and those which are goods of aggregates rather than of individuals. Agency values include liberty and autonomy; welfare values include preference satisfaction and equality of resources; and aggregate values include communal solidarity, racial harmony and the like.

The second distinction we wish to mention divides asocial and social values: values such that individuals could enjoy them in the absence of community – being as we said before goods *in* individuals – and values of which this is not true. Asocial values include liberty in the traditional negative sense, and also utility. Social values include equality of resources and, a less commonly mentioned value, the right of individuals to participate in collective decision-making processes. They also include all aggregate goods, since these can not be realized without society.

Our two distinctions cross to form a matrix.

	Agency	Welfare	Aggregate
Asocial	1	2	–
Social	3	4	5

It is instructive to try to situate any particular normative theory of the state within this matrix. We leave the exercise to the reader.

In this section we have tried to give some indication of the variety of approaches to be found within the normative analysis of the state. This variety is rich and we hope that our brief discussion has conveyed something of this wealth. But, even if we have failed in that respect, the essays collected in this volume ought certainly to compensate.

Notes

1 We ignore the individuation question as to what makes a set of rules at one time the same apparatus, and therefore the same state, as a set of rules at another; the question may be determined by their diachronic relations to one another or the preservation of certain intrinsic or relational properties between the two times.

2 See, for example, Nozick (1974), pp. 23–5.

3 On this variety see Macdonald and Pettit (1981), ch. 3; and Pettit (forthcoming a). For a survey of alternative interpretations of individualism, see Lukes (1973).

4 For more extensive discussion of supervenience, see Macdonald and Pettit (1981), and Currie (1984).

5 For a characterization see James (1984), ch. 4.

6 On the principle of personal good, see Broome (1986); on the humanistic principle, see Raz (1986), p. 194.

7 For discussion of the relationship between utilitarianism and Paretianism, see Hamlin (1986a), ch. 3, and Sen (1987), ch. 2, and references therein.

8 A certain subjectivist might extol equality without denying the in-individuals doctrine. He would say that what matters is that everything is with the individual *as if* he were equal to his fellows; see Jackson (1986).

9 This is similar to the distinction between the humanistic principle and individualism made by Raz (1986), pp. 198–203.

10 In addition to those referred to above, see Harsanyi (1976) and Habermas, whose work is expounded in McCarthy (1978). For a discussion of alternative approaches to contractarianism, see Hamlin (1986a), ch. 3.

11 For discussion of the issue in the context of Habermas, see Pettit (1982).

12 The strategy can vary in other ways too. For example, it may be pursued directly, as when certain values are defended on grounds of intuitive plausibility/reflective equilibrium, or dialectically, as when they are shown to require endorsement by anyone who endorses some more agreed values. For examples of the dialectical strategy see Hart (1955) and Goodin (1985).

Part I

Democracy

2

Deliberation and Democratic Legitimacy

Joshua Cohen

In this essay I explore the ideal of a 'deliberative democracy'.[1] By a deliberative democracy I shall mean, roughly, an association whose affairs are governed by the public deliberation of its members. I propose an account of the value of such an association that treats democracy itself as a fundamental political ideal and not simply as a derivative ideal that can be explained in terms of the values of fairness or equality of respect.

The essay is in three sections. In section I, I focus on Rawls's discussion of democracy and use that discussion both to introduce certain features of a deliberative democracy, and to raise some doubts about whether their importance is naturally explained in terms of the notion of a fair system of social co-operation. In section II, I develop an account of deliberative democracy in terms of the notion of an *ideal deliberative procedure*. The characterization of that procedure provides an abstract model of deliberation which links the intuitive ideal of democratic association to a more substantive view of deliberative democracy. Three features of the ideal deliberative procedure figure prominently in the essay. First, it helps to account for some familiar judgements about collective decision-making, in particular about the ways that collective decision-making ought to be different from bargaining, contracting and other market-type interactions, both in its explicit attention to considerations of the common advantage and in the ways that that attention helps to form the aims of the participants. Second, it accounts for the common view that the notion of democratic association is tied to notions of autonomy and the common good. Third, the ideal deliberative procedure provides a distinctive structure for addressing institutional questions. And in section III of the paper I rely on that distinctive structure in responding to four objections to the account of deliberative democracy.

I

The ideal of deliberative democracy is a familiar ideal. Aspects of it have been highlighted in recent discussion of the role of republican conceptions of self-government in shaping the American constitutional tradition and contemporary public law.[2] It is represented as well in radical democratic and socialist criticisms of the politics of advanced industrial societies.[3] And some of its central features are highlighted in Rawls's account of democratic politics in a just society, particularly in those parts of his account that seek to incorporate the 'liberty of the ancients' and to respond to radical democrats and socialists who argue that 'the basic liberties may prove to be merely formal'. In the discussion that follows I shall first say something about Rawls's remarks on three such features, and then consider his explanation of them.[4]

First, in a well-ordered democracy, political debate is organized around alternative conceptions of the public good. So an ideal pluralist scheme, in which democratic politics consists of fair bargaining among groups each of which pursues its particular or sectional interest, is unsuited to a just society (Rawls 1971, pp. 360–1).[5] Citizens and parties operating in the political arena ought not to 'take a narrow or group-interested standpoint' (p. 360). And parties should only be responsive to demands that are 'argued for openly by reference to a conception of the public good' (pp. 226, 472). Public explanations and justifications of laws and policies are to be cast in terms of conceptions of the common good (conceptions that, on Rawls's view, must be consistent with the two principles of justice), and public deliberation should aim to work out the details of such conceptions and to apply them to particular issues of public policy (p. 362).

Second, the ideal of democratic order has egalitarian implications that must be satisfied in ways that are manifest to citizens. The reason is that in a just society political opportunites and powers must be independent of economic or social position – the political liberties must have a fair value[6] – and the fact that they are independent must be more or less evident to citizens. Ensuring this manifestly fair value might, for example, require public funding of political parties and restrictions on private political spending, as well as progressive tax measures that serve to limit inequalities of wealth and to ensure that the political agenda is not controlled by the interests of economically and socially dominant groups (Rawls 1971, pp. 225–6, 277–8; 1982, pp. 42–3). In principle, these distributional requirements might be more stringently egalitarian than those fixed by the difference principle (1982, p. 43).[7] This is so in part because the main point of these measures is not simply to ensure that democratic politics proceeds under fair conditions, nor only to encourage just legislation, but also to ensure that the equality of citizens is manifest and to declare a commitment to that equality 'as the public intention' (1971, p. 233).

Third, democratic politics should be ordered in ways that provide a basis for self-respect, that encourage the development of a sense of political competence, and that contribute to the formation of a sense of justice;[8] it should fix 'the foundations for civic friendship and [shape] the ethos of political culture' (Rawls 1971, p. 234). Thus the importance of democratic order is not confined to its role in obstructing the class legislation that can be expected from systems in which groups are effectively excluded from the channels of political representation and bargaining. In addition, democratic politics should also shape the ways in which the members of the society understand themselves and their own legitimate interests.

When properly conducted, then, democratic politics involves *public deliberation focused on the common good*, requires some form of *manifest equality* among citizens, and *shapes the identity and interests* of citizens in ways that contribute to the formation of a public conception of common good. How does the ideal of a fair system of social co-operation provide a way to account for the attractiveness and importance of these three features of the deliberative democratic ideal? Rawls suggests a formal and an informal line of argument. The formal argument is that parties in the original position would choose the principle of participation[9] with the proviso that the political liberties have their fair value. The three conditions are important because they must be satisfied if constitutional arrangements are to ensure participation rights, guarantee a fair value to those rights, and plausibly produce legislation that encourages a fair distribution according to the difference principle.

Rawls also suggests an informal argument for the ordering of political institutions, and I shall focus on this informal argument here:

> Justice as fairness begins with the idea that where common principles are necessary and to everyone's advantage, they are to be worked out from the viewpoint of a suitably defined initial situation of equality in which each person is fairly represented. The principle of participation transfers this notion from the original position to the constitution . . . [thus] preserv[ing] the equal representation of the original position to the degree that this is feasible. (Rawls 1971, pp. 221–2)[10]

Or, as he puts it elsewhere: 'The idea [of the fair value of political liberty] is to incorporate into the basic structure of society an effective political procedure which *mirrors* in that structure the fair representation of persons achieved by the original position' (1982, p. 45; emphasis added). The suggestion is that, since we accept the intuitive ideal of a fair system of co-operation, we should want our political institutions themselves to conform, in so far as it is feasible, to the requirement that terms of association be worked out under fair conditions. And so we arrive directly at the requirement of equal liberties with fair value, rather than arriving at it indirectly, through a hypothetical choice of that requirement under fair conditions. In this informal argument, the original position serves as an *abstract model* of what fair conditions are, and of what we should strive to mirror in our political institutions, rather than as an initial-choice situation in which regulative principles for those institutions are selected.

I think that Rawls is right in wanting to accommodate the three conditions. What I find less plausible is that the three conditions are natural consequences of the ideal of fairness. Taking the notion of fairness as fundamental, and aiming (as in the informal argument) to model political arrangements on the original position, it is not clear why, for example, political debate ought to be focused on the common good, or why the manifest equality of citizens is an important feature of a democratic association. The pluralist conception of democratic politics as a system of bargaining with fair representation for all groups seems an equally good mirror of the ideal of fairness.

The response to this objection is clear enough: the connection between the ideal of fairness and the three features of democratic politics depends on psychological and sociological assumptions. Those features do not follow directly from the ideal of a fair system of co-operation, or from that ideal as it is modeled in the original position. Rather, we arrive at them when we consider what is required to preserve fair arrangements and to achieve fair outcomes. For example, public political debate should be conducted in terms of considerations of the common good because we cannot expect outcomes that advance the common good unless people are looking for them. Even an ideal pluralist scheme, with equal bargaining power and no barriers to entry, cannot reasonably be expected to advance the common good as defined by the difference principle (1971, p. 360).

But this is, I think, too indirect and instrumental an argument for the three conditions. Like utilitarian defences of liberty, it rests on a series of highly speculative sociological and psychological judgements. I want to suggest that the reason why the three are attractive is not that an order with, for example, no explicit deliberation about the common good and no manifest equality would be unfair (though of course it might be). Instead it is that they comprise elements of an independent and expressly political ideal that is focused in the first instance[11] on the appropriate conduct of public affairs – on, that is, the appropriate ways of arriving at collective decisions. And to understand that ideal we ought not to proceed by seeking to 'mirror' ideal fairness in the fairness of political arrangements, but instead to proceed by seeking to mirror a system of ideal deliberation in social and political institutions. I want now to turn to this alternative.

The notion of a deliberative democracy is rooted in the intuitive ideal of a democratic association in which the justification of the terms and conditions of association proceeds through public argument and reasoning among equal citizens. Citizens in such an order share a commitment to the resolution of problems of collective choice through public reasoning, and regard their basic institutions as legitimate in so far as they establish the framework for free public deliberation. To elaborate this ideal, I begin with a more explicit account of the ideal itself, presenting what I shall call the 'formal conception' of deliberative democracy. Proceeding from this formal conception, I pursue a more substantive account of deliberative democracy by presenting an account of an *ideal deliberative procedure* that captures the notion of justification through public argument and reasoning among equal citizens, and serves in turn as a model for deliberative institutions.

The formal conception of a deliberative democracy has five main features:

D1   A deliberative democracy is an ongoing and independent association, whose members expect it to continue into the indefinite future.

D2   The members of the association share (and it is common knowledge that they share) the view that the appropriate terms of association provide a framework for or are the results of their deliberation. They share, that is, a commitment to co-ordinating their activities within institutions that make deliberation possible and according to norms that they arrive at through their deliberation. For them, free deliberation among equals is the basis of legitimacy.

D3   A deliberative democracy is a pluralistic association. The members have diverse preferences, convictions and ideals concerning the conduct of their own lives. While sharing a commitment to the deliberative resolution of problems of collective choice (D2), they also have divergent aims, and do not think that some particular set of preferences, convictions or ideals is mandatory.

D4   Because the members of a democratic association regard deliberative procedures as the source of *legitimacy*, it is important to them that the terms of their association not merely *be* the results of their deliberation, but also be *manifest* to them as such.[13] They prefer institutions in which the connections between deliberation and outcomes are evident to ones in which the connections are less clear.

D5   The members recognize one another as having deliberative capacities, i.e. the capacities required for entering into a public exchange of reasons and for acting on the result of such public reasoning.

A theory of deliberative democracy aims to give substance to this formal ideal by characterizing the conditions that should obtain if the social order is to be manifestly regulated by deliberative forms of collective choice. I propose to sketch a view of this sort by considering an ideal scheme of deliberation, which I shall call the 'ideal deliberative procedure'. The aim in sketching this procedure is to give an explicit statement of the conditions for deliberative decision-making that are suited to the formal conception, and thereby to highlight the properties that democratic institutions should embody, so far as possible. I should emphasize that the ideal deliberative procedure is meant to provide a model for institutions to mirror – in the first instance for the institutions in which collective choices are made and social outcomes publicly justified – and not to characterize an initial situation in which the terms of association themselves are chosen.[14]

Turning then to the ideal procedure, there are three general aspects of deliberation. There is a need to decide on an agenda, to propose alternative solutions to the problems on the agenda, supporting those solutions with reasons, and to conclude by settling on an alternative. A democratic conception can be represented in terms of the requirements that it sets on such a procedure. In particular, outcomes are democratically legitimate if and only if they could be the object of a free and reasoned agreement among equals. The ideal deliberative procedure is a procedure that captures this principle.[15]

I1   Ideal deliberation is *free* in that it satisfies two conditions. First, the participants regard themselves as bound only by the results of their deliberation and by the preconditions for that deliberation. Their consideration of proposals is not constrained by the authority of prior norms or requirements. Second, the participants suppose that they can act from the results, taking the fact that a certain decision is arrived at through their deliberation as a sufficient reason for complying with it.

I2   Deliberation is *reasoned* in that the parties to it are required to state their reasons for advancing proposals, supporting them or criticizing them. They give reasons with the expectation that those reasons (and not, for example, their power) will settle the fate of their proposal. In ideal deliberation, as Habermas puts it, 'no force except that of the better argument is exercised' (1975, p. 108). Reasons are offered with the aim of bringing others to accept the proposal, given their disparate ends (D3) and their commitment (D2) to settling the conditions of their association through free deliberation among equals. Proposals may be rejected because they are not defended with acceptable reasons, even if they could be so defended. The deliberative conception emphasizes that collective choices should be *made in a deliberative way*, and not only that those choices should have a desirable fit with the preferences of citizens.

I3   In ideal deliberation parties are both formally and substantively *equal*. They are formally equal in that the rules regulating the procedure do not single out individuals. Everyone with the deliberative capacities has equal standing at each stage of the deliberative process. Each can put issues on the agenda, propose solutions, and offer reasons in support of or in criticism of proposals. And each has an equal voice in the decision. The participants are substantively equal in that the existing distribution of power and resources does not shape their chances to contribute to deliberation, nor does that distribution play an authoritative role in their deliberation. The participants in the deliberative procedure do not regard themselves as bound by the existing system of rights, except in so far as that system establishes the framework of free deliberation among equals. Instead they regard that system as a potential object of their deliberative judgement.

I4　Finally, ideal deliberation aims to arrive at a rationally motivated *consensus* – to find reasons that are persuasive to all who are committed to acting on the results of a free and reasoned assessment of alternatives by equals. Even under ideal conditions there is no promise that consensual reasons will be forthcoming. If they are not, then deliberation concludes with voting, subject to some form of majority rule.[16] The fact that it may so conclude does not, however, eliminate the distinction between deliberative forms of collective choice and forms that aggregate non-deliberative preferences. The institutional consequences are likely to be different in the two cases, and the results of voting among those who are committed to finding reasons that are persuasive to all are likely to differ from the results of an aggregation that proceeds in the absence of this commitment.

Drawing on this characterization of ideal deliberation, can we say anything more substantive about a deliberative democracy? What are the implications of a commitment to deliberative decisions for the terms of social association? In the remarks that follow I shall indicate the ways that this commitment carries with it a commitment to advance the common good and to respect individual autonomy.

Common good and autonomy

Consider first the notion of the common good. Since the aim of ideal deliberation is to secure agreement among all who are committed to free deliberation among equals, and the condition of pluralism obtains (D3), the focus of deliberation is on ways of advancing the aims of each party to it. While no one is indifferent to his/her own good, everyone also seeks to arrive at decisions that are acceptable to all who share the commitment to deliberation (D2). (As we shall see just below, taking that commitment seriously is likely to require a willingness to revise one's understanding of one's own preferences and convictions.) Thus the characterization of an ideal deliberative procedure links the formal notion of deliberative democracy with the more substantive ideal of a democratic association in which public debate is focused on the common good of the members.

Of course, talk about the common good is one thing; sincere efforts to advance it are another. While public deliberation may be organized around appeals to the common good, is there any reason to think that even ideal deliberation would not consist in efforts to disguise personal or class advantage as the common advantage? There are two responses to this question. The first is that in my account of the formal idea of a deliberative democracy, I stipulated (D2) that the members of the association are committed to resolving their differences through deliberation, and thus to providing reasons that they sincerely expect to be persuasive to others who share that commitment. In short, this stipulation rules out the problem. Presumably, however, the objection is best understood as directed against the plausibility of realizing a deliberative procedure that conforms to the ideal, and thus is not answerable through stipulation.

The second response, then, rests on a claim about the effects of deliberation on the motivations of deliberators.[17] A consequence of the reasonableness of the deliberative procedure (I2) together with the condition of pluralism (D3) is that the mere fact of having a preference, conviction or ideal does not by itself provide a reason in support of a proposal. While I may take my preferences as a sufficient reason for advancing a proposal, deliberation under conditions of pluralism requires that I find reasons that make the proposal acceptable to others who cannot be expected to regard my preferences as sufficient reasons for agreeing. The motivational thesis is that the need to advance reasons that persuade others will help to shape the motivations that people bring to the deliberative procedure in two ways. First, the practice of presenting reasons will contribute to the formation of a commitment to the deliberative resolution of political questions (D2). Given that commitment, the likelihood of a sincere representation of preferences and convictions should increase, while the likelihood of their strategic misrepresentation declines. Second, it will shape the content of preferences and convictions as well. Assuming a commitment to deliberative justification, the discovery that I can offer no persuasive reasons on behalf of a proposal of mine may transform the preferences that motivate the proposal. Aims that I recognize to be inconsistent with the requirements of deliberative agreement may tend to lose their force, at least when I expect others to be proceeding in reasonable ways and expect the outcome of deliberation to regulate subsequent action.

Consider, for example, the desire to be wealthier come what may. I cannot appeal to this desire itself in defending policies. The motivational claim is the need to find an independent justification that does not appeal to this desire and will tend to shape it into, for example, a desire to have a level of wealth that is consistent with a level that others (i.e. equal citizens) find acceptable. I am of course assuming that the deliberation is known to be regulative, and that the wealth cannot be protected through wholly non-deliberative means.

Deliberation, then, focuses debate on the common good. And the relevant conceptions of the common good are not comprised simply of interests and preferences that are antecedent to deliberation. Instead, the interests, aims and ideals that comprise the common good are those that survive deliberation, interests that, on public reflection, we think it legitimate to appeal to in making claims on social resources. Thus the first and third of the features of deliberative democracy that I mentioned in the discussion of Rawls (pp. 18–19 above) comprise central elements in the deliberative conception.

The ideal deliberative scheme also indicates the importance of autonomy in a deliberative democracy. In particular, it is responsive to two main threats to autonomy. As a general matter, actions fail to be autonomous if the preferences on which an agent acts are, roughly, given by the circumstances, and not determined by the agent. There are two paradigm cases of 'external' determination. The first is what Elster (1982) has called 'adaptive preferences'.[18] These are preferences that shift with changes in the circumstances of the agent without any deliberate contribution by the agent to that shift. This is true, for example, of the political preferences of instinctive centrists who move to the median position in the political distribution, wherever it happens to be. The second I shall call 'accommodationist preferences'. While they are deliberately formed, accommodationist preferences represent psychological adjustments to conditions of subordination in which individuals are not recognized as having the capacity for self-government. Consider Stoic slaves, who deliberately shape their desires to match their powers, with a view to minimizing frustration. Since the existing relations of power make slavery the only possibility, they cultivate desires to be slaves, and then act on those desires. While their motives are deliberately formed, and they act on their desires, the Stoic slaves do not act autonomously when they seek to be good slaves. The absence of alternatives and consequent denial of scope for the deliberative capacities that defines the condition of slaves supports the conclusion that their desires result from their circumstances, even though those circumstances shape the desires of the Stoic slaves through their deliberation.

There are then at least two dimensions of autonomy. The phenomenon of adaptive preferences underlines the importance of conditions that permit and encourage the deliberative formation of preferences; the phenomenon of accommodationist preferences indicates the need for favorable conditions for the exercise of the deliberative capacities. Both concerns are met when institutions for collective decision-making are modelled on the ideal deliberative procedure. Relations of power and subordination are neutralized (I1, I3, I4), and each is recognized as having the deliberative capacities (D5), thus addressing the problem of accommodationist preferences. Further, the requirement of reasonableness discourages adaptive preferences (I2). While preferences are 'formed' by the deliberative procedure, this type of preference formation is consistent with autonomy, since preferences that are shaped by public deliberation are not simply given by external circumstances. Instead they are the result of 'the power of reason as applied through public discussion'.[19]

Beginning, then, from the formal ideal of a deliberative democracy, we arrive at the more substantive ideal of an association that is regulated by deliberation aimed at the common good and that respects the autonomy of the members. And so, in seeking to embody the ideal deliberative procedure in institutions, we seek, *inter alia*, to design institutions that focus political debate on the common good, that shape the identity and interests of citizens in ways that contribute to an attachment to the common good, and that provide the favourable conditions for the exercise of deliberative powers that are required for autonomy.

III

I want now to shift the focus. While I shall continue to pursue the relationship between the ideal deliberative procedure and more substantive issues about deliberative democratic association, I want to do so by considering four natural objections to the conception I have been discussing, objections to that conception for being sectarian, incoherent, unjust and irrelevant. My aim is not to provide a detailed response to the objections, but to clarify the conception of deliberative democracy by sketching the lines along which a response should proceed. Before turning to the objections, I enter two remarks about what follows.

First, as I indicated earlier, a central aim in the deliberative conception is to specify the institutional preconditions for deliberative decision-making. The role of the ideal deliberative procedure is to provide an abstract characterization of the important properties of deliberative institutions. The role of the ideal deliberative procedure is thus different from the role of an ideal social contract. The ideal deliberative procedure provides a model for institutions, a model that they should mirror, so far as possible. It is not a choice situation in which institutional principles are selected. The key point about the institutional reflection is that it should *make deliberation possible*. Institutions in a deliberative democracy do not serve simply to implement the results of deliberation, as though free deliberation could proceed in the absence of appropriate institutions. Neither the commitment to nor the capacity for arriving at deliberative decisions is something that we can simply assume to obtain independent from the proper ordering of institutions. The institutions themselves must provide the framework for the formation of the will; they determine whether there is equality, whether deliberation is free and reasoned, whether there is autonomy, and so on.

Second, I shall be focusing here on some requirements on 'public' institutions that reflect the ideal of deliberative resolution. But there is of course no reason to expect as a general matter that the preconditions for deliberation will respect familiar institutional boundaries between 'private' and 'public' and will all pertain to the public arena. For example, inequalities of wealth, or the absence of institutional measures designed to redress the consequences of those inequalities, can serve to undermine the equality required in deliberative arenas themselves. And so a more complete treatment would need to address a wider range of institutional issues (see Cohen and Rogers 1983, chs 3, 6; Cohen 1988).

Sectarianism

The first objection is that the ideal of deliberative democracy is objectionably sectarian because it depends on a particular view of the good life – an ideal of active citizenship. What makes it sectarian is not the specific ideal on which it depends, but the (alleged) fact that it depends on some specific conception at all. I do not think that the conception of deliberative democracy suffers from the alleged difficulty. In explaining why not, I shall put to the side current controversy about the thesis that sectarianism is avoidable and objectionable, and assume that it is both.[20]

Views of the good figure in political conceptions in at least two ways. First, the *justification* of some conceptions appeals to a notion of the human good. Aristotelian views, for example, endorse the claim that the exercise of the deliberative capacities is a fundamental component of a good human life, and conclude that a political association ought to be organized to encourage the realization of those capacities by its members. A second way in which conceptions of the good enter is that the *stability* of a society may require widespread allegiance to a specific conception of the good, even though its institutions can be justified without appeal to that conception. For example, a social order that can be justified without reference to ideals of national allegiance may none the less require widespread endorsement of the ideal of patriotic devotion for its stability.

A political conception is objectionably sectarian only if its *justification* depends on a particular view of the human good, and not simply because its stability is contingent on widespread agreement on the value of certain activities and aspirations. For this reason the democratic conception is not sectarian. It is organized around a view of political justification – that justification proceeds through free deliberation among equal citizens – and not a conception of the proper conduct of life. So, while it is plausible that the stability of a deliberative democracy depends on encouraging the ideal of active citizenship, this dependence does not suffice to show that it is objectionably sectarian.

Incoherence

Consider next the putative incoherence of the ideal. We find this charge in an important tradition of argument, including Schumpeter's *Capitalism, Socialism, and Democracy* and, more recently, William Riker's work on social choice and democracy. I want here to say a word about the latter, focusing on just one reason that Riker gives for thinking that the ideal of popular self-government is incoherent.[21]

Institutionalizing a deliberative procedure requires a decision rule short of consensus – for example, majority rule. But majority rule is globally unstable: as a general matter, there exists a majority-rule path leading from any element in the set of alternatives to any other element in the set. The majority, standing in for the people, wills everything and therefore wills nothing. Of course, while anything can be the result of majority decision, it is not true that everything will be the result. But, because majority rule is so unstable, the actual decision of the majority will not be determined by preferences themselves, since they do not constrain the outcome. Instead decisions will reflect the particular institutional constraints under which they are made. But these constraints are 'exogenous to the world of tastes and values' (Riker 1982, p. 190). So the ideal of popular self-government is incoherent because we are, so to speak, governed by the institutions, and not by ourselves.

I want to suggest one difficulty with this argument that highlights the structure of the deliberative conception. According to the argument I just sketched, outcomes in majority-rule institutions reflect 'exogenous' institutional constraints, and not underlying preferences. This suggests that we can identify the preferences and convictions that are relevant to collective choices apart from the institutions through which they are formed and expressed. But that is just what the deliberative conception denies. On this conception, the relevent preferences and convictions are those that could be expressed in free deliberation, and not those that are prior to it. For this reason, popular self-government *premises* the existence of institutions that provide a framework for deliberation; these arrangements are not 'exogenous constraints' on the aggregation of preferences, but instead help to shape their content and the way that citizens choose to advance them. And, once the deliberative institutions are in place, and preferences, convictions and political actions are shaped by them, it is not clear that instability problems remain so severe as to support the conclusion that self-government is an empty and incoherent ideal.

Injustice

The third problem concerns injustice. I have been treating the ideal of democracy as the basic ideal for a political conception. But it might be argued that the ideal of democracy is not suited to the role of fundamental political ideal because its treatment of basic liberties is manifestly unacceptable. It makes those liberties dependent on judgements of majorities and thus endorses the democratic legitimacy of decisions that restrict the basic liberties of individuals. In responding to this objection I shall focus on the liberty of expression,[22] and shall begin by filling out a version of the objection which I put in the words of an imagined critic.[23]

'You embrace the ideal of a democratic order. The aim of a democratic order is to maximize the *power of the people* to secure its wants. To defend the liberty of expression you will argue that that power is diminished if the people lack the information required for exercising their will. Since expression provides information, you will conclude that abridgements of expression ought to be barred. The problem with your argument is that preventing restrictions on expression also restricts the power of the people, since the citizens may collectively prefer such restrictions. And so it is not at all clear as a general matter that the protection of expression will maximize popular power. So while you will, of course, not want to prevent everyone from speaking all the time, you cannot defend the claim that there is even a presumption in favour of the protection of expression. And this disregard for fundamental liberties is unacceptable.'

This objection has force against some conceptions on which democracy is a fundamental ideal, particularly those in which the value of expression turns exclusively on its role as a source of information about how best to advance popular ends. But it does not have any force against the deliberative conception, since the latter does not make the case for expression turn on its role in maximizing the power of the people to secure its wants. That case rests instead on a conception of collective choice, in particular on a view about how the 'wants' that are relevant to collective choice are formed and defined in the first place. The relevant preferences and convictions are those that arise from or are confirmed through deliberation. And a framework of free expression is required for the reasoned consideration of alternatives that comprises deliberation. The deliberative conception holds that free expression is required for *determining* what advances the common good, because what is good is fixed by public deliberation, and not prior to it. It is fixed by informed and autonomous judgements, involving the exercise of the deliberative capacities. So the ideal of deliberative democracy is not hostile to free expression; it rather presupposes such freedom.

But what about expression with no direct bearing on issues of public policy? Is the conception of deliberative democracy committed to treating all 'non-political expression' as second-class, and as meriting lesser protection? I do not think so. The deliberative conception construes politics as aiming in part at the formation of preferences and convictions, not just at their articulation and aggregation. Because of this emphasis on reasoning about preferences and convictions, and the bearing of expression with no political focus on such reasoning, the deliberative view draws no bright line between political speech and other sorts of expression. Forms of expression that do not address issues of policy may well bear on the formation of the interests, aims, and ideals that citizens bring to public deliberation. For this reason the deliberative conception supports protection for the full range of expression, regardless of the content of that expression.[24] It would violate the core of the ideal of free deliberation among equals to fix preferences and convictions in advance by restricting the content of expression, or by barring access to expression, or by preventing the expression that is essential to having convictions at all. Thus the injustice objection fails because the liberties are not simply among the topics for deliberation; they help to comprise the framework that makes it possible.[25]

Irrelevance

The irrelevance objection is that the notion of public deliberation is irrelevant to modern political conditions.[26] This is the most important objection, but also the one about which it is hardest to say anything at the level of generality required by the present context. Here again I shall confine myself to one version of the objection, though one that I take to be representative.

The version that I want to consider starts from the assumption that a direct democracy with citizens gathering in legislative assemblies is the only way to institutionalize a deliberative procedure. Premising that, and recognizing that direct democracy is impossible under modern conditions, the objection concludes that we ought to be led to reject the ideal because it is not relevant to our circumstances.

The claim about the impossibility of direct democracy is plainly correct. But I see no merit in the claim that direct democracy is the uniquely suitable way to institutionalize the ideal procedure.[27] In fact, in the absence of a theory about the operations of democratic assemblies – a theory which cannot simply stipulate that ideal conditions obtain – there is no reason to be confident that a direct democracy would subject political questions to deliberative resolution, even if a direct democracy were a genuine institutional possibility.[28] In the absence of a realistic account of the functioning of citizen assemblies, we cannot simply assume that large gatherings with open-ended agendas will yield any deliberation at all, or that they will encourage participants to regard one another as equals in a free deliberative procedure. The appropriate ordering of deliberative institutions depends on issues of political psychology and political behaviour; it is not an immediate consequence of the deliberative ideal. So, far from being the only deliberative scheme, direct democracy may not even be a particularly good arrangement for deliberation. But, once we reject the idea that a direct democracy is the natural or necessary form of expression of the deliberative ideal, the straightforward argument for irrelevance no longer works. In saying how the ideal might be relevant, however, we come up against the problem I mentioned earlier. Lacking a good understanding of the workings of institutions, we are inevitably thrown back on more or less speculative judgements. What follows is some sketchy remarks on one issue that should be taken in this spirit.

At the heart of the institutionalization of the deliberative procedure is the existence of arenas in which citizens can propose issues for the political agenda and participate in debate about those issues. The existence of such arenas is a public good, and ought to be supported with public money. This is not because public support is the only way, or even the most efficient way, of ensuring the provision of such arenas. Instead, public provision expresses the basic commitment of a democratic order to the resolution of political questions through free deliberation among equals. The problem is to figure out how arenas might be organized to encourage such deliberation.

In considering that organization, there are two key points that I want to underscore. The first is that material inequalities are an important source of political inequalities. The second point – which is more speculative – is that deliberative arenas which are organized exclusively on local, sectional or issue-specific lines are unlikely to produce the open-ended deliberation required to institutionalize a deliberative procedure. Since these arenas bring together only a narrow range of interests, deliberation in them can be expected at best to produce coherent sectional interests, but no more comprehensive conception of the common good.

These two considerations together provide support for the view that political parties supported by public funds play an important role in making a deliberative democracy possible.[29] There are two reasons for this, corresponding to the two considerations I have just mentioned. In the first place, an important feature of organizations generally, and parties in particular, is that they provide a means through which individuals and groups who lack the 'natural' advantage of wealth can overcome the political disadvantages that follow on that lack. Thus they can help to overcome the inequalities in deliberative arenas that result from material inequality. Of course, to play this role, political organizations must themselves be freed from the dominance of private resources, and that independence must be manifest. Thus the need for public funding. Here we arrive back at the second point that I mentioned in the discussion of Rawls's view – that measures are needed to ensure manifest equality – though now as a way of displaying a shared commitment to deliberative decisions, and not simply as an expression of the commitment to fairness. Second, because parties are required to address a comprehensive range of political issues, they provide arenas in which debate is not restricted in the ways that it is in local, sectional or issue-specific organizations. They can provide the more open-ended arenas needed to form and articulate the conceptions of the common good that provide the focus of political debate in a deliberative democracy.

There is certainly no guarantee that parties will operate as I have just described. But this is not especially troubling, since there are no guarantees of anything in politics. The question is how we can best approximate the deliberative conception. And it is difficult to see how that is possible in the absence of strong parties, supported with public resources (though, of course, a wide range of other conditions are required as well).

IV

I have suggested that we take the notion of democratic association as a fundamental political ideal, and have elaborated that ideal by reference to an ideal deliberative procedure and the requirements for institutionalizing such a procedure. I have sketched a few of those requirements here. To show that the democratic ideal can play the role of fundamental organizing ideal, I should need to pursue the account of fundamental liberties and political organization in much greater detail and to address a wide range of other issues as well. Of course, the richer the requirements are for institutionalizing free public deliberation, the larger the range of issues that may need to be removed from the political agenda; that is, the larger the range of issues that form the background framework of public deliberation rather than its subject matter. And, the larger that range, the less there is to deliberate about. Whether that is good news or bad news, it is in any case a suitable place to conclude.

Notes

I have had countless discussions of the subject matter of this paper with Joel Rogers, and wish to thank him for his unfailingly sound and generous advice. For our joint treatment of the issues that I discuss here, see Cohen and Rogers (1983), ch. 6. The main differences between the treatment of issues here and the treatment in the book lies in the explicit account of the ideal deliberative procedure, the fuller treatment of the notions of autonomy and the common good, and the account of the connection of those notions with the ideal procedure. An earlier draft of this paper was presented to the Pacific Division Meetings of the American Philosophical Association. I would like to thank Loren Lomasky and the editors of this collection for helpful comments on that draft.

1   I originally came across the term 'deliberative democracy' in Sunstein (1985). He cites (n. 26) an article by Bessette, which I have not consulted.

2   For some representative examples, see Sunstein (1984, 1985, 1986), Michelman (1986), Ackerman (1984, 1986).

3   I have in mind, in particular, criticisms which focus on the ways in which material inequalities and weak political parties restrict democracy by constraining public political debate or undermining the equality of the participants in that debate. For

discussion of these criticisms, and of their connections with the ideal of democratic order, see Cohen and Rogers (1983), chs 3, 6; Unger (1987), ch. 5.

4 In the discussion that follows, I draw on Rawls (1971, esp. sections 36, 37, 43, 54; 1982).

5 This rejection is not particularly idiosyncratic. Sunstein, for example, argues (1984, 1985) that ideal pluralism has never been embraced as a political ideal in American public law.

6 Officially, the requirement of fair value is that 'everyone has a fair opportunity to hold public office and to influence the outcome of political decisions' (Rawls 1982, p. 42).

7 Whatever their stringency, these distributional requirements take priority over the difference principle, since the requirement of fair value is part of the principle of liberty; that is, the first principle of justice (Rawls 1982, pp. 41–2).

8 The importance of democratic politics in the account of the acquisition of the sense of justice is underscored in Rawls (1971), pp. 473–4.

9 The principle of participation states that 'all citizens are to have an equal right to take part in, and to determine the outcome of, the constitutional process that establishes the laws with which they are to comply' (Rawls 1971, p. 221).

10 I assume that the principle of participation should be understood here to include the requirement of the fair value of political liberty.

11 The reasons for the phrase 'in the first instance' are clarified below at pp. 22–3.

12 Since writing the first draft of this section of the paper, I have read Elster (1986a) and Manin (1987), which both present parallel conceptions. This is especially so with Elster's treatment of the psychology of public deliberation (pp. 112–13). I am indebted to Alan Hamlin for bringing the Elster article to my attention. The overlap is explained by the fact that Elster, Manin and I all draw on Habermas. See Habermas (1975, 1979, 1984). I have also found the discussion of the contractualist account of motivation in Scanlon (1982) very helpful.

13 For philosophical discussions of the importance of manifestness or publicity, see Kant (1983), pp. 135–9; Rawls (1971), p. 133 and section 29; Williams (1985), pp. 101–2, 200.

14 The distinction between the ideal procedure and an initial-choice situation will be important in the later discussion of motivation formation (see pp. 24–5) and institutions (pp. 26–7).

15 There are of course norms and requirements on individuals that do not have deliberative justification. The conception of deliberative democracy is, in Rawls's term, a 'political conception', and not a comprehensive moral theory. On the distinction between political and comprehensive theories, see Rawls (1987), pp. 1–25.

16 For criticism of the reliance on an assumption of unanimity in deliberative views, see Manin (1987), pp. 359–61.

17 Note the parallel with Elster (1986a) indicated in note 12. See also the discussion in Habermas (1975), p. 108, about 'needs that can be communicatively shared', and Habermas (1979), ch. 2.

18 For an interesting discussion of autonomous preferences and political processes, see Sunstein (1986 pp. 1145–58; 1984, pp. 1699–700).

19 Whitney *vs*. California, 274 US 357 (1927).

20   For contrasting views on sectarianism, see Rawls (1987); Dworkin (1985), pt 3; MacIntyre (1981); Sandel (1982).

21   See Riker (1982); for discussion of Riker's view see Coleman and Ferejohn (1986); Cohen (1986).

22   For discussion of the connection between ideals of democracy and freedom of expression, see Meikeljohn (1948), Tribe (1978; 1985, ch. 2) and Ely (1980, pp. 93–4, 105–16). Freedom of expression is a special case that can perhaps be more straightforwardly accommodated by the democratic conception than liberties of conscience, or the liberties associated with privacy and personhood. I do think, however, that these other liberties can be given satisfactory treatment by the democratic conception, and would reject it if I did not think so. The general idea would be to argue that other fundamental liberties must be protected if citizens are to be able to engage in and have equal standing in political deliberation without fear that such engagement puts them at risk for their convictions or personal choices. Whether this line of argument will work out on the details is a matter for treatment elsewhere.

23   This objection is suggested in Dworkin (1985), pp. 61–3. He cites the following passage from a letter of Madison's: 'And a people who mean to be their own Governors, must arm themselves with *the power which knowledge gives*' (emphasis added).

24   On the distinction betweeen content-based and content-neutral abridgements, the complexities of drawing the distinction in particular cases, and the special reasons for hostility to content-based abridgements, see Tribe (1978), pp. 584–682; Stone (1987), pp. 46–118.

25   I am not suggesting that the deliberative view provides the only sound justification for the liberty of expression. My concern here is rather to show that the deliberative view is capable of accommodating it.

26   For an especially sharp statement of the irrelevance objection, see Schmitt (1985).

27   This view is sometimes associated with Rousseau, who is said to have conflated the notion of democratic legitimacy with the institutional expression of that ideal in a direct democracy. For criticism of this interpretation, see Cohen (1986a).

28   Madison urges this point in the *Federalist Papers*. Objecting to a proposal advanced by Jefferson which would have regularly referred constitutional questions 'to the decision of the whole of society', Madison argues that this would increase 'the danger of disturbing the public tranquillity by interesting too strongly the public passions'. And 'it is the reason, alone, of the public that ought to control and regulate the government . . . [while] the passions ought to be controlled and regulated by the government'. I endorse the form of the objection, not its content. (*Federalist Papers* 1961, pp. 315–17.)

29   Here I draw on Cohen and Rogers (1983), pp. 154–7. The idea that parties are required to organize political choice and to provide a focus for public deliberation is one strand of arguments about 'responsible parties' in American political-science literature. My understanding of this view has been greatly aided by Perlman (1987), and, more generally, by the work of my colleague Walter Dean Burnham on the implications of party decline for democratic politics. See, for example, Burnham (1982).

3

The Limits of Democracy

Albert Weale

Among democratic theorists one debate has been of particular importance: that between so-called 'participatory' theorists on the one hand and so-called 'elitist' theorists on the other. Although the terms of the debate are often imprecise and the evidence to which appeal is made is capable of different interpretations, the debate is clearly one that touches on a problem that is central to democratic theory. All sides to the debate accept that representative democracy is a desirable form of government as a general principle of political organization. The question that is being posed in the debate concerns the limits of popular government. How far should popular control be extended? Elitists are prone to say, as little as is consistent with satisfying irrefutable popular demands; participationists are prone to say, as much as possible. Between the two there are a great many intermediate positions, and as many points of disagreement.

Sometimes the argument will turn on practicalities. Sometimes the constraints of time are stressed as a limit on effective participation. Dahl (1970, 1982) has been especially successful in exploring this limitation, arguing, in effect, that participatory democracy is rather like the socialism to which Oscar Wilde referred when he said that its trouble was that it took far too many evenings. Another source of constraint explored by Dahl (Dahl and Tufte 1973) has been size of place. Direct participation in decision-making presumes the possibility of face-to-face contact, and so the geographical extent of political control becomes an important variable determining the scope for increased participation. Although these points are well taken, they do not by themselves settle the argument as to the limits of democracy. For within the constraints of time and place it is still possible to choose different forms of government among which there will be varying degrees of participation. It was political choice and tradition, rather than the limits of time and geography, that led the French until recently to operate with a system of appointed prefects in each department rather than fully empowered local authorities, and similar considerations of political ideology led the United Kingdom to operate with appointed health authorities rather than placing the government of hospital-based health services under direct democratic control.

There are, in fact, likely to be four restrictions on a form of government that limit the extent to which it is democratic. The first is a restriction of *scope*. Certain public decisions are removed from the control of representative or direct assemblies and placed in the hands of other decision-makers. The most familiar example of scope restrictions of this kind is the constitutional protection given to certain basic rights. When civil and political rights are constitutionally entrenched, then it is not possible for the government of the day to pass certain types of legislation or to adopt certain policies. A clear example of this restriction of scope occurs in the First Amendment of the US Constitution, where Congress is forbidden to pass any law that abridges freedom of speech. The second restriction is related to the first, but is logically distinct and it is one of *source*. Sometimes a public policy is adopted not because it has the sanction of popular support, but because the authority to make the decision derives from an alternative source. The best example here is probably judicial decision-making in the English courts, which has common law origins rather than a basis in democratically determined statue. The third limit is one of *constituency*. Even when the policy is one which falls within the scope of democratic decision-making, and even when the source of power to make the decision may be identified with the popular will, the relevant demos may be more or less narrowly circumscribed, as is the case, for example, with a property qualification on the right to vote. Finally, the restrictions may be ones of *decision rule*. Constitutionally entrenched protections may often be removed by democratic decision, but only after a special decision rule has been followed – for example, by satisfying the requirement that two thirds of those voting support the amendment.

Those who advocate restrictions on democracy are free to stress one or more of the above features as a method for achieving their aims. Perhaps the argument with the longest lineage concerns the limits to be placed on the constituency. From Aristotle to Kant it was argued that the possession of property was a necessary condition for effective and responsible participation in government. Even a philosophical radical such as James Mill, suspicious of the misuse of power that a property-based franchise involved, argued for restricting the constituency to males over the age of forty (J. Mill 1820). Mill's argument is interesting because it explicitly recognises the costs of political participation – a feature of political participation that Downs (1957) was later to stress. Citizens are excluded from the vote not because Mill thought they would act irresponsibly, but because Mill was sensitive to the fact that political participation involves effort and therefore cost. The utility-maximizing arrangement would not necessarily be the one in which everyone participated, for, if someone's interests could be adequately protected by the participation of another, then they would have effectively gained the benefits without incurring the costs. We may express this point in the language of modern utilitarianism by saying that democracy is a practice that requires general but not universal participation for its maintenance.

Mill's argument is valid even if its premise is mistaken. It might be thought that it was an error to use a utilitarian argument to impose a restriction on categories of people. After all, if political participation is a cost, then on utilitarian assumptions citizens should recognize the fact and participate only up to the point where the marginal gains equal the marginal costs. The correct utilitarian rule would then appear to be one in which all citizens were granted the right of participation and decided the limits of participation according to their own judgement. However, this ignores the fact that for Mill power is a zero-sum relationship: when A gains power B loses it. It follows from this conception of power that, if one member of a certain category exercises the right to participate in decision-making, then all other members of the same category are potentially obliged to participate even if they have a net utility loss, since the costs of failing to participate when others are doing so is an even greater loss. The logic of imposing a categorical restriction on participation is therefore exactly analogous to the logic by which established firms seek price regulation. By putting *themselves* under a restriction, they avoid the costs of protecting themselves from predatory price-cutting by *others*.

From our perspective, of course, it is simply fatuous to believe that the interests of wives, daughters and younger male offspring would be adequately protected by the male head of household. But this is to question Mill's premise, not the form of argument he used. As an argument Mill's approach is valid, and it can be used as an argument for extending the franchise once an alternative premise is granted. In this respect James Mill's argument is more liberal than that of his son, since it imposes a less stringent test of voter competence in allocating the vote. John Stuart Mill's proposal for increased votes depending on educational qualifications (J. S. Mill 1861) requires that equality of political participation depend on *two* tests: the demonstration of an interest and the attainment of educational qualifications. James Mill, by contrast, merely requires the demonstration of an otherwise unrepresented interest.

If utilitarian arguments about the size of the relevant constituency have been important, thinkers in the tradition of rights have sought to limit the *scope* of democratic decision-making in an attempt to protect certain fundamental components of the lives citizens lead. One of the earliest and most eloquent expositions of this viewpoint can be found in the *Federalist Papers*, particularly those whose authorship is ascribed to Madison. John Stuart Mill, too, identified the problem of the conflict of majority opinion and minority pursuit of experiments in living. More recently, Fishkin (1979) has identified a logical contradiction between the principle of majority rule and the protection of rights which he interprets in terms of the avoidance of 'severe deprivations'. And a striking feature of Nozick's account of the minimal state (Nozick 1974), the most consistent attempt to draw out the political implications of the rights position, is that it contains no features that would make democracy a preferred form of government: limited government might be democratic government, but it need not be. Dworkin (1978), too, has sought to explore the conflict between democratic preference and the protection of individual rights.

A further source of criticism of democratic politics comes from the public choice tradition. In this tradition two principal types of difficulty are identified. The first of these is the problem that in any complex world there is no mechanism adequately to translate a statement of individual preferences over available alternatives into a coherent statement of public choice. Once we move outside simple worlds of binary alternatives and well-structured preference profiles, there is no set of rules for translating a statement of individual preferences into a social choice without violating attractive properties of a choice rule. In particular, we run up against the problem of the 'disequilibrium of majority rule'. Briefly stated, this means that, with three or more alternatives to choose from, a majority-voting procedure will result in the selection of an alternative that is in fact less preferred by a majority than some rejected alternative. Not only does this result make it difficult to asign any meaning to statements about what 'society prefers' or what 'the public wants'; it is also the basis for other problematic features of democratic decision-making. For example, it has long been observed that vote-trading in legislative bodies throws up results that are Pareto-inferior to some alternative tax–benefit package. It turns out on analysis that the conditions under which this can happen are identical with the conditions creating the disequilibrium of majority rule. Breaking the cycle of majority preference can be an expensive business. (For the above results, see Riker 1982.)

The second line of attack on democratic procedures coming from the public choice tradition stresses the dangers that voting procedures create for those who are in the minority. In *The Calculus of Consent* (1965), Buchanan and Tullock argued that any voting rule on public projects that required less than unanimity was likely to create 'external costs' for the minority that was outvoted. However, since a unanimity rule involved its own costs, the rational decision at the stage of a constitutional contract was to accept some qualified majority procedure.

Summarizing these approaches, we can see that each offers some reason for modifying the operation of popular government. The utilitarian argument originating with James Mill draws attention to the costs of political participation and raises via its modern discussion in Downs the problems associated with the extent to which mass publics can be expected to become involved in political decision-making. The argument from the disequilibrium of majority rule draws attention to the problems of assuming that the same voting rule can be used in all circumstances. The argument from rights or external costs raises the issue of whether the scope of majority rule should be limited in particular ways. All the criticisms raise implicitly the question of what the alternative source of public decision-making might be if it is not some form of popular government.

I A principle of constitutional choice

It is easy to see that there are considerable problems with the use of democratic procedures; it is less easy to determine a method by which those problems may be solved. It is a commonplace of modern political science (though by no means insignificant for that reason) that democratic procedures are necessary to achieve a peaceful reconciliation of competing conceptions of the public good. In this sense the modern state can only secure legitimacy by adopting popular government as its fundamental principle of decision-making. Yet, in the face of the difficulties identified, it becomes difficult to determine the limits of democratic procedures.

The principle whose significance I should like to explore in this context has been stated by Habermas. After noting that the modern paradigm of procedural legitimacy is to be found in Rousseau's notion of the *volonté generale*, Habermas claims that this paradigm has confused the modern discussion of democracy leading to a preference for a particular organizational form rather than a particular mode of justification.

> If one calls democracies precisely those political orders that satisfy the procedural type of legitimacy, then questions of democratization can be treated for what they are: as organizational questions. For it depends on the concrete social and political conditions, on scopes of disposition, on information, and so forth, which types of organization and which mechanisms are in each case better suited to bring about procedurally legitimate decisions and institutions ... It is a question of finding arrangements which can ground the presumption that the basic insof society and the basic political decisions would meet the unenforced agreement of all those involved, if they could participate, as free and equal, in discursive will-formation. Democratization cannot mean an a priori preference for a specific type of organization, for example, for so-called direct democracy. (Habermas 1979, p. 186)

The claim in this passage is that democratic theory rests not upon a preference in favour of particular organization forms, but instead upon a commitment to political institutions that can be justified in the light of critical reflection upon their operation and performance. In so far, then, as the problems that we have identified raise critical problems for the operation of popular government, they need to be incorporated into any coherent democratic theory.

The intellectual device that Habermas favours for systematizing these critical reflections is that of the 'ideal speech situation', a mode of interaction in which there is unenforced and informed communication between the participants in a dialogue whose aim is consensus on the truth. The similarity between this notion and the agreements that might be supposed to emerge from a Rawlsian 'original position' or 'constitutional contract' have often been noted (see, for a particularly clear discussion, Lukes 1982). More surprising, perhaps, is the fact that a similar criterion for the evaluation of political organizations has been urged within the public choice tradition by Buchanan, who has argued that we should think of constitutional disputes as a 'dialogue in which all persons are assigned equal values' (Buchanan 1986, p. 63), where the search is for an agreed set of constitutional choices that respect the long-term interests of those who are party to the dialogue. In other words, we have a convergence of argument on the thought that the democratic attitude is tied not to particular organizational arrangements but to a critical mode of justification of political institutions.

It may be thought that appeal to constitutional dialogue is metaphorical in character and that the real work in the argument is being done by the assumptions made as to the nature of the parties to the constitutional dialogue. It is a familiar observation in the discussion of Rawls that different presumed motivational accounts of the contracting parties will yield different conclusions on the terms of the social contract, and a similar point has been made by Lukes in respect of Habermas's theory. If this line of criticism is pursued, it might seem as though all that the metaphor of a constitutional dialogue embodied was the requirement that one prescribe solutions to political conflicts that are somehow impartial between competing conceptions of the good. However, I should like to contend that there is more to the theory of constitutional dialogue than is implied by this criticism. In particular, I shall suggest, the theory of constitutional dialogue incorporates assumptions about the nature of persons that in turn imply conclusions about the limits of democracy.

The most important of these assumptions is contained within the principle of critical justification by means of a constitutional dialogue itself. Why should a theory presume the need for critical justification unless it is also assumed that potential members of a political community are autonomous creatures deserving of the respect that a reasoned account of the political order contains? In other words, the theory of constitutional dialogue conceives of citizens not as bundles of preferences to be maximally satisfied, but as reasoning creatures whose desires and motivations can be modified in the light of rational argument. Moreover, within the constitutional dialogue no perspective is given privileged status. Persons are to be regarded as free *and* equal.

Following Lindley (1986) I shall refer to the concern for autonomy embodied in the theory of constitutional dialogue as an 'autonomy interest'. The important point to note about this form of constitutional theory is that it presupposes the crucial role of a person's autonomy interests, rather in the way that Dworkin (1978, pp. 150–83) wished to argue that the contractarian theory in general presupposes a theory of rights. The interests are logically prior to the interests that may be furthered by the adoption of particular democratic procedures or organizational forms. My contention, then, is that it is this logical priority that provides the first ground for limiting the scope of democratic procedures. Protection of autonomy interests is the first condition that must be satisfied in the operation of political systems, and this in turn implies limits on what democracies may do.

The point may be illustrated by the example of the principles of the rule of law. These principles require that laws be made in conformity with certain conditions, including that they should be cast as general rules; they should be made public; they should not be retrospective; they should be intelligible; they should not be contradictory; they should not require conduct beyond the abilities of the affected party; they should be sufficiently stable to provide a basis by which those affected can orient their conduct; and the administration of the laws should coincide with the announced laws (Fuller 1969, p. 39). There are many reasons why it is desirable to respect the principles of the rule of law in the making of legislation, but fundamental among such reasons is that it is only by acting in accordance with the principles of the rule of law that the state shows respect for persons as creatures capable of self-regulation in their lives by their taking into account the purposes served by the law. To fail to make law in accordance with these principles is therefore to override the autonomy interests of members of the community.

It is, of course, an open question as to what the precise political conditions might be for the maintenance of the rule of law. There has been a tendency in contemporary political theory to assume that the strict separation of powers and the system of Madisonian checks and balances is the most natural way to achieve protection of these autonomy interests in the form of constitutionally entrenched civil and political rights (see, for example, Ackerman 1980; Dworkin 1978; Rawls 1971). However, this conclusion risks putting the matter too firmly. Protection of political and civil rights exists in political systems which do not have the sharp separation between the legislature and the executive contained within the US Constitution. The reason for this is probably to be found in one of the results of public choice theory referred to above, namely the difficulty of identifying stable legislative majorities. In such a situation minorities who are potentially vulnerable to majority tyranny have the possibility of detaching some subset of the majority coalition from their partners and helping to form a new majority coalition. Hence the political basis for the protection of rights comprises just that fluidity of democratic politics to which critics of popular government have appealed.

The case is no doubt stronger for the clear separation of judicial functions and the identification of the set of basic civil and constitutional liberties in a documentary constitution, as critics of the United Kingdom's failure to implement a bill of rights have noted. In this case a remedy that is thought to protect citizens from governments of whatever type can be used to protect them against the potential harms of democratic government.

Should there also be limits on a democracy's ability to legislate on matters of property? As Buchanan (1986, pp. 255–6) has noted, it is this issue that tends to divide liberals or libertarians from social democrats. Both may agree that there should be minimal interference with the liberties of citizens, but they disagree on the extent to which the acquisition and use of property should be included within those liberties. Hence there is dispute whether important questions of public policy are properly matters that fall within the scope of popular government or should be assigned to the protected sphere of constitutional liberties. These issues include such matters as the role of government in environmental protection, anti-monopoly policy, health and safety legislation, the control of pension funds, the relief of poverty, and the achievement of equality of opportunity.

It is surely difficult to defend property as a constitutional liberty on a par with other political and civic rights. One obvious reason why there is a disanalogy between property and the conventional list of constitutional liberties is that there is a rivalness implicit in the exercise of property rights that is not present in the other cases. Thus, if I exercise my freedom of religion that does not necessarily impair your exercise of your freedom of religion; if I express my political opinions, that does not prevent you from expressing your political opinions; and, if I am protected by the principles of the rule of law, that does not prevent you from being protected by the same principles. The exercise of property rights, by contrast, does involve excluding others from exercising the same rights. If I lay claim to a piece of property, then you cannot lay claim to the same piece of property. There may be cases, of course, where exercising one's constitutional liberties does prevent others from exercising those same liberties, as with the well-known example of everyone exercising their right to freedom of expression in the same room simultaneously, thus rendering nugatory the value of the right. However, these are cases where circumstances militate against the general exercise of the right. Property rights by contrast are intrinsically rival claims, since the right to property comprises such rights as exclusive use, possession and disposal.

It is difficult to see, therefore, how a limitation could be imposed on the scope of popular government to prevent it from interfering with property if such a limitation were to be justified in terms of autonomy. Indeed, if such policies as the development of social security schemes are viewed as creating a form of 'new' property, and if the provision of adequate income maintenance can be viewed as a necessary condition for preserving autonomy, then the taxation necessary to finance extensive schemes of social security may well be justified by appeal to the value of autonomy rather than conflict with it (Weale 1983, pp. 60–1). A similar point may be made in respect of environmental or health and safety regulation. If there is no right to property of the same class as a right to constitutional freedoms, then the regulation of the employment of property for productive purposes cannot be outwith the legitimate sphere of government activity. To allege that such regulation may reduce marketed output below the level that would otherwise have occurred with a system of free contract between property-owner and worker is irrelevant in this context. Efficiency considerations are consequent upon the definition of property rights; to regulate matters of environmental amenity or occupational health and safety is to modify the definition of property rights and not simply to limit their exercise.

II Generalized interests other than autonomy

Autonomy interests have pride of place among the generalized interests that are invoked in a constitutional dialogue. However, they are not the only interests that may be invoked. The question naturally arises, therefore, as to what other generalized interests may be appealed to. In this section I wish to develop the suggestion that these interests, whatever they might be, can be described by reference to one or more of three properties: namely, that they are long-term, universalizable among members of a given population group, and common to members of that population group.

The notion that it is long-term interests that are part of a community's generalizable interests is one that needs some defence, not least because it has been an ancient criticism of popular decision-making that it leads to a neglect of such interests. Why should one's interests not be identified with what is to one's benefit in the short term? After all, it has been argued (Parfit 1984, pp. 117–94) that a 'critical present aims' theory is the best account of rationality.

Suppose, however, that one can make a valid distinction between long- and short-term interests (it is difficult to see how the phenomenon of regret is possible unless this distinction is allowed). Then, although it may be possible for persons to act on their short-term interests, it is difficult to see how an appeal to short-term interests could be more potent in a constitutional dialogue than long-term interests. The latter, by definition, pick out relatively permanent features of human welfare, and this alone suggests that they represent interests that are generalizable in a way that short-term interests are not.

A common technique for protecting one's long-term interests is to put the attainment of short-term objectives beyond one's reach – the case of Ulysses binding himself to the mast, in the various forms that Elster (1979) has discussed. It might seem, therefore, as though one of the ways in which democracies might protect their long-term interests would be by putting certain decisions beyond their own reach, rather in the way that individual autonomy is protected by preventing popular governments from legislating in normal or standard ways on matters of constitutional liberties. Such an argument has been advanced in a specific form by Buchanan (1986, pp. 187–226), who claims that there is a persistent bias in democracy towards attention to the short term. The vote motive of politicians seeking to be elected makes it difficult to face the hard choices that governments need to make when they encounter economic setbacks. Consequently there is a tendency for democracies to use deficit financing to cushion themselves against short-term deterioration in economic prosperity. The consequence is erosion of the capital assets on which the long-term prosperity of the society depends. The solution, as Buchanan sees it, is to impose a constitutional restriction upon the ability of governments to finance their spending programmes by means of deficits.

There is much technical detail in this argument. To some extent one's attitude will depend on whether one thinks the depreciation of capital assets is a logical consequence of the use of deficits, as Buchanan himself believes, or whether it is a putative empirical consequence arising from a 'crowding-out' effect. However, such technical questions are in a sense secondary to the philosophical issue of whether this is the sort of consideration that would be allowed at the stage of a constitutional convention or dialogue. In principle, it is difficult to see why it should not be allowed. If appeal is to be made to generalized interests, then the long-term consequences of a decision procedure appear to fall into that category. If it is a genuine empirical truth that democracies are prone to the temptation of the short term, then it would seem relevant to identify this as a problem at the stage of constitutional design.

The test to be applied in deciding the weight the point should bear can also be established in terms of a theory of dialogue. Presumably, if appeal is to be made to generalized interests, then it needs to be established that those generalized interests are threatened by adopting or failing to adopt a particular procedure, and the way to do this is to show how those interests are affected by intersubjectively usable empirical procedures. Hence, it is *prima facie* evidence for the proponents of balanced budgets that high welfare spending appears to be associated with relatively low levels of capital formation and consequently higher rates of unemployment (Cameron 1985). Whether the evidence is so compelling as to provide a watertight case for balance-budget constitutional restriction is, of course, an open question. What matters in the present context is that the appeal to putative generalized interests must rest upon presumed empirical claims. *Ex hypothesi*, such claims are refutable in terms of potential empirical evidence.

However, it has been asserted (Brennan and Buchanan 1985, p. 59) that all such evidence must be discounted to allow for the effect of Hume's principle, which states that, even if politicians are not rogues, we should design our political institutions on the assumption that they are, to avoid the dangers associated with tyranny. Yet this appeal to Hume is difficult to allow in the case of constitutional dialogue. It rests upon one of two assumptions. Either it is a generalization from experience, in which case it is no better founded than the original proposition about the tendency of democratic governments to damage their own long-term interests, or it rests upon a particular attitude to risk, requiring that we weigh the worst case option in our deliberations more heavily than the others. Yet, as a number of discussions of contract theory have established (for example, Barry 1973; Harsanyi 1975; Sen 1970, p. 140) risk aversion is not a generalizable interest. Appeal to Hume's principle cannot, therefore, be an uncontentious move within a constitutional dialogue, and it cannot, therefore, form a sound principle of constitutional design.

It is plausible to believe that universalizable interests might also be invoked at the stage of constitutional dialogue. If the purpose of the dialogue is to persuade participants to accept certain reasons for restraining their conduct by reference to constitutional norms, then universalizable interests are by definition those which appeal to all members of the dialogue. Yet this apparently self-evident truth has striking consequences. Consider James Mill's argument that the existence of costs to political participation entails a limit on the franchise as it applies to members of a population. Although the application of Mill's argument to categories of persons leads to absurdities, the form of the argument is none the less valid. Since political participation involves a cost, those for whom the costs are high will seek to avoid a situation in which issues are determined contrary to their interests by virtue of the participation of others in the political process. It is not implausible to suppose, therefore, that, if the costs of participation are high, it is appropriate to limit participation in the making of decisions.

The argument seems absurd when it is applied to categories of persons. Is it absurd, however, when it is applied to categories of activities? Suppose, for example, that there were certain policy decisions that could either be decided by the participation of those who were directly affected by the policy or instead by appointed officials accountable to representatives with a broad range of responsibilities. Policies on the location or funding of schools or hospitals might fall into this category. Suppose one had an interest in these matters, but that the cost of political participation as the price of promoting that interest was high, and that one was without the prospect of success. Then it might be preferable, as a second best, to avoid the option of participation and delegate much of the decision-making to appointed officials who were none the less accountable, in the sense of having to answer for, their decisions. Such an example is not fanciful. The vast bulk of decision-making in the welfare state takes this form, contrary to the prediction of Myrdal (1960), who saw 'beyond the welfare state' to a form of policy in which decision-making by citizens would be central and widespread.

The crucial point in the argument, however, is that one would prescribe absence of participation not only for oneself but for others as well. It has seemed obvious for these who favour participation to say what they are demanding is participation as a right rather than as a duty. Yet the effective exercise of such a right is not universalizable, since it excludes the participation of those for whom the relevant costs are high. An inflation of the claim of participation might well not be echoed widely in a constitutional dialogue by those who anticipated that participation would be expensive of time and energy best spent elsewhere. This argument from the non-universalizability of the interest of participation would complement those of a more general kind that are sceptical of participatory claims on such grounds as the need to ensure that governments retain a functional capacity to deliver public services, which can only be ensured if they remain free from day-to-day political pressures (Sharpe 1973, pp. 129–68)

The third property of generalizable interests is that they should be common to members of a group. It hardly needs arguing that interests of this kind might acceptably be introduced into a constitutional dialogue. To point out that there is an interest whose promotion would benefit all is the simplest way of appealing to a generalized interest. Paradoxically, its implementation may be the most difficult to achieve. To say that there is an arrangement that if adopted would promote everyone's interests is to say that existing arrangements leave members of the community inside the Pareto frontier. Yet it may prove impossible to identify such arrangements. The simplest example is provided by the phenomenon of vote-trading. It has been shown that situations in which vote-trading will arise are just those in which the Arrow problem of social intransitivity exists, yet the pervasiveness of the latter suggests that the former may be difficult to eradicate.

III Acceptability

Do the conclusions to which the above arguments lead survive the test of reflective equilibrium? This is a difficult question to answer, since there is always likely to be a high degree of subjective assessment in the response. What is in accord with my settled convictions may not be in accord with yours, and fighting another round of the theoretical dialectic may simply leave us both exhausted. So the test of acceptability is going to be irreducibly personal. Certainly the problem of the relationship between constitutional rights and majority rule has been present in modern democratic theory from Schumpeter's allusions to the problem of minorities and Dahl's elegant exposition of the problem of intense preferences (Dahl 1956). Here the difficulty surely is to identify a theory that will explain and account for the conflict of two *prima facie* attractive principles rather than dispute the conclusion that they are in conflict. The appeal to generalizable interests other than autonomy interests seems more open-textured. I find it difficult to see how it could be irrelevant to point out that certain types of decision procedure can lead to a sacrifice of long-term interests to short-term ones. Naturally the empirical evidence on which this claim rests may be disputed, but that is not to question the validity of the theory, merely to question whether it holds under the conjectured circumstances. Similarly, I find it difficult to see how it can be denied that democracy may be limited if participation costs are high or outcomes Pareto-inferior. The extent to which these are genuine problems will vary with the political culture of different societies. And even ardent democrats find it difficult to change political cultures by prescription.

4

Politics *with* Romance: Towards a Theory of Democratic Socialism

Geoffrey Brennan

It is a central tenet of the democratic-socialist theory of politics that majoritarian collective decision-making with universal franchise can be depended upon to produce social outcomes that are generally both egalitarian and in the 'public interest'. Or at least I shall take this to be so, and for the purposes of this essay shall treat such a tenet as democratic socialism's characteristic feature. The question that I shall be concerned with is how this tenet might be grounded.

That some such grounding is required may not seem obvious. The common view of democracy is manifestly a heroic one – we are, after all, all democrats now. To brand a person or an attitude or a policy as 'undemocratic' is commonly seen as being a self-evidently decisive critique: it is to remove that person or attitude or policy from the domain of discourse among reasonable people.

Yet the possibility of a heroic view of democratic politics *has* been questioned explicitly in recent times – at least at the level of political theorizing. Scholars within the increasingly influential 'public choice' tradition have argued that the heroic view of democratic process has never been properly argued or supported, and indeed that subjecting democratic process to proper analytic scrutiny reveals just how precarious any such heroic view must be.

In fact, the title of this essay derives from the title of one written by the central figure in public choice scholarship, James Buchanan. The title of that earlier paper (Buchanan 1984) is 'Politics *without* Romance', a phrase that is seen by Buchanan to characterize the central thrust of public choice theory. As Buchanan there describes it, 'Public choice theory has been the avenue through which a romantic and illusory set of notions about the workings of government and the behaviour of persons who govern has been replaced by a set of notions that embody more skepticism about what governments can do and what governors will do, notions that are surely more consistent with the political reality that we may all observe around us . . .' (p. 11). And he goes on to identify the assumption 'that the state, that politics, somehow works its way toward some transcendent "public good" ' as the 'socialist mystique' (p. 12). So construed, public choice appears as an explicit, calculated attack on democratic-socialist doctrine. Moreover, Buchanan is not the only person who so identifies it. This is a perception that is also shared by many of public choice theory's most vigorous critics. One notable line of criticism in this connection is precisely that public choice is more oriented towards anti-government rhetoric than truth, and its proponents are more interested 'in economics as an ideology than as a science' (Quiggin 1987, p. 10). This line runs in the face of public choice theory's own vigorous defence of its 'scientific' status. As Buchanan puts it in 'Politics without Romance',

> I do not want to appear to place too much emphasis on the normative implications of public choice theory. These implications can stand on their own, and they can be allowed to emerge as they will (or will not) from the positive analysis. The *theory* of public choice, as such, is or can be a wholly positive theory, wholly scientific and *wertfrei* in the standard meanings of these terms. The implications for the comparative evaluation of institutions have to do with methods of making such comparisons, not with specific results. . . . It seems to be nothing more than simple and obvious wisdom to compare social institutions as they might be expected actually to operate rather than to compare romantic models of how such institutions might be hoped to operate. (Buchanan 1984, p. 12)

In this essay I shall attempt to show how public choice theory and its method of analysis might be used to develop a heroic theory of democratic politics – or at least to show that the sort of heroic view that social-democratic theory requires is not necessarily undermined by the public choice approach. There are two aspects of that approach that will be most relevant here. One is that public choice theory offers a procedure for normative political theorizing that is somewhat different from the standard one. It is a procedure that I basically endorse and which I shall argue for in section I. The second issue involves the assumptions about human motivation that are appropriate in political analysis. The standard motivational assumption made in public choice theory is that all political agents are best modelled as if they act so as to maximize their incomes. That is, public choice imports its motivational assumptions directly from the conventional economics of markets. This has proved to be the most controversial aspect of the whole public choice programme and is often seen to be the aspect of the theory that is most significant ideologically: in other words, the assumption that political agents are predominantly self-interested is seen to be primarily responsible for the political scepticism to which public-choice analysis allegedly gives rise. In what follows, I shall indicate the grounds on which public choice theorists have justified the use of *homo economicus* in politics and the grounds on which its use has been attacked (section III). My general argument is that the line of argument that public choice theorists have used is conceptually correct, but has been inappropriately applied – a position that I justify in section IV. Specifically I shall argue that public choice theory, properly understood, need not rule out a heroic view of democratic politics, and furthermore that the possibility of this heroic view can be interpreted as constituting the analytic basis for a democratic-socialist theory of politics. Alternatively put, public choice theory does leave much room for romance in politics. Indeed, as I shall argue, politics *without* romance is like no democratic politics we know.

The two strands of argument at stake here are interconnected in interesting ways. In the first place, the conception of normative political theory that public choice theory advances depends on certain assumptions about human motivation that are worth exposing – not least because there is some question as to the coherence of some sorts of normative theorizing given the *homo economicus* construct. I shall explore this connection in section II. In the second place, the particular model of political behaviour that I shall develop has implications for normative political theory and how this is to be under- stood – implications that I shall point up in section IV. Section V offers a brief summary and conclusion.

I Two notions of political theory

Economists believe that a good sense of what is feasible in social affairs is a crucial prerequisite of proper ethical judgement.[1] A major part of the economist's social function, as the profession perceives it, is to remind the public at large of generalized scarcity, of the necessity of making hard choices, of the absence of free lunches. Economists hold (correctly in my view) that, if there is to be anything at all to the idea of social theory, it must be the case that not all imaginable worlds are feasible. They also hold that a proper understanding of *which* worlds are feasible is absolutely crucial to any normative social theory: if one's understandings of the world are wrong, one's ethical judgements about the whole range of social issues can be right only by accident. There is indeed a conjecture, argued vigorously by Milton Friedman in 'The Methodology of Positive Economics', and probably widely accepted within the profession, that most disagreements in practical politics arise from disagreements about how the world works rather than from differences in values. The implication is that intellectual attention should be directed towards understanding the way the world works, rather than exploring values. Disagreements about how the world should be may well turn out to be irrelevant because the possibilities being compared turn out to be infeasible: much waste of time and energy in pointless disagreements about values could, so the line goes, be avoided if only we took the trouble to attend first to understanding the way the world works. And, in achieving such understanding, attention to the *constraints* – natural, institutional and human – on possible social outcomes is crucial.

This position is to some extent informed by the intellectual history of economics, and it may be useful here to offer a simple illustration. Consider the medieval notion of the 'just price'. This notion no longer plays any role in the economist's theory of markets. Virtually all economists regard its demise as a 'good thing'. They argue that any *proper* explanation of why prices (and outputs) are what they are must make appeal to the interaction of forces of demand and supply. Whether the price so generated is 'just' or not, or, indeed, what exactly a 'just price' would be, is simply irrelevant. Or, at least, such questions do not help explain *how* the market works. They might well bear on the evaluation of the market as an institution, but this is a second-level question and one, moreover, that can only be answered once the way the market works is properly understood. Further, once that understanding is gained, the normative significance of any particular price is itself seen in a different light: ethical attention tends to be redirected towards the 'justice' of the market system as a whole, and away from the idea of a just price for each traded good.

Public choice theorists tend to interpret their enterprise in much the same terms as the replacement of the medieval just-price doctrine by demand-and-supply analysis. They see public choice analysis as an attempt to *explain* what has hitherto been treated solely as a matter of ethics – a sort of triumph of science over superstition. For, if political processes *can* be analysed in terms of the demand – supply apparatus in its relevant political reformulation, then the ethical element in explaining *how* political processes work is very substantially diminished if not obliterated entirely. Of course, ethical elements will reappear to the extent that alternative political arrangements are to be evaluated – but, in the public choice view, it is simply a mistake to introduce those elements as part of the explanatory account. Particular public policies are to be seen as emerging from the interactions of rational agents, all pursuing their particular and partially conflicting goals within the framework imposed by democratic political institutions: 'just policy' is about as relevant in explaining what occurs as the 'just price' is in market interactions.

In short, then, public choice theorists insist on applying to politics the same sort of two-stage evaluative procedure that economists apply to markets: at the first stage, we are to apply our objective analysis to the explanation of political outcomes; at the second stage, we can evaluate those outcomes and *thereby* assess the institutional process by which those outcomes are generated. The first task is necessarily positive in character; the second, necessarily normative. Moreover, the public choice line is that this two-stage evaluation procedure gives rise to a normative political theory very different from that traditionally offered in political philosophy or political science. The latter sort of 'political theory' involves little more, as public choice theorists see it, than spelling out the normative criteria by which particular political outcomes (policies, candidates or whatever) or political institutions should be evaluated. Political theory, so interpreted, is simply a branch of social ethics (much like just-price doctrine): it involves a minimal analytic component, and even that minimal component tends to be subsumed under considerations of how the normative criteria are to be properly specified, rather than being offered as an independent piece of analysis and available for explicit examination. Public choice theorists are inclined to scoff at this approach on the grounds that it presumes a 'benevolent despot' model of government. And it is not difficult to see the force of this description: the mere fact of applying normative criteria directly to policy outcomes seems to imply that governments possess both the *power* to change policies in the direction the criteria indicate and the *inclination* to do so. Even so, normative theorizing does not in itself necessarily imply any particular model of government, and it seems doubtful whether the benevolent-despot model is one that traditional political theorists would endorse. The particular contribution of the public choice conception of normative political theory is not so much the attack on the benevolent-despot model *per se* as it is the characteristic *separation* of positive analysis from ethical evaluation, and the greatly expanded *role* of the positive analytic component.

Two aspects of this public choice conception are worth noting at this point. The first is that politics and political institutions are to be evaluated *instrumentally*, by reference to the outcomes or pattern of outcomes that the institutions generate. The evaluative system must therefore be consequentialist in style.[2] This is perhaps not surprising given the utilitarian origins of much welfare economics.[3] And it is an approach so natural to economists that many might feel it unthinkable that any other approach could be legitimate. It is therefore worth emphasizing that normative theories of politics of a deontological kind are by no means unknown and, as I shall argue in section IV, may have a certain relevance that consequentialist theories lack.

The second point about this two-tier evaluation procedure is that it naturally invites what Buchanan has called a 'constitutional' approach. That is, the domain of normative evaluation is not so much particular policies as the political institutions from which those policies emerge. This is because policies are naturally 'packaged' together under the political institutions from which they arise: policy A can only be altered by altering the rules of the political game of which policy A is the solution, and such a change in the rules will also alter the equilibrium policy outcomes across the whole range of government activities. Of course, the evaluative criteria may be applied to particular policies, but only as an input to the more general exercise of institutional evaluation: ultimately, one can only change the rules of the game, not who wins each play.[4]

II The two-tier theory and motivational assumptions

The two-tier theory of normative evaluation which public choice endorses involves a clear separation of positive analysis and normative evaluation. It should be clear that any such separation rests on assumptions concerning human motivation. Consider the 'just price' analogy yet again. Suppose specifically that all individuals in their market transactions were strongly motivated by considerations of justice. Then individual buyers and sellers would be constrained by internal motivational considerations only to buy and sell at prices that were not too far from those that justice required. If this were so, no satisfactory account of the way that markets work could proceed without some understanding of prevailing notions of justice: the 'just price' doctrine would be, in some measure, revivified. It is, however, important to distinguish between the explanatory and evaluative uses of the concept of justice here. Justice in the explanatory setting becomes relevant only to the extent that it does, as a matter of fact, motivate agents in their market roles. And the concept of justice relevant to this exercise is the one those agents actually use. Whether that is the 'correct' notion of justice is immaterial. By contrast, in *evaluating* market outcomes, justice is (or is not) relevant independently of whether it actually motivates agent behaviour; and the relevant concept of justice is the 'correct' one, so far as it can be discerned.

Now, as is well known, public choice theory adopts, in most applications, the motivational assumptions used most commonly in the economic theory of markets. In fact, the motivational apparatus used in economics is somewhat complex. For certain purposes (and most notably for deriving propositions about the normative properties of alternative institutions) *relatively* modest assumptions (namely, that agents act purposively and that their purposes are in conflict) are all that is required. In making positive predictions, however, it is necessary to specify something concrete about what those agents' purposes (or 'utility functions') are, but again the assumptions required vary according to the nature of the predictions at stake. For many comparative static propositions (i.e. propositions that seek to explain why the world changes in the way it does) the assumption that wealth is *one* of the arguments in agents' utility functions is all that is required. Propositions of a stronger kind which attempt to explain why the world is as it is typically require stronger assumptions – and specifically that wealth is the *only* argument in agents' utility functions.

A simply example may help here. Consider the proposition that individuals choose their asset portfolios so that the net-of-risk, net-of-tax rates of return on all assets are equalized. This is a proposition of the stronger kind, and requires the assumption that net expected wealth is the only argument in agents' utility functions. This proposition may turn out to be false – but a weaker proposition may still hold: namely, that changes in relative rates of return (net-of-tax and risk premia) will induce agents to demand more of the more profitable asset and less of the less profitable one. This weaker proposition requires the weaker motivational assumption that wealth is one argument (among potentially many others) in agents' utility functions.

By and large, public choice theorists have been inclined to adopt motivational assumptions of the strong form: they have generally taken agents to be egoistic in the simple wealth-maximizing sense. This *homo economicus* postulate has a distinguished pedigree in economics, and despite its simplicity and possible implausibility has been shown to work tolerably well for a wide range of applications in conventional market analysis. It is, economists claim, a matter of empirical record that this motivational postulate works very much better in explaining why prices are what they are than any comparably general and empirically convenient assumption, including specifically the postulate that agents are primarily (or even significantly) concerned with the *justice* of particular prices. On this basis, public choice theorists have simply absorbed *homo economicus* into political analysis, with very little in the way of further argument. I intend to explore the argument that seems to underlie such extrapolation in the next section.

At *this* point it is worth exposing a possible logical difficulty that the two-tier evaluative procedure, with its obliteration of normative considerations at the explanatory level, seems to confront. If it is correct that all agents can be satisfactorily assumed to be motivated in their market and political roles by predominant self-interest, how can any place for normative evaluation remain? To retain a consistent motivational scheme, it would seem necessary to postulate self-interest at the level of institutional evaluation, as elsewhere in human choice. The public choice response to this charge, among those few who have taken the difficulty seriously, is to emphasize that the normative analysis in their two-step procedure occurs at a different level of abstraction from that of ordinary choice – whether market or political. Decisions on alternative policies take place at an 'in-period' level in which agents know their particular interests and hence can be modelled more or less in *homo economicus* terms. The evaluation of alternative *institutions*, however, takes place at a more abstract 'constitutional' level, in which individuals are uncertain as to what their particular positions will be over the long future in which the institutions are in place. Such uncertainty about one's own future position induces each to take a more general view of what is desirable – outcomes must be good in the relevant *expected* sense, which involves taking account of the valuations of that outcome in any of the positions in which the agent could find himself. Self-interest thus remains the basic motivation but is transformed into *general* interest by radical uncertainty about which future role will be occupied. This concern with general interest is, then, to be interpreted as proxying for normative evaluation.

Whether this line of argument is entirely persuasive depends on the extent to which one believes that normative categories can be subsumed under generalized notions of self-interest. On this matter I am sceptical. It seems to me that, if normative political theory is to be a genuinely interesting enterprise, it must be the case that ethical considerations make some claim on one's attentions independent of self-interest. When I describe a policy or political arrangement as a 'good' one, it is not obvious that I am saying merely that it is a good one for *me*, or even for all *like* me, and even with my own good interpreted in the relevant constitutional terms.

However, this whole issue can to some extent be finessed by assigning *homo economicus* motivations a rather more modest role. Suppose we allow that wealth-maximizing considerations constitute the predominant concern at the 'in-period' level of actual choice, but that independent ethical considerations weigh also, though in a rather minor way. By contrast, at the constitutional level, precisely because of uncertainty about what institutions would promote self-interest best, these ethical considerations would tend to play a rather more significant role. We could then see the constitutional 'veil of ignorance' construction as tending to modify the conflict between self-interest and ethics without arguing necessarily that that conflict is obliterated, or that ethics can be ultimately reduced to generalized self-interest. Moreover, the motivational structure assumed here would be sufficient to generate all the comparative static results in standard market analysis. The modest shift away from the very strong form of the *homo economicus* assumption typically used in public choice theory takes little away from conventional economics, and enables us to avoid possible conceptual difficulties in admitting the relevance of any normative considerations (beyond those derived from the agent's self-interest). As I shall attempt to show in what follows, however, this apparently modest motivational shift has significant implications for the possible role of normative considerations in collective decision-making contexts, and for the possibility of a heroic view of politics. Because the motivational assumptions are so crucial, it is worthwhile briefly examining the reasoning that has led public choice analysis to incorporate *homo economicus* into politics. We shall then turn to the main analytic proposition in this essay, and to its implications for the role of ethics in in-period politics.

III The public choice case for *homo economicus* in politics and the standard response

The standard argument used in public choice theory for the use of *homo economicus* in politics is essentially a methodological one. The central proposition is that the same basic motivational structure must be applied in analysing individual behaviour in all institutional settings and specifically in both political and market contexts. To assume that individuals behave by reference to one set of motives in collective decision-making contexts and to another in decentralized decision-making contexts has seemed to public choice theorists both to postulate an implausible schizophrenia in human behaviour and to risk introducing ideological bias into institutional comparisons. In particular, if individuals in their market choices are to be treated as if totally self-interested and in their political choices as if predominantly public-interested then there does appear to be a bias towards collective as against decentralized action (towards government over markets) automatically built into the analysis. Since a major concern of public-choice theory has been with precisely this question (i.e. with the normative properties of collective as opposed to decentralized decision-making devices[5]), any such in-built bias is clearly unsatisfactory. In short, there is a clear methodological requirement of 'motivational neutrality', and it is on this basis that *homo economicus* is imported into politics. Any attack on the use of *homo economicus* in politics is seen equally to be an attack on its use in market analysis: the case for *homo economicus* stands or falls across the board. And the usefulness of the *homo economicus* construction in the market context is well attested from the record in conventional economics. *Ergo*, the case for *homo economicus* in politics is taken to be unexceptionable.

The standard attack on this line (apart from blank horror, charges of 'undemocratic sentiment', and the like) is predominantly empirical. There is occasional opposition to the motivational neutrality premise as such (including foreshadowings of the line that I shall develop in the next section[6]), but for the most part the argument is focused on evidence *against homo economicus* in the political context specifically. The *prima facie* evidence involves, *inter alia*, the following points.

1 Political advertising, political debate and political rhetoric make much appeal to ethical and ideological categories ('justice', 'efficiency', 'moral probity', and so on) and relatively little to the particular interests of particular voters. Standard political aphorisms of the Kennnedy kind (such as 'Do not ask what your country can do for you: ask rather what you can do for your country') seem to have some political potency, but are the very reverse of what a *homo economicus* treatment would lead us to expect.

2   If voters were rational egoists, it seems unlikely that turn-out would be anything like as large in large electorates as it actually is. The probability that the vote of a single individual will prove decisive (i.e. of a tie among all other voters under simple majority rule) becomes quite small as the voting population increases, so that, even if the income stakes are quite high for particular voters, the expected return to voting remains negligible unless turn-out is expected to be unhistorically low (rather less than 1 per cent in a US presidential election, say).

3   Studies of individual voting behaviour seem to indicate little support for the *homo economicus* postulate. Many voters appear to vote habitually, or in the way their parents voted, or in such a way as to locate themselves in the social structure, or in a manner they think best for the community as a whole. Few appear to be motivated predominantly by narrow self-interest, even where there are issues that might affect that interest significantly.

4   There is some evidence that politicans' ideological positions explain their voting behaviour better than do constituent interests.[7]

It is not appropriate here to attempt to weigh all the evidence and provide a careful evaluation. As in most contexts, there are major problems of interpretation even where the data are good – which they often are not. However, what does at least seem totally clear is that *in politics* the balance of the evidence in favour of *homo economicus* is not as decisive as it appears to be in market settings. The methodological principle of motivational neutrality seems to be under empirical attack.

The attack may be more apparent than real, however. As I have already noted, the strict *homo economicus* construction in the strong form used in standard public choice analysis is not necessary to generate the comparative static results that make up the major part of conventional market economics. The fact that such comparative static results are empirically robust cannot then be adduced as evidence in favour of *homo economicus*. Much in conventional economics would survive intact if agent motivations were assumed to *include*, but not be *restricted* to, wealth maximization. Specifically, one could allow for considerable altruism and/or ethical concern on the part of agents without undermining much in the traditional corpus. In this event, however, behaviour in the market setting may be expected to diverge from political behaviour to the extent that the altruism is collective in nature or ethical principles are defined over *social* as distinct from individual outcomes. For familiar free-rider reasons, individuals in decentralized choice settings will not necessarily find it rational to make unilateral transfers to the poor, or possible to act to bring about some 'social outcome' that is effectively inaccessible to individual action. Confronted with relevant alternatives in the collective context, however, individuals will rationally vote to give effect to their altruism or their ethically informed references over social outcomes. In this way, it might be argued, public choice theorists, in applying strict *homo economicus* motivations in politics, compound three errors. First, they fail to recognize that their application of the egoistic assumption in politics is much more demanding than the analogous application in conventional market settings. Second, they fail to see that an apparently modest change in that assumption could involve quite significant differences in market and political behaviour without any sacrifice of the general 'rational actor' apparatus. And, third, they fail to recognize that the assumption gives a distinct anti-collectivist bias to institutional comparison.[8]

This line of reasoning is worth taking seriously, but it is not entirely compelling. For one thing, it cannot explain all the puzzles that the critics of public choice pose. In particular, it cannot give a satisfactory account of the level of turn-out, because, if each voter knows others to be 'rationally' altruistic or otherwise motivated by public interest, then he has *less* incentive to vote. Moreover, it is not clear how important the alleged anti-collectivist bias that *homo economicus* assumptions are supposed to establish really are. Any altruism or instrumental social ethic can be expected to influence individuals' market behaviour to some extent, and hence moderate the degree of 'market failure' as conventionally measured.

Equally, provided agents remain self-interested to any significant extent, then much of the flavour of standard public choice results will remain. If a genuinely heroic view of politics is to be mounted – one of the kind that democratic-socialist theory would seem to require – something more than a gesture in a direction away from egoistic political behaviour is needed. It will not be enough simply to throw a bit of altruism into individuals' utility functions. In what follows, I shall sketch briefly what I believe to be a more satisfactory line.

IV Ethics in politics

If we are to give an account of the role and significance of ethics as an element in political process, we shall need something that carries us further than merely assuming agents to be ethically motivated in some measure: we shall want an account of why ethical matters become *disproportionately* more significant in collective than in decentralized decision-making contexts. And such an account, to be persuasive to conventional public choice scholars, must be consistent with basic axioms of rational conduct. It is such an argument that I here seek to provide.

Because I have stated the line of reasoning involved at some length in other settings,[9] the discussion here can be brief. It is an argument about the nature of voting, and, in particular, an explanation of why ethical considerations are likely to weigh much more than self-interest does in the voter's 'rational calculus' as to how to vote. The crucial observation is that, just as an individual's interests cannot explain his going to the polls, neither can it explain the individual's vote once he gets there. Unless the individual's casting his vote for candidate/position A induces others to do so, the only situation in which the individual can influence electoral outcomes is one in which there is an exact tie among all other voters. Clearly, then, the probability that a single voter will have a decisive influence on the outcome is very small in large electorates, and neither the individual's presence at the polls nor the direction of his vote can be explained (solely) in instrumental terms. Focusing on the latter aspect, it is clear that there is a crucial difference between the electoral context and some corresponding market choice, in that in the market context the chooser is decisive – the opportunity cost of choosing A is B forgone. In the electoral setting, by contrast, the outcome is *detached* from the individual's expression of preference. The opportunity cost of voting for A is not B forgone, but merely a *vote* for B forgone: whether A wins depends negligibly on how I vote, and almost entirely on how everyone else votes. Hence, voting is to be construed as an 'expression of support', not as an act of choice among candidates or policies. And there may be any number of reasons why an individual may express support for a candidate or policy that he would not *choose*. One obvious such case is where the voter preceives the candidate or policy to be good or desirable overall and thereby 'worthy of support' on that voter's own ethical reckoning, but inimical to his own particular interests. It is entirely rational for the voter to vote for that policy even though he would not choose it in an analogous market setting. If an individual has *any* inclination to express support for A, then the expected cost to him (in terms of personal wealth forgone) of indulging that inclination is negligible. Interests will be relatively significant in the market where individual agents are decisive: at the ballot box, what predominates is better described as 'expressive considerations', the things that weigh in inducing a voter to express support for one candidate or policy rather than another. It is worth emphasizing here that there is no change in the underlying utility function as we move from maket place to ballot box, and certainly no repudiation of the basic axioms of rational choice theory. What changes is the institutional gearing that translates that same underlying motivational structure into different behavioural patterns.

Moving from this general observation to a theory of electoral behaviour requires us to say something further about those attributes of rival candidates/policies that seem most likely to engage the expressive dimension in voters' minds. Several possibilities suggest themselves. The candidate may have attributes (colourful personality, good looks – a generally 'attractive' persona) with which voters seek to identify. Or the candidate or policies or party may project an image which can be used by the voter to locate himself socially or ideologically. Or, most important for the argument here, the candidate or policies may in some way engage the ethical passions of the voter.

That is, the voter may endorse ethical or political *principles* for which he seeks to express support in the casting of his vote. Such possibilities are the *result*, not the rejection, of rational electoral conduct.

A simple example from Tullock (1971) illustrates. Our representative voter, J, values transfers to a clearly identifiable set of needy persons, 'the poor', at five cents for every dollar that the poor's income rises. The poor number one eleventh of the population, so that a dollar transferred to all members of the poor costs each member of the rest of the population, J included, ten cents. Consequently, J will not make any transfers to any poor persons unilaterally: it would cost him one dollar for something he values at only five cents. Moreover, J will not voluntarily enter any co-opertaive deal to transfer from everyone to the poor: that collective transfer programme would cost him ten cents for something he values at only five cents. Hence, if he knew he was to be decisive on the collective decision regarding the transfer programme, J would vote against it. However, J knows that there is little chance that he will be decisive – so little, in fact, that it hardly pays him to work out what the collective programme would cost him (in extra taxes, say) or even what precise value he places on having the lot of the poor improved. There is no point in entertaining some irrelevant calculus. What is relevant is that J likes to think of himself as a generous person. He believes people ought, in principle, to support the poor. The notion that he might, by his own action, cause his own taxes to rise hardly seems relevant – and if he *did* allow such considerations to inhibit his own generosity he would doubtless feel rather guilty about it. Faced with one candidate who stands for generosity and sensitivity towards the poor, and another who stands for callousness towards the poor and parsimony in the use of welfare funds, J finds himself drawn to support the former: Scrooge *after* his brush with the Christmas ghosts is surely a more *attractive* candidate than Scrooge *before*. Expressed in terms of a hypothetical decision calculus, the expected cost involved in voting for the post-ghost Scrooge is negligible: it is the net five cents per dollar transferred (five cents benefit minus ten cents cost) multiplied by the probability that there will be an exact tie among all other voters. If the number of voters is at all large, that expected cost cannot be greater than a few cents, whereas the expected *benefit* is the value J places on acting in accord with the dictates of his conscience – acting so as to express the principles which would lie unexpressed in other settings where the cost of expressing them is much higher.

Now, it is clear that, if voters vote according to their moral principles, then electoral competition will tend to constrain politicians to articulate those moral principles as an important part of their policy platforms. In order to secure support, politicians will have to be seen to embrace those principles – and this not so much because voters vote to bring about outcomes in accordance with their ethical norms as because the public expression of those ethical norms calls forth voter support (a little like cheering for a favoured team in a sporting event). The politician or party must be seen clearly to represent or instantiate those principles: policies will then be selected that reflect those principles; political rhetoric must uphold those principles and politicians' 'private' conduct must not be inconsistent with them. The politician who is involved in sex scandals, or lies about qualifications or plagiarizes other politicians' speeches[10] is unlikely to be elected, even though his continued capacity to produce goodies for supportive constituents is in no way doubted.

Ethics thus enters the political process. Being elected involves, among other things, articulating attractive ethical principles. And it may even be that the best route to being successful in such an exercise is genuinely to believe the moral principles one articulates. An electorally successfully statesman – one who calls the citizenry back to their own ethical convictions – is not a contradiction in terms (though, for reasons I shall mention shortly, is not necessarily typical either). A heroic view of the *possibilities* of politics is *not* incoherent, and does not call for either a sacrifice of basic rationality axioms or for a totally implausible psychology.

However, while ethical principles are among the things that might generate expressions of electoral support, they do not exhaust the set by any means. Voters may, given that the consequences of their actions are divorced from the action itself, simply vote inconsequentially – from whimsy, or fancy, or convenience (as in numbering candidates in the order they appear on the ballot paper). Or it may be that passions other than moral passions predominate in voters' decisions – anger, xenophobia, spite, hatred.[11] In other words, the possibility of politics as an ethical exercise should not encourage complacency. There is no guarantee that ethical considerations will predominate. It is, however, possible – and plausible – that ethical considerations will bear in electoral politics in a way and to an extent that they will not bear in settings where the individual's choice over outcome is decisive: the market place is the notable exemplar.

If this is accepted, a further point follows. The way in which ethics bears in politics is not neutral among different kinds of ethical theory. Furthermore, this non-neutrality maps roughly onto a very familiar distinction in moral philosophy – that between deontological and consequentialist ethical systems. This distinction is between those ethical theories that are defined directly over the domain of actions (deontological) and those that are defined over the outcomes that those actions generate (consequentialist). Assuming, plausibly, that voting is one of the actions that a deontological theory includes as ethically relevant, the deontological ethical system provides its adherents with reasons both to vote and to vote in a particular way once the voter's moral passions are engaged. Suppose, however, that someone holding a strictly consequentialist theory sees his principles to be at stake in a particular election. It *may* be that he will be moved to express those principles electorally by voting for the candidate/policy that articulates them, but nothing in the ethical system itself would encourage him to do so unless either he expects to influence the emergent outcome (which is hopelessly implausible) or his conduct has other desirable consequences such as winning adherents to his ethic. It should be noted that some – possibly most – variants of 'consequentialism' in the literature (rule consequentialism, restrictive consequentialism,[12] and so on) contain deontological elements. But it is not to be thought that the set of strictly consequentialist doctrines is empty. Consider the simplest forms of utilitarianism, for example. The utilitarian, like the rational egoistic agent, may well have insufficient reason to vote. If many other voters are utilitarians, he may well not need to; and, if few others are, the chances of influencing the outcome along utilitarian lines will be negligible. The value of the time and effort taken to vote may thus be ill-spent, given the utilitarian scheme: the voter's time and energy will, plausibly, be better spent earning income to be given to the poorest or in some yet more pleasurable pursuit. Of course, this is not an *ethical* argument against this variant of utilitarianism unless one believes somehow independently that everyone *should* vote. It is, rather, a positive argument that deontological systems are more likely than consequentialist ones to survive electorally – or, at least, are likely to be more electorally relevant than their acceptance among the enfranchised would suggest.

Further, recall that it is not enough for an ethical view to be seen to be '*correct*': it must also motivate and activate the voter. Certain moral theories that emphasize the virtues of objective and dispassionate reflection, although intellectually persuasive, may by their very nature fail to engage the passions of the voter sufficiently to be electorally effective. It may be that something of a Gresham's law operates in electoral politics – that bad ethics (bad because instinctive, unreflective, excessively engaged) will tend to drive out good (good because the opposite). Politics may often be an arena for ethical debate, but it is not a moral-philosophy seminar – supposing, for the purpose of illustration, that a moral-philosophy seminar can be seen as a context where participants are engaged in some common quest for moral truth.

V Conclusion

First, a brief summary. In this essay, I have argued, against public choice orthodoxy,

1   that there is a predictable difference between behaviour in market and behaviour in electoral settings – a difference that is itself grounded in rational choice theory, and involves no retreat from the principle of motivational neutrality appropriately interpreted;
2   that, specifically, while *homo economicus* may predominate in markets, he is very substantially muted in the electoral setting;

3   that, furthermore, ethical considerations seem certain to play a correspondingly enlarged role in political *process* – that is, ethical considerations seem likely to be electorally potent, and therefore to constrain the whole conduct of politics within an ethical frame;

4   that, accordingly, it is possible to take a heroic view of democratic politics, as articulating and promoting policies that instantiate 'justice', 'efficiency', 'public interest', 'fairness', 'decency' and the 'American [or whatever] way of life', instead of accepting the orthodox public choice view of politics as simply another arena for the pursuit of interests.

With this as background, I wish to return to the rival conceptions of normative political theory that public choice theorists have tended to emphasize: their own two-tier one, with its strong analytic component and more abstract 'constitutional' evaluation; and the conventional 'political theory' alternative, which is best understood as a piece of social ethics, with relatively little analytic component at all. I remain persuaded that the public choice procedure is an appropriate one for *evaluative* purposes, even though certain motivational assumptions predominant in the orthodoxy require substantial modification. But evaluation of social outcomes is one thing and motivation to act is another. There is no guarantee that the procedure used to evaluate social outcomes will be appropriate or relevant in *motivating* individuals within collective decision-making contexts.

Let me use a parable to explain what I mean here. There were once two social democrats. Both enjoyed some measure of electoral success and became active and successful politicians. Both were faithful to their principles. But one day one of them read a succinct and comprehensible review of public choice theory, and found it utterly persuasive. He realized that, if this was how politics *really* worked, he had better adjust his behaviour. First, he had best reorient his political speeches away from the articulation of social-democratic principle (to which he fundamentally adhered) and towards a systematic analysis of how his policies would increase the incomes of certain key voters. Otherwise, he would not be maximizing his chances of being elected to implement the principles in which he still believed. Second, however, in the party room among his social-democrat colleagues, he would have to encourage them to focus their attention not on day-to-day policies, which he now saw would have to be altered to meet the realities of electoral constraints, but on the more abstract rules of the political game, which provided the only feasible means of getting his normative principles implemented. All this seemed to him essential given his new-found understanding of political process. The saga has a sad ending. The public choice devotee failed to be elected next time around. Electors were not, it seems, too impressed with his detailed calculations of dollars and cents. And, the election after that, he failed to get pre-selection. The party was not at all attracted by the abstract and somewhat arcane rule changes that were his new preoccupation. They preferred a more conventional candidate, who would spout the aphorisms of social-democrat doctrine with convincing fervour and try to push through the standard social-democrat policies. And so, as it turned out, did the voters. So the ignorant social democrat flourished, while the one acculturated to public choice doctrine failed.

My point here is the following. Suppose that the picture of political process that underlies this parable is correct – and, as I have argued in this paper, nothing in basic public choice logic would lead us to suppose otherwise. Then it is not merely the case that a politician who follows the standard public choice line at the level of policy choice will tend to do less well electorally than one who does not. It is also the case that the moral agent who adopts the public choice evaluative procedure will tend to be less successful politically than one who relies on a more traditional conception of 'political theory' to do the relevant normative work. Conventional political theory seems to be much closer than is the public choice alternative to the sort of ethical reflection that the political system demands. I do not necessarily mean here to paint a picture of conventional political theory as a sort of 'up-market ideology'. But it may be that the public choice line, with its characteristically instrumental view of political institutions (or policies or candidates) is susceptible to the charge of political naïveté – a charge which much conventional political theorizing could be seen to avoid, precisely because it is connected to its ethical base more directly and without the mediation of complex, abstract and often counter-intuitive analysis.

Notes

1   It is somewhat self-serving of them to hold this view, because it is precisely a 'good sense of what is feasible' that they see their discipline as providing. However, being good students of Smith and Mandeville, they tend to be tolerant of self-serving behaviour: at least in certain settings, it may have optimific results. Moreover, for familiar free-rider problems, the fact that behaviour is profession-ally self-serving does not provide adequate motive for that behaviour: almost all the benefits from my promoting economics go to other economists. In any case, it is the content of, not the reason for, the view that is crucial here.

2   For a discussion of consequentialism in its various guises, see Pettit and Brennan (1986).

3   Although utilitarianism in its traditional form has been rejected by many economists, vestiges of the utilitarian perception remain in the modern 'Paretian' welfare criteria and even in some versions of contractarianism. See, for example, Coleman (1980) for relevant discussion.

4   For an extended discussion of this line of reasoning, see Brennan and Buchanan (1985).

5   'I have often said that public choice offers a "theory of governmental failure" that is fully comparable to the "theory of market failure" that emerged from the theoretical welfare economics of the 1930's and 1940's. . . . The private

sector–public sector decision that each community must make is now more likely to be discussed in meaningful terms, with organizational arrangements analyzed by comparisons between realistically modelled alternatives' (Buchanan 1984, p. 12).

6   See, for example, Barry (1970); Goodin and Roberts (1975); and Meehl (1977).
7   There is, however, an alternative explanation here that does not violate *homo economicus*: namely, that representatives are participants in log-rolling exercises. This means that representatives will vote against constituent interests in some cases in order to promote constituent interests overall.
8   For a vigorous presentation of this latter proposition, see Quiggin (1987).
9   See, for example, Brennan and Buchanan (1984); Brennan and Lomasky (1985); and Brennan and Pincus (1987).
10   All notable instances in the (1987) lead-up to the Democratic primaries in the US presidential race.
11   For example, malice towards the rich can be as potent a force for redistributive policies as compassion for the poor.
12   See Pettit and Brennan (1986).

Part II

Contract and Compliance

5

Maximizing Social Welfare: Is it the Government's Business?

Robert Sugden

The question 'What is the source of the legitimacy of government?' is central to political theory but may seem peripheral to economics. But in their normative work economists typically think of themselves as advisers to a government which (it is assumed, often more in hope than expectation) will be interested in the 'policy implications' of economic research. To be able to give such advice, the economist must appeal to some ideas about the proper functions of government. Most of the theories that economists use to derive their 'policy implications' start from the assumption that the government is (or ought to be) concerned to maximize the overall welfare of society. To treat this as self-evident is to suppose that the answer to the question about the legitimacy of government is also self-evident: the proper function of government is the maximization of welfare, and, to the extent that government seeks to maximize welfare, its use of coercion is legitimate. In this essay, I shall argue for a different view, in which government is not seen as maximizing anything, and in which the maximization of the overall welfare of society is, quite simply, not the government's business. The general approach I shall argue for is *contractarian*.

I The maximizing tradition

The idea that the government's proper function is to maximize social welfare derives from the utilitarian tradition in which economics developed in the nineteenth century, and which provided the intellectual foundation for early work in welfare economics. To classical utilitarians, the welfare of a whole society was simply the sum of the happiness or utility of the individuals who comprised it. Political institutions were legitimate to the extent that they were consistent with the maximization of this total. An enlightened and rational government, therefore, would try to maximize the welfare of society.

One significant feature of this approach is that it depends on what I shall call a *synoptic* viewpoint. A society is made up of individuals, each with his or her own interests, preferences and moral beliefs; we may say that each has a different viewpoint on society. The utilitarian tries to view society not from these individual viewpoints, but as though from a single distant vantage point. To take an analogy: the best viewpoint for judging the relative sizes of different peaks in a block of mountains is from as far away as possible, so as to reduce the distorting effects of perspective. Similarly, the utilitarian argues, any individual's view of society is distorted by his or her personal interests and biases; the judgements of a rational government ought to be made from an impartial standpoint. The idea of an infinitely distant viewpoint is represented in utilitarian thinking by the concept of an Ideal Spectator who sympathizes impartially with the pleasures and pains of all individuals. A good government, the utilitarian believes, would base its decisions on the Ideal Spectator's view of society. Such a government may be personified as the Ideal Decision-Maker.

A second important feature of the utilitarian approach is its *maximizing* structure. The objectives of a good government can be formulated as a problem of maximization, the maximum being the sum of individuals' utilities. This connects with the first feature, because economists in the utilitarian tradition model individuals as maximizers of their own utilities. Thus to treat a government as a maximizer is to treat it as though it were a kind of individual. And this idea also lies behind the insistence that the government should take the viewpoint of the Ideal Spectator. What each individual's pleasures and pains are to him, *all* pleasures and pains are to the impartial sympathies of the Ideal Spectator; just as a rational individual evaluates alternative courses of action against the criterion of maximizing his own utility, so the Ideal Decision-Maker evaluates them against the criterion of maximizing the sum of utilities.

The years since the 1920s have seen a watering-down of the utilitarian element in welfare economics, but these two features are still recognizable in the way economists think about how governments ought to behave. The first major mutation in utilitarian welfare economics came when economists began to doubt whether the concept of utility had any meaning other than as way of describing preferences (or, on a more extreme view, as a way of describing choices). While the concepts of pleasure and pain seem to offer at least some hope of objective definition and measurement, preferences are incurably subjective. If person 1's utility function was simply a statement of person 1's preferences, how could person 1's utility be compared with person 2's? In response to these difficulties Bergson (1938) and Samuelson (1947) proposed a new approach, which has come to be known as *welfarism*. This approach accepts that individual utility functions are merely representations of preferences, and does not attempt to make any kind of objective comparisons between individuals' utilities. However, it is open to any person to make judgements about the overall good of society, provided that it is clear that these are value judgements, with no pretensions to being statements of fact. A view of the overall good of society is expressed in the form of a (Bergson–Samuelson) *social welfare function*, according to which the social welfare in any given 'social state' x is $f[u_1(x), \ldots, u_n(x)]$. Here $u_1(.), \ldots, u_n(.)$ are the utility functions of the n individuals who make up society and $f[.]$ is the social welfare function. The precise specification of the function will determine how one person's utility is to be traded off against another's; these trade-offs represent the ethical judgements of anyone who accepts the function as defining the social good. Arrow (1967) suggests that the social welfare function should be understood as a representation of the ethical judgements of an impartial 'public official' – someone whose role requires him to make, and to act on, judgements about the overall good of society.

The implications of the Bergson–Samuelson approach have been made clearer as a result of the decades of debate about Arrow's impossibility theorem (1951). Arrow argued that it was not enough to assert that, for any given profile of individuals' preferences in society, the public official would be able to come up with a social welfare function. There would have to be some procedure (locted, presumably, in the official's head) for generating social welfare functions from information about the preference profile. Arrow showed that it was impossible to specify such a procedure if it was required to satisfy a number of apparently reasonable conditions. It would be rash to suggest that there is any consensus about how this result should be coped with, but many economists, I think, have come to agree with Sen (1979a) that the problem is one of excessive 'informational constraints'. Arrow's formulation requires that the public official use no other information than is contained in the n preference orderings of individuals. In particular, he is not allowed to take as external data any information about the interpersonal comparability of utilities. In addition, Arrow's 'independence of irrelevant alternatives' condition prevents the public official from forming his own judgements about how one person's utility should be traded off against another's and then treating these judgements as data for his procedure. On Sen's view, the solution to Arrow's problem is to admit 'information' – even if only in the form of subjective judgements – about the interpersonal comparability of utility. The implication of this is that the Bergson–Samuelson approach does not do away with the need for interpersonal comparisons, but simply changes their status: they are to be understood as normative judgements and not, as in classical utilitarianism, as statements of fact.

This approach, then, is essentially a refined form of utilitarianism, based on information about preferences rather than utilities. It clearly retains the maximizing feature of utilitarianism: the whole point of the social welfare function is that it is there to be maximized. It also retains the synoptic viewpoint. The social welfare function is a representation of a special kind of preference-ordering – the preference-ordering of someone who is taking an impartial rather than egoistical view of society. For Arrow this is the public official. Harsanyi (1955) offers a more formal characterization of impartiality that has been very influential. On this view, a person forms his 'ethical preferences' by imagining himself in a position where he has an equal probability of becoming any individual in society and has to make choices between social states *before* finding out who he is to be. Whatever preferences would guide his choices in this position are his ethical preferences. This imaginary position is essentially that of the Ideal Spectator of classical utilitarianism; the only difference is that Harsanyi's disembodied person is motivated by self-interest (since he is going to *become* an individual in society) rather than by sympathy.

In recent years, economists have begun to contemplate more radical breaks with utilitarianism. Here again Sen has been very influential. In a series of papers he has urged economists to relax another type of informational constraint by admitting 'non-utility information'. In the Bergson–Samuelson approach, the overall good of society – the entity that ought to be maximized by government – is a function only of individuals' utilities. Sen argues that there are important moral principles – for example, principles concerned with liberty or discrimination – that cannot be formulated solely in terms of propositions about utility (see, for example, 1979a). If we are to be able to specify social welfare functions that embody widely held moral principles, he argues, we may be forced to make use of information about features of social states other than the utilities they generate.

This criticism of welfarism is also beginning to be taken on board by economists. (Witness the almost obsessive interest that social choice theorists have taken in Sen's 'Paretian liberal' paradox.) However, the synoptic viewpoint and the maximizing structure of utilitarianism remain almost intact.

In the Bergson–Samuelson approach, the maximizing structure appears as the requirement that social choices ought to be those that maximize the value of the social welfare function. But this function is simply a representation of an ordering of social states – a 'social welfare ordering'. There is an equivalence, then, between the idea that social choices ought to maximize the value of some function and the idea that they ought to be consistent with some ordering of social states. Social choice theorists – and Sen (for example, 1969, 1977) in particular – have devoted a great deal of energy to analysing different formal conditions of 'consistency' for social choices and have been prepared on occasion to allow weaker concepts of consistency than the existence of a social ordering. But the fundamental idea that social choices ought to satisfy *some* formal consistency conditions has rarely been questioned. Why not? Part of the answer, I think, is that the problem of social choice is being looked at from a synoptic viewpoint. To take this viewpoint is to reduce the problem of social choice to a problem faced by some kind of Ideal Decision-Maker; and then it is natural to require the same kind of consistency on the part of the Ideal Decision-Maker as we would of any other rational individual.

Let me give one example of what I mean by using a synoptic viewpoint in a non-utilitarian way. Sen (1976) discusses Nozick's view that rights should be construed as constraints on the domain of social choice. Nozick (1973, p. 62) says, 'If I have a right to choose to live in New York or Massachusetts, and I choose Massachusetts, then alternatives involving my living in New York are not appropriate objects to be entered in a social ordering.' Sen's reply is this:

> But one can also argue that, if I believe it is a better society which – given other things – lets Nozick decide where he wishes to live, then I must *assert* that it is socially *better* that Nozick should be permitted to live in Massachusetts as desired by him. If Nozick is forced out of Massachusetts, then one would wish to say not only that Nozick's rights have been violated, but that society is worse off – given other things – by stopping Nozick from living where he wishes.

Notice the difference between what Sen is saying and what Nozick is saying. Nozick is saying that, if he chooses to live in Massachusetts, then it is no business of society's to ask whether this is good or bad. He is not trying to persuade us that any social purpose is being served by his being free to choose where he lives. He is not concerned with how things might look to an Ideal Spectator, but only with how they look to him: he has a right to choose where he lives, and society must respect it. Sen, in contrast, is claiming that Nozick's freedom is a component of the overall good of society, that it is good *from a social point of view* that Nozick is free to choose where he lives. This is a non-utilitarian but synoptic view of rights. The contractarian view of rights is much closer to Nozick's.

II The contractarian viewpoint

I shall not be arguing for any one contractarian theory, but for the general approach that is common to a family of contractarian theories that derives from Hobbes's *Leviathan* (1651) and Locke's *Two Treatises of Government* (1690). Rawls's *A Theory of Justice* (1971), Buchanan's *The Limits of Liberty* (1975) and Gauthier's *Morals by Agreement* (1986) are important modern works in this tradition.

I shall begin by considering the argument for contractarianism that is presented by Rawls. I start from Rawls because he has presented the case for contractarianism with particular force and eloquence and because I find his presentation of this case so persuasive. It must be admitted, however, that Rawls's long and rich book is open to various readings. The particular form of contractarianism embodied in Rawls's own theory has many similarities with Harsanyi's form of welfarism. On some readings,[1] the parties to Rawls's contract, like the disembodied individuals of Harsanyi's theory, are no more than thinly disguised Ideal Spectators. Here, however, I wish to identify the genuinely contractarian strand in Rawls's argument.

Rawls see utilitarianism as the main alternative to contractarianism (1971, p. 22); and so his argument for contractarianism is largely presented in the form of a critique of utilitarianism. However, as I shall try to show, many of his criticism apply not merely to utilitarianism, but to synoptic and maximizing theories in general.

Rawls's central objection to utilitarianism is that it 'does not take seriously the distinction between persons' (p. 27). Utilitarianism treats the welfare of society as an *aggregate* of the welfares of individuals, and then views the maximization of this aggregate as the proper object of social choice. It takes no account of the *distribution* of welfare:

> The striking feature of the utilitarian view of justice is that it does not matter, except indirectly, how this sum of satisfactions is distributed among individuals any more than it matters, except indirectly, how one man distributes his satisfactions over time. The correct distribution in either case is that which yields the maximum fulfilment. (p. 26)

It might seem from this that Rawls's critique of utilitarianism is directed merely at the idea that social welfare must be the *sum of* individuals' utilities. The idea that utilities must be summed is an essential feature of classical utilitarianism, but this is not required in the welfarist approach: this is just one of many views about the distribution of welfare which could be incorporated into the specification of a Bergson–Samuelson social welfare function. But Rawls continues in a way that implies he is objecting to the whole concept of a social welfare function, and not just to the particular form of function associated with classical utilitarianism: 'Thus [for utilitarians] there is no reason in principle why the greater gains of some should not compensate for the lesser losses of others; or more importantly, why the violation of the liberty of a few might not be made right by the greater good shared by many' (p. 26).

Here the objection seems to be to any attempt to trade off one person's losses against another person's gains in order to reach an assessment of social welfare. Such trade-offs are part of all welfarist theories.[2] To make such trade-offs,

Rawls says, is to treat a society of separate individuals as though it were a single person: it amounts to adopting 'for society as a whole the principle of rational choice for one man', the one man being the Ideal Spectator (pp. 26–7). By this construction 'many persons are fused into one'; and it is to this attempt to fuse individual persons into a social mass that Rawls fundamentally objects:

> On this conception of society separate individuals are thought of as so many different lines along which rights and duties are to be assigned and scarce means of satisfaction allocated in accordance with rules so as to give the greatest fulfilment of wants. The nature of the decision made by the ideal legislator is not, therefore, materially different from that of an entrepreneur deciding how to maximize his profit by producing this or that commodity, or that of a consumer deciding how to maximize his satisfaction by the purchase of this or that collection of goods. In each case there is a single person whose system of desires determines the best allocation of limited means. The correct decision is essentially a question of efficient administration. (p. 27)

Rawls returns to this criticism when he argues that utilitarianism lacks 'psychological stability'. A set of principles of justice is psychologically stable if it generates its own support – that is, if people living in a society organized according to those principles can be expected to develop the desire to uphold them. Rawls claims that this is true of his own principles of justice because they can be seen to work to everyone's advantage. But

> When the principle of utility is satisfied, however, there is no such assurance that everyone benefits. Allegiance to the social system may demand that some should forgo advantages for the sake of the greater good of the whole. . . . We are to accept the greater advantages of others as a sufficient reason for lower expectations over the whole course of our life. This is surely an extreme demand. In fact, when society is conceived as a system of co-operation designed to advance the good of its members, it seems quite incredible that some citizens should be expected, on the basis of political principles, to accept lower prospects of life for the sake of others. (pp. 177–8)

In other words, a conception of justice that allows one person's losses to be traded off against another person's gains is not psychologically stable.

It is tempting to reply that a theory of justice cannot avoid the necessity to make trade-offs between individuals' welfares. If we insist that the welfares of different individuals are incommensurable with one another, we seem to be left with the Paretian position: that, whenever there are two social states, neither of which Pareto-dominates the other, these are non-comparable. Such a position would have nothing to say about the issues of distribution that surely should be central to any theory of economic justice. But this is to assume that the purpose of a theory of justice is to generate a ranking of social states in terms of their overall goodness – to assume that a theory of justice must be synoptic.

Rawls's objection to utilitarianism (which, I suggest, can be extended to all synoptic theories of the social good) must be understood in contractarian terms.[3] In a contractarian theory, each individual is regarded as having a set of entitlements or rights that exist prior to any process of social choice. This pre-social position forms a fixed reference point with which alternative social arrangements can be compared. Thus, for example, when Rawls asks whether everyone benefits from a society organized on utilitarian principles, he is asking whether everyone is better off in the utilitarian society than in the pre-social position. If someone is worse off, then the utilitarian society cannot be regarded as a voluntary association of individuals for mutual benefit: someone has been deprived of advantages to which he is entitled, and this is unjust. In the language of social choice theory, for Rawls it seems to be a necessary condition for a society to be just that it is a Pareto improvement over the pre-social reference point.

The starting point for a contractarian theory, then, is a specification of individuals' rights. By using this starting point, contractarians insist on the priority of the individual over society: society is seen as the creation of individuals who could have lived without it, and its purposes are those of the individuals who create it. Thus, as Gauthier (1986, p. 222) puts it, rights 'are what each person brings to the bargaining table, not what she takes from it'. This is very different from the role of rights in a synoptic theory. Take the passage I quoted from Sen in section I. For Sen, rights are a source of (non-utilitarian) social value: it is good for society that they exist and are respected.[4] Perhaps (for Sen does not go into detail) he has in mind something like Mill's belief (J.S. Mill 1859, ch. 1) that it is only through choosing their own plans of life that human beings can fully develop their faculties, and that 'it really is of importance, not only what men do, but also what manner of men they are that do it'.[5] At any rate, he must have in mind some way in which respect for rights is good from a social point of view. On the contractarian view, in contrast, rights do not serve any social purpose. It is the other way round: the purpose of social co-operation is to benefit individuals, and the concept of benefit is defined in terms of the reference point provided by a system of rights.

To this it might be objected that many rights have no meaning outside society. Take the right to vote, for example. It would be absurd to imagine individuals *in a state of nature* coming to Gauthier's bargaining table equipped with rights to vote, and much more plausible to suppose that they would leave the table with such rights. (Each might agree to an arrangement by which certain matters could be determined collectively; but each might make his agreement conditional on his having a vote whenever collective decisions were made.) My reply is that contractarian forms of reasoning can be used at various levels. If we are looking for a contractarian justification for the existence of government at all – the problem addressed by Hobbes and Locke – then we must start from a state of nature in which there is no government and thus are no politics and no political rights. But if we are looking for a contractarian justification for a particular change in the rules by which collective decisions are made, we may take as our starting point a system of constitutional rights among which the right to vote would be included.

Different contractarian theories differ in the way the initial system of rights is specified. Hobbes's specification of the state of nature (Hobbes 1651, ch. 13) represents contractarianism in its purest and most uncompromising form. In Hobbes's state of nature individuals are effectively unconstrained by any obligations to one another: each may do whatever he judges most likely to preserve his own life, whatever the consequences for others. I shall follow Hobbes in regarding this as a system of rights: everyone has the right to do whatever will preserve his own life or, as Hobbes puts it, every man has a right to every thing. In the modern contractarian literature, the approach of Buchanan (1975) is essentially Hobbesian.

A second major strand in contractarian thinking derives from Locke. In Locke's state of nature (Locke 1960, *Second Treatise*, chs 1–5), individuals are subject to a system of natural law, the content of which is supposed to be evident to the natural reason of man. Natural law gives each person a right to his own body, to the produce of his own labour, and to property justly acquired. (I shall not go into the difficulties surrounding Locke's theory of just acquisition.) These rights, unlike Hobbes's, have corresponding duties: each person has a duty to allow each other person to use his own body how he chooses, and so on. In the modern contractarian literature, Gauthier (1986) presents perhaps the most Lockean theory. Gauthier's contractarian reasoning starts from a system of natural rights very similar to Locke's. The main difference concerns the derivation of these rights. Locke's individuals reason their way to these rights from the premise that we are all the handiwork of God, put into the world to carry out God's purposes; Gauthier's individuals reason only from a concern to further their own interests. Nozick (1974) is another modern writer who has used a Lockean state of nature, but Nozick is not quite a contractarian in the sense relevant for this essay: he asks what institutions would evolve in an on-going Lockean state of nature, rather than imagining some once-and-for-all contract.

Rawls (1971, p. 11) sees his theory of justice as being in the Lockean tradition, but his starting-point is much more abstract than Locke's. For Rawls, principles of justice are those that would be agreed by rational and self-interested persons in an 'original position' of equality. In this original position, a 'veil of ignorance' prevents anyone from knowing his position in society, his endowment of natural ability, or even his tastes – anything, in fact, that could allow him to identify a difference between his own interests and those of the other parties to the contract. The contracting parties seek to reach agreement on principles of justice to which all will be bound. Rawls sees his original position as the counterpart of the state of nature in traditional contract theory (p. 12). There is a major difference, however: Hobbes's and Locke's states of nature represent forms of human life that, however solitary, poor, nasty and brutish (in the Hobbesian case) or inconvenient (in the Lockean case), could be lived. We can imagine what it would be like to live in the worlds Hobbes and Locke describe. Rawls's original position is simply a thought experiment; it is not any form of human life at all. It is clear that Hobbes's and Locke's states of nature constitute specifications of rights, in the sense that each person comes to the bargaining table knowing that he is not obliged to make any agreement at all: he has the option of making do with life in the state of nature. But how can Rawls's original position be interpreted in this way? Such an interpretation can be given only if we know what life would be like for the contracting parties if they failed to agree. In fact, nothing in Rawls's theory turns on the answer to this question, but nevertheless Rawls answers it. The contracting parties are trying to agree on a set of principles of justice. In the absence of agreement, he says, they will be stuck with egoism (p. 136). I take this to mean that the veil of ignorance will be lifted and they will all have to live in a society that is unconstrained by any notions of justice. This amounts to saying that Rawls's contracting parties come to the bargaining table with the right to be egoistic.

After specifiying the rights that individuals bring to the bargaining table, a contractarian theory must provide a model of bargaining. Typically, contractarian theories assume that the parties to the bargaining are rational and that they are all equally well informed. Some theories, such as Rawls's, impose strict limits on the amount of information that the contracting parties are allowed to have; others impose no restrictions at all. Something must also be said about the enforceability of agreements. In some theories, ensuring that an agreement can be enforced is part of the problem faced by the contracting parties. This, for example, is an important aspect of Hobbes's argument for absolute government. In other theories, it is assumed that agreements will be kept. Here Rawls occupies a middle position, generally expecting his contracting parties to live up to the principles of justice that they have chosen, but making some allowance for the 'strains of commitment' (p. 145).

The fundamental idea is not to predict what would in fact happen if people lived in a state of nature or could somehow be placed in Rawls's original position, but to arrive at propositions about *what it would be rational for them to do*. This is because the conclusions of contractarian reasoning are to be used to *justify* particular social arrangements, and the justification is to be addressed to rational persons.

The nature of justification provided by a contractarian theory is very different from that provided by a synoptic theory. A contractarian theory justifies a particular outcome by showing every individual that this is the best he can rationally expect, given his entitlements and given the fact that he is dealing with other rational individuals who also have entitlements. In this sense the outcome is shown to be good for each individual taken separately. There is no trading-off of one person's welfare against another's; the outcome is justified *to everyone*. There is no attempt to make judgements from the viewpoint of the Ideal Spectator: contractarian theories use as many viewpoints as there are persons in society.

In synoptic theories, I have argued, the model of good government is the Ideal Decision-Maker – a public official who chooses in the light of impartial judgements about the overall good of society. The corresponding figure in contractarian theories may be thought of as the Ideal Chairman. The Ideal Chairman presides over the contractarian bargaining table. His responsibility is to guide the contracting parties to an outcome that is acceptable, not to him, but to each of them. He must ensure that each person is fully aware of the consequences of his decisions, so that no one is manoeuvred by other people's debating skills, tactics or superior information into an agreement he will later see to have been contrary to his interests. In other words, it his responsibility to guide the contracting parties to an outcome that each can recognize as the best he can rationally expect. A contractarian justification for a particular outcome, then, is one that could be used by the Ideal Chairman to persuade all individuals to accept it. But the outcome is not chosen by the Ideal Chairman and he is not responsible for it. It has been chosen by the individual contracting parties, and it is they who are responsible for it.

III Contractarianism and collective rationality

Gauthier (1986, pp. 206–8) gives a simple example of a state of nature. Joanna and Jonathan are castaways on a small and otherwise uninhabited island. According to Gauthier's specification of natural rights, each is free to take whatever food grows naturally on the island without considering the other person's interests. Suppose some tree yields nutritious fruit, and that food is scarce. Then Joanna may take whatever she needs – if she gets the chance before Jonathan takes it. (Gauthier's argument is that, by taking the fruit, Joanna does not make herself any better off than she would have been if Jonathan had never appeared on the island; thus she is not *using* Jonathan to gain advantages for herself. If, however, the fruit was the product of Jonathan's labour in cultivating the tree, then Joanna would *not* be free to take it: to take the fruit then would be to be a parasite, which Gauthier's natural law forbids.) I shall not try to defend this ingenious justification of a basically Lockean system of rights, but simply take these rights as given. My purpose is to examine the logical structure of contractarian arguments, and any such argument must start from *some* specification of rights.

Any economist will instantly recognize that this system of rights is likely to generate prisoner's dilemma problems. Suppose the fruit on the tree takes time to ripen. It can be eaten as soon as it appears, but it is tastier and more nutritious if left a few weeks on the tree. If Joanna decides to wait until the fruit is ripe, it will pay Jonathan to take it all before it ripens; and *vice versa*. If each thinks only of his or her own interests, and if no agreement is made between them, the result will be a scramble to eat unripe fruit. This is the tragedy of the commons (G. Hardin 1968). Or perhaps Joanna will arm herself and guard the tree until the fruit is ripe. (This, I think, would be permissible under Gauthier's natural law. In fighting off Jonathan she is not trying to get anything that wouldn't be available to her in his absence.) Jonathan may respond by arming himself so that he can penetrate Joanna's defences. (This, too, is permissible. Jonathan is not trying to get anything that wouldn't be available to him in Joanna's absence.) The result is a wasteful diversion of effort into the accumulation of weapons and defensive systems. This is the tragedy of the arms race.

Either of these types of problem can be modelled as a prisoner's dilemma game. As many other writers have done, I shall treat this game as a model of the problems that might generate a case for government, and then use it to illustrate the differences between contractarian and synoptic theories. To prevent the discussion from becoming too abstract, I shall compare a particular contractarian theory – that proposed by Gauthier – with a particular synoptic one: Bergson–Samuelson welfarism.

In the prisoner's dilemma game, each person has a choice of two strategies, 'defect' (take the fruit as soon as you get the chance, accumulate weapons and try to take possession of the tree) and 'co-operate' (wait until the fruit is ripe, then take a half share of whatever is on the tree). Table 1 presents this game in its classic form. The numbers in the cells are utility indices, defined according to the logic of expected utility theory; the first number in each cell is Joanna's utility, the second Jonathan's. It is important to realize that these indices are *not* interpersonally comparable: there is one scale for Joanna's utility and another for Jonathan's.

Table 1   The prisoner's dilemma game

		Jonathan	
		Co-operate	Defect
Joanna	Co-operate	2, 2	0, 3
	Defect	3, 0	1, 1

If this game is played non-co-operatively – that is, if the players cannot make agreements to co-ordinate their strategies – the outcome of rational play must be (1, 1). Each knows that, whatever the other does, his or her own best strategy is to defect: so both will defect. The essence of contractarian reasoning, however, is to treat problems of human interaction as *co-operative* games.

For a contractarian analysis, we may begin by assuming that both players are rational, that both know each other to be rational, that both are fully informed about the nature of the game, and that any agreement that they reach will be enforced. The first three of these assumptions correspond with my notion of a bargaining process presided over by an Ideal Chairman. The fourth may be interpreted in any of three ways. One interpretation makes it an assumption about the technology of enforcement in the state of nature: once an agreement is made, each person is able to enforce it. A second interpretation is closer to Gauthier's own. Whatever it would be rational for individuals to agree to do, in a situation in which agreements can be enforced, is morally required of individuals even when enforcement is not possible. Or, at least, each individual is morally required to act in this way provided he can expect those with whom he interacts to do the same. (Gauthier says all this, but goes further: he argues that it is rational to aquire the disposition to behave morally.) The third (and Hobbesian) interpretation is most relevant for a discussion of government.

Enforcement of agreements, we might say, requires the existence of some common power set over both individuals – a government. This assertion is a little artificial for a two-person problem, since we might expect two individuals to be able to enforce their own agreements without any external machinery: if the game is played repeatedly, any breach of an agreement by one player in one round can be punished by the other in subsequent rounds. But in many-person prisoner's dilemma problems, agreements are much more fragile (Sugden 1986, ch. 7). So we might conceive of our individuals as trying to agree on the constitution of a government which is to have the power to coerce them. Then the analysis will lead to a contractarian conclusion about the legitimate functions of government.

We now need some principle of rational play in a co-operative game. For my present purpose, a very weak principle will do: that, if a game has a unique *core solution*, this is the outcome that will be chosen as the result of rational play. Let me explain this concept. Consider any possible outcome x of a co-operative game (i.e. any cell in the matrix that describes the game). Then x is *blocked* if there exists some group (or *coalition*) of players who, by co-ordinating their own strategies, can guarantee themselves an outcome better than x, irrespective of what the other players in the game do (and this includes the possibility that the other players may behave irrationally). Here 'better than x' means 'better for at least one member of the coalition and at least as good for all members'. The concept of a coalition includes at one extreme a single individual and at the other, the set of all individuals. An outcome is in the core if it is not blocked by any coalition. To see the point behind all this, suppose that some outcome x is blocked. Then there must be some group of players who, by agreeing to co-ordinate their strategies, can be sure of improving on x. How, then, could it be rational for them to acquiesce in an arrangement that produced x? The implication is that (at least if any core outcomes exist) non-core outcomes cannot come about if all players are fully informed and rational. Hence, if there is only one core outcome, this must be the consequence of rational play.

Applying this principle to the prisoner's dilemma game, there is a unique core solution. This is (2, 2), the outcome of both Joanna and Jonathan playing co-operative strategies. The outcome of their both defecting, (1, 1), is blocked because they both prefer (2, 2) and they have the power to produce (2, 2) by agreeing to co-operate. The outcome in which Joanna defects and Jonathan co-operates, (3, 0), is blocked by Jonathan: he has the power to guarantee himself a utility of at least 1 by defecting. Similarly, (0, 3) is blocked by Joanna. But (2, 2) cannot be blocked. The most that either player can guarantee himself or herself by acting in isolation is a utility level of 1, and, since there is no way that (2, 2) can be improved on for both of them, a coalition of the two of them cannot block it.

This argument may be put more intuitively by considering how the Ideal Chairman might advise Joanna and Jonathan to settle for (2, 2). He can say to Joanna, 'There is only one outcome that is better for you than (2, 2) and that is (3, 0). But how can you possibly expect to be able to hold out for an outcome that requires Jonathan to co-operate while you defect? Jonathan can be sure of getting an outcome better for him than (3, 0), simply by defecting himself. It will not be rational for him to co-operate unless you offer him something in return, namely your own co-operation.' And he can give similar advice to Jonathan. Thus the Ideal Chairman can recommend (2, 2) to both individuals as the best that each can rationally expect to achieve.

Compare this with a welfarist analysis of the same problem. To a welfarist, the problem is to rank the four outcomes in terms of the overall welfare of society. In welfarist terms, (2, 2) is clearly better than (1, 1): remember that welfarists use only information about utilities in ranking social states. But which of (2, 2), (0, 3) and (3, 0) is best depends on the specification of the social welfare function (that is, on the particular value judgements about the distribution of welfare made by the 'public official'). So it is possible that a welfarist Ideal Decision-Maker might choose, say, (3, 0) rather than (2, 2). Suppose Joanna is ill while Jonathan is healthy. Then, from the Ideal Decision-Maker's vantage point, the overall good of society may be best served by favouring Joanna. To choose (3, 0) is to require Jonathan to put up with a worse outcome than the (1, 1) he could expect in a state of nature; but Jonathan can be told that, from a social point of view, Joanna's greater gain compensates for his lesser loss. The Ideal Chairman, in contrast, cannot use this kind of argument. He has to find an outcome that he can recommend both to Joanna *and* to Jonathan, neither of whom is concerned with the social point of view.

Suppose, however, that (2, 2) *is* the outcome that maximizes social welfare, so that the Ideal Decision-Maker chooses the same outcome as the Ideal Chairman would recommend. Then welfarist and contractarian arguments are leading to the same conclusion: they both legitimate the existence of a government with the power to coerce both individuals to play co-operative strategies.

However, the nature of the justification is very different in the two cases. This can be seen by considering a variant of the story of Joanna and Jonathan in which the strategies of 'co-operate' and 'defect' remain open to Joanna, but Jonathan is unable to play the 'defect' strategy. (Perhaps the unripe fruit can be gathered only by climbing the tree, which Joanna is able to do but Jonathan is not, whereas ripe fruit falls from the tree and can be gathered by either. Or perhaps Joanna has the skill to make a lethal weapon against which Jonathan has no defence.) Then the game takes what from an analytical point of view is a trivial form, which is shown in Table 2.

Table 2 A second version of the game

		Jonathan Co-operate
Joanna	Co-operate	2, 2
	Defect	3, 0

It is immediately clear that this game has a unique core solution, and that this is (3, 0). Joanna is free to choose whether to co-operate or to defect, either choice being permissible in terms of Gauthier's natural law. Whatever she does, Jonathan will co-operate, being simply unable to defect. If Joanna co-operates, she gets a utility of 2 whereas by defecting she can get 3. Clearly it pays her to defect. (In the language of game theory, she blocks (2, 2).) The Ideal Chairman must recommend (3, 0) to the two individuals as the best outcome each can rationally expect, given the rationality and the rights of the other. There is, then, no contractarian justification for a government that compels Joanna to co-operate.

Compare the implications of the welfarist approach. If there is a welfarist justification for government in the first case, it is because the social welfare function ranks (2, 2) above (3, 0), (0, 3) and (1, 1): the outcome in which both co-operate is the best of the four possible outcomes in terms of overall social welfare. But then (2, 2) must be the better of the two feasible outcomes in the second version of the story, and so the justification for compelling Joanna to co-operate remains.

The point of this example is that the contractarian argument for government is one of *mutual advantage*. In the classic prisoner's dilemma problem, where both individuals have the power to defect, it is legitimate to coerce Joanna and Jonathan because (at least under certain ideal bargaining conditions) this is something to which they would both rationally agree. The restriction placed on Joanna – that she is prevented from defecting – is justified because it is part of a larger arrangement that benefits her. In justifying this restriction to Joanna, the benefit to Jonathan is neither here nor there. Thus, if, as in the second version of the story, Jonathan has nothing to offer in return for Joanna's co-operation, the justification for restricting Joanna disappears. In contrast, the welfarist argument is one of *overall advantage*. The justification for coercing Joanna is that the costs this imposes on her are outweighed, in the scale of social welfare, by the benefits to Jonathan. Equally, the justification for coercing Jonathan is that the costs imposed on him are outweighed by the benefits conferred on Joanna. If the second of these arguments is made redundant by Jonathan's inability to defect, the validity of the first is unaffected. It is purely incidental that in the original version of the story the introduction of government happens to work out to the benefit of both individuals.

This example illustrates the difference between the maximizing structure of a synoptic theory and the non-maximizing structure of a contractarian one. As I pointed out above, social choice theorists have investigated properties of consistency that might be required of patterns of choice, and have sometimes been prepared to relax the strict requirements of maximization (i.e. that choices should derive from an ordering of alternative options). One of the most basic axioms of consistency of choices is the axiom of contraction consistency that Sen (1969) calls 'Property α'. This is used very widely in social choice theory as a minimal requirement of consistency. It is a property of a 'choice function', a choice function being a rule which specifies what may be chosen from every possible feasible set. Let S be a feasible set (i.e. a set of elements, one and only one of which must be chosen) and let $C(S)$ be the set of 'choosable' elements. (The idea that there may be more than one choosable element in the feasible set is to allow for the possibility of indifference. Thus $C(S) = \{x\}$ represents the idea that, from the set S, x should be chosen, while $C(S) = \{x, y\}$ represents the idea that, from the set S, either x or y ought to be chosen but it doesn't matter which.) Let x and y be any two elements that are both members of each of the sets S and S' where S' is a subset of S. Then Property α requires that, if x is a member of $C(S)$, it must also be a member of $C(S')$. As Sen puts it, 'if the world champion in some game is a Pakistani, then he must also be the champion in Pakistan'. In Sugden (1985) I present a vestigial form of Property α which I call 'minimal consistency'. This requires that, if x alone is chosen from S (i.e. $C(S) = \{x\}$), then it is not the case that y alone is chosen from the set $\{x, y\}$. As I show in that essay, this minimal property is common to almost all the consistency requirements that have been put forward in social choice theory.

Now consider the story of Joanna and Jonathan. In the first version of the story, the feasible set is {(1, 1), (2, 2), (3, 0), (0, 3)}. Contractarian and (I have assumed) welfarist arguments both lead to recommendations in favour of (2, 2). In the second version of the story, the feasible set shrinks to {(2, 2), (3, 0)}. The principle of minimal consistency requires that, if (2, 2) was uniquely recommended in the first case, (3, 0) cannot be uniquely recommended in the second. The welfarist analysis satisfies this condition, recommending (2, 2) in both cases. But the contractarian analysis does not satisfy the condition of minimal consistency, recommending (2, 2) in the first case and (3, 0) in the second.

What are we to make of this? It seems we must recognize that contractarian forms of reasoning can violate even the most fundamental conditions of 'consistency'. The reason for this, I suggest, is that these consistency conditions derive from a maximizing model of choice. Such a model may be appropriate for the choices of a single individual, and for synoptic theories in which the problem of social choice is effectively reduced to the choice problem of an Ideal Decision-Maker. But, on the contractarian approach, there is no single chooser to whom 'collective rationality' could be attributed.

IV Conclusion

I have been analysing a state-of-nature problem and considering how, at the most fundamental level, government might be justified. It might be objected that this has little relevance to issues of day-to-day political decision-making. In most contractarian theories it is the basic rules of the political process that are viewed as the outcomes of contract, and then day-to-day decision making is carried out within the constraints of these rules. Perhaps, it might be suggested, the parties to a social contract would agree to establish a government which was given the objective of maximizing some social welfare function. Certainly there may be circumstances in which a principle of maximization might serve as an acceptable rule of thumb for a contractarian government – acceptable because it could be expected to work to the benefit of everyone in the long run. But, even so, principles of maximization would have no ultimate status: underlying any day-to-day use of such principles is an implicit appeal to a non-maximizing argument of mutual advantage.

To see this point more clearly, consider a mirror-image case: the place of rights in utilitarian theories. Most utilitarians accept that in some circumstances it is appropriate for governments to treat individuals as though they had natural rights: this is seen as a convenient rule of thumb for achieving utilitarian ends. For the utilitarian, however, rights have no ultimate status: underlying any utilitarian argument for respecting rights there is an implicit appeal to a principle of maximization.

For someone who has learned to think about economic and political questions within a synoptic framework, it is hard to make the shift of perspective required to see things in the contractarian way. The contractarian insistence on mutual benefit appears to come down to the implausible claim that the right of any one individual not to suffer a loss outweighs any amount of benefit that the others might gain: that an individual's rights have infinite value. But this is not at all what the contractarian is saying. The contractarian may accept that, from a social point of view – from the viewpoint of the Ideal Spectator – the gains of some can compensate for the losses of others. What is at issue is whether this is the proper viewpoint for a government to take. If, as the contractarian insists, government is to be seen as the creation of individuals, then the government has only those functions that individuals would choose to give it. No individual is concerned with the maximization of social welfare, and so no individual would choose that this should be the function of government. Maximizing social welfare, then, is not the government's business.

Notes

I have presented earlier versions of this essay to an Economic and Social Research Council-supported symposium on rights and rationality at the University of Uppsala, to seminars at the University of Cambridge, the University of East Anglia and University College, London, and to a meeting of the Society for Applied Philosophy. The paper has benefited from the comments of many people, but particularly Bob Goodin, Martin Hollis, Alan Hamlin, Nick Nathan, Prasanta Pattanaik, Philip Pettit and Albert Weale. It has also been improved as a result of more general discussions with Jim Buchanan, David Gauthier and John Rawls at a recent Liberty Fund conference.

1   In some of my earlier work, I have interpreted Rawls's argument in this way: see Sugden (1981). I now think this was a mistake.
2   Strickly speaking, this is true only for those welfarist theories that generate a complete ranking of all social states. One might propose that social states should be ranked in terms of social welfare only when they are Pareto-comparable; this would generate an incomplete ranking that might be called 'welfarist' and that would not require any interpersonal comparisons.
3   I am not suggesting that contractarian theories are the only sort of non-synoptic theories that there are. For example, Nozick's theory of justice (Nozick 1974) is not synoptic but arguably is not contractarian either (see later).
4   This approach is developed more fully in Sen (1981).
5   Mill, of course, saw the development of human potential as an element of 'utility in the largest sense, grounded on the permanent interests of a man as a progressive being' (J. S. Mill 1859, ch. 1). On a more conventional definition of utility, however, Mill's argument for liberty must surely be interpreted as non-utilitarian.

6

Liberty, Contract and the State

Alan Hamlin

In this essay I examine the specifically contractarian strategy for linking liberty and the state. This concentration on the contractarian strategy is motivated by a distinction that can be drawn between a liberal theory of the state and a theory of the liberal state. The former label will apply to any theory which takes liberty (perhaps of a particular type) as a central value and proceeds to flesh out the implications of this value for the state. The latter label will apply to any theory of the state that concludes that liberty (perhaps of a particular type) must be the central or only concern of the good polity. The obvious question is, then, does a liberal theory of the state necessarily imply a liberal state? Certainly this has been claimed, most forcibly by Nozick (1974), who argues that, under suitable constraints, a liberal or minimal state will emerge by an invisible-hand process from the interaction of free individuals. In contrast I shall contend that the contractarian method provides a better vehicle for the explication of the liberal theory of the state than is afforded by the invisible-hand approach; and that a commitment to liberal theory in its contractarian form does not entail a commitment to a liberal state.

A second theme of this essay concerns the relationship between the contractarian strategy and individual rights. The grounding of substantial individual rights and their role in the normative theory of the state is, of course, an area of major and continuing debate, and this is true even within the recently revived contractarian tradition.[1] I shall investigate the status of rights relative to the contractarian strategy and, in particular, the question of whether rights should be seen as an input into the contract process or an outcome of that process, in order to assess the possibility of a distinctively contractarian theory of rights.

The main body of this essay is divided into four sections. Section I sketches some of the defining characteristics of the contractarian strategy for the normative appraisal of states. Section II compares the contractarian and invisible-hand forms of the liberal theory of the state and contends that the contractarian strategy provides the more promising prospect. Section III is concerned with the relationship between contractarianism and individual rights. Finally, section IV brings the various arguments together so as to address the question of whether the liberal theory of the state must amount to a theory of the liberal state.

I The contractarian strategy

The contractarian strategy supports a wide variety of tactical variants. The purpose of this section is not to catalogue and classify this variety but rather to identify some of the fundamental characteristics common to all contractarian arguments and make two distinctions that partition the set of all contractarian positions in a manner that will be of some importance in what follows. In respect of the first purpose I shall mention just five key concerns of contractarianism, which may be summarized under the headings 'moral individualism', 'mutuality', 'rationality', 'proceduralism' and 'the *status quo ante* problem'.[2]

An obvious starting point from which to characterize contractarianism is its conception of society as 'a cooperative venture for mutual advantage' (Rawls 1971, p. 4; see also Gauthier 1986, pp. 10–13). A direct implication of this view of society is that the criterion by which social institutions are to be judged must be related directly to the advantages those institutions provide for the constituent individuals, with the additional proviso that mutuality of advantage must be ensured. This specification immediately identifies a commitment to a form of moral individualism. The exact extent of this commitment varies from one contract theory to another, but there is a common requirement for a commitment to at least the position identified elsewhere as the principle of individual relevance (see ch. 1 above). This principle involves the idea that social institutions must be justified by reference to their effects on individuals, but does not require that institutions be accountable to individuals' present perceptions of their own interests. It is individuals in hypothetical situations that are of central importance within the contractarian strategy.

At a minimal level, mutuality of advantage can be seen to relate directly to unanimity. If an institution offers advantages to all relative to some well-defined alternative, then we can expect unanimous support for that institution relative to that alternative, at least in so far as 'advantage' is related to expressed preference in the normal way. It is clearly a move of this type that provides the link between the specification of society as 'a cooperative venture for mutual advantage' and voluntary, unanimous agreement or contract as the key to normative analysis.

A third essential characteristic of the contractarian viewpoint to set alongside the principle of individual relevance and the requirement of mutuality of advantage is already clear from the above. If agreement is to provide the assurance of mutuality of advantage, then we must be assured that agreement is related to advantage in the normal way. This is a basic role of rationality in the contractarian perspective. Of course, the details of the way in which a rationality postulate influences the form of the contract, or the principles that emerge from that contract, will depend upon the precise notion of rationality that is employed; but, whatever the precise notion may be, rational agreement rather than agreement *per se* is the lynchpin of any contractarian theory (Rawls 1971, pp. 142–9, 416–24).[3]

A fourth aspect of contractarianism to be stressed here is the emphasis on an ultimately procedural normative criterion rather than substantive or end-state criteria. To be sure, some contractarians argue that their procedure identifies a unique set of end-state principles, but even in these cases it is the procedural argument that takes pride of place. Thus Rawls (1971, p. 15) is at pains to distinguish his argument for the contractarian method from the derivation of the particular principles of justice, viewing the former as more basic than the latter; and Buchanan (1975, ch. 1) eschews all end-state principles in arguing that the outcome of contractual bargaining at what he terms the pre-constitutional level carries normative significance regardless of its substantive content.

The fifth and final aspect of contractarianism to be mentioned here is the concern with the *status quo ante* problem that arises directly out of the emphasis on procedural justification. The essential question here is whether contractarianism can ever offer an entirely self-contained normative account. The outcome of any agreement must reflect not only the process of agreement but also the initial conditions or circumstances of agreement. Any conceivable outcome could be agreed by rational individuals starting from some artificially designed *status quo*. If contractarianism is to pass the 'so what' test associated with the question 'Why should I care that this outcome could have arisen from a particular type of agreement?' it must restrict the set of allowable initial conditions. The question is, then, whether this search for the appropriate initial conditions or Archimedean point can be conducted from within the resources of contractarianism itself, or whether some additional and external normative argument is required to ground the contract.

I have suggested that contractarianism entails moral individualism in the form of the principle of individual relevance, a commitment to mutuality of advantage, the explication of normative principles from the starting point of rationality, the adoption of an essentially procedural criterion as the ultimate touchstone of normative analysis, and a concern over the specification of the *status quo ante* relevant to the contract procedure. Before developing or deploying any of these aspects of the contractarian strategy, it is necessary to make two distinctions each of which identifies important sub-classes of contemporary contractarian thought: the first distinction hinges on an ambiguity in the notion of agreement, whilst the second concerns the intended range of application of the contract argument.

The ambiguity in the notion of agreement involves the distinction between consensual agreement and compromise agreement, and mirrors the distinction between co-ordination games and mixed-motive games (see Schelling 1960). Consensual agreement occurs when the individuals concerned share a common objective, or hold objectives that are directly co-possible, whereas compromise agreement arises when the individuals concerned have conflicting interests which nevertheless allow trade-offs that provide some mutual benefit. The consensual and compromise views of agreement each support a line of contractarian argument.

The consensual view of contract stresses the co-operative aspect of society and looks to evaluate social institutions from the point of view of that which is common or basic to all individuals. The Rawlsian specification of contractarianism is clearly consensual in this sense with the original position being the formal device that strips individuals of all those aspects which might provide sources of interpersonal conflict. From the consensual perspective the principles that should govern social institutions are derived by considering the rational choice of a 'representative' individual in the knowledge that the relevant agreement is guaranteed by the construction.

By contrast, the compromise view of contract stresses interpersonal bargaining as the appropriate paradigm, where conflict over the division of the socially generated surplus is of at least as great significance as co-operation. Buchanan and Gauthier both provide examples of compromise- or bargaining-based contractarianism, although the two cases vary significantly in many other respects.

The second distinction to be made identifies two views of the range of contractarianism: the global and the local. At its most ambitious, contractarianism can be seen as a theory of ethics, with the normative evaluation of social institutions dropping out as just one aspect of the overall social contract. Such a global contract is committed to the idea that contractarianism can provide a totally self-contained normative argument, which will involve, *inter alia*, a solution to the *status quo ante* problem.

Alternatively, contractarianism can be seen as being restricted to a local sphere – for example, the political sphere concerned solely with questions of social organization. If this more limited view of contractarianism is taken, then it is possible to resort to non-contract arguments in characterizing the background against which the local, political contract is set, and in particular in resolving the *status quo ante* problem. Thus, to offer an example which will be relevant later, the global view of contract must take individual rights to be grounded in the contract process, rather than the other way around, whereas the local view of contract may be able to accept rights and the contract process as independent inputs into normative political analysis.[4]

The distinction between global and local contractarianism cross-cuts with the distinction between consensual and compromise approaches to contract to yield four possibilities. A consensual–global view seeks to construct morality from within the resources that are argued to be common to all rational individuals without recourse to any claim regarding the positive moral significance of this starting point – although, of course, the starting point must still satisfy the requirements of neutrality or impartiality necessary to identify the truly common aspects of individuals. The Rawlsian contract argument may fall into this category with the fundamental nature of the individual providing the ultimate source or morality. It is in this sense that the theory can be seen most clearly to be Kantian, since it is the Kantian view of the nature of the individual that ultimately drives the argument.

In sharp contrast, Buchanan's contractarianism is of the compromise–local variety, with the constitution of social institutions, and particularly the state, being the subject matter of bargaining between individuals that takes place against a state-of-nature background.

II Contractarianism and liberal theory

The classic liberal argument moves directly from the value of liberty to the specification of the form and limitations of the liberal state (see, for example, Gray 1986, ch. 6). This form of argument constitutes what I have termed the theory of the liberal state. But such a theory invites this question: if individual liberty is the driving force of the theory, why should individuals not be at liberty to choose or agree the form and type of state that they prefer, provided of course that agreement is understood in a way which protects individual liberty and does not, for example, submerge some individuals in a tide made up of the majority? This question shifts attention back from the theory of the liberal state to the liberal theory of the state.

In this section I shall consider two possible lines of argument that might qualify as liberal theories of the state. The first possibility is that appropriate social institutions, including the state, will arise from the interaction of free individuals provided that those individuals act in ways that respect the liberty of others. This is the implicit or invisible-hand approach to the liberal theory of the state exemplified in the work of Nozick. The second possibility is the explicit or contractarian strategy in which individuals hypothetically confront direct choices about the principles that are to govern their social institutions.[5] I shall argue that, contrary to Nozick, the implicit or invisible-hand approach does not succeed in establishing a criterion by which social institutions can be evaluated, and that this failure renders Nozick's argument inappropriate as a liberal theory of the state. I shall then suggest that the contractarian strategy avoids the problems confronted by Nozick's argument and embodies a number of other characteristics that suit it to the task of providing a liberal theory of the state.

Nozick's invisible-hand argument hinges on the historical entitlement principle in which justice in acquisition and justice in transfer define justice in end-states. The procedural commitment manifest in this principle mirrors the proceduralism of contractarianism and lays the basis for the argument that social institutions that emerge from the operation of liberal or voluntary processes such as those involved in market exchange are to be approved as liberal. Nozick's argument that the liberal theory of the state conceived in this way results in a theory of the liberal state then requires only an argument that the liberal state will actually emerge from the operation of liberal processes.[6]

Nozick's defence of the entitlement principle is limited to an analogy with the logic of inference where the truth of the premises together with the truth-preserving properties of the rules of inference are sufficient to ensure the truth of the conclusion (Nozick 1974, p. 151). Much of the criticism of the entitlement principle has focused on the absence of a substantial theory of justice in acquisition in Nozick or elsewhere. However, as Reiman (1981) has argued, it is doubtful that the entitlement principle is valid – at least for repeated applications of the process of transfer – even if the justice of the initial position is granted.

In place of the analogy with the rules of inference, Reiman considers the following statement: if you are healthy and engage in a health-preserving activity then you will be healthy. This statement is of the same form as the entitlement principle and is true for single applications, but there can be no presumption of validity in the case of repeated application since there are many activities that are health-preserving (or even health-promoting) when performed once but fatal when repeated sufficiently often.

The question is, then, whether the rules of justice in transfer are subject to the sort of cumulative threshold effects which arise in Reiman's health example and which potentially invalidate the entitlement principle. This seems likely. For example, the accumulation of private property in small amounts may be fully consistent with the liberty of others in the way Nozick suggests, but if such accumulation is carried beyond a certain point it may begin to encroach upon the liberty of others as monopoly power is created. It is perhaps significant that Nozick's famous discussion of the Wilt Chamberlain example, which is intended to display the superiority of procedural principles over end-state principles, is restricted to a single application of the justice-in-transfer rule. Even if we share Nozick's intuition that Chamberlain is entitled to his high income since it is derived from a just starting point by voluntary means, would this intuition survive a continuation of the story in which Chamberlain used his income to acquire monopoly power over some important commodity (without violating any individual rights) and then used his monopoly power to restrict supplies and so make still higher incomes and acquire greater monopoly power (and so on)? Perhaps it is more plausible to suggest that, even if we agree with Nozick that a purely end-state principle of justice would involve unacceptable interference with procedures, we must also accept that a purely procedural principle such as the entitlement principle would involve at least the risk of collectively unacceptable end-states.

It is doubtful, then, that the liberal theory of the state as conceived by Nozick gives rise to any coherent criterion for the appraisal of social institutions, since an institution that arises by a sequence of individually just moves from a just starting point may or may not be just in itself. The problem here is essentially that the weight of a procedural normative criterion is being placed on market contracts which are not themselves indicative of individuals' considered evaluations of alternative social arrangements. Indeed, market contracts are simply one form of social institution about which individuals might have considered views, and it is clearly inappropriate to filter views about the comparative merits of different social institutions through one of the institutions under consideration. Put in other words, whilst Nozick's argument certainly gives pride of place to individual choice in a manner that respects liberty, the choices made are only choices concerning the allocation of goods within the society, not choices explicitly concerned with the form of society itself. Whilst the argument does constitute a particular version of the liberal theory of markets, it is not appropriately cast as a liberal theory of the state.[7]

Turning now to the contractarian strategy as a possible setting for the liberal theory of the state, the most obvious merit of this strategy is that it explicitly formulates the selection and evaluation of the constitutional and institutional structure of society as being directly responsive to the constituent individuals. The principle of individual relevance, the commitment to mutuality of advantage and the specification of full rationality all play a part in ensuring that the contractarian strategy reflects the evaluation of social institutions from the perspective of free and rational individuals, even though the circumstances of agreement are hypothetical. Thus the explicit or contractarian approach seems more appropriate to the task of providing a normative theory of the state than the implicit or invisible-hand argument concerning the evolution of social institutions.

The normative appeal of the claim that a given social arrangement is what free and rational individuals would agree is strong, but there are two further characteristics of the contractarian strategy that may seem to diminish the strength of this appeal: the procedural nature of the contractarian criterion and the resultant concern with the *status quo ante* problem. If the procedural nature of contractarianism is similar to Nozick's justice-in-transfer criterion, might we not expect to find potential threshold effects in the contractarian case which threaten the coherence of the criterion? And, even if this is not the case, are we not left with a problem of identifying the appropriate initial conditions that is parallel to the problem of establishing justice in acquisition?

The answer to the first of these questions is clearly no. The essence of any contractarian argument is that the agreement criterion (whether in its consensual or its compromise interpretation) operates at the level of a single conceptual contract rather than at the level of a sequence of actual contracts with potentially unanticipated cumulative effects. Given a suitable specification of the initial circumstances of agreement, the contractarian version of the procedural criterion successfully avoids the problem encountered by the entitlement principle.

The second question is much more problematic for contractarians. Indeed, this question is widely regarded (see, for example, Harsanyi 1987) as exposing the Achilles' heel of contractarianism. We have already noted that the *status quo ante* problem is particularly relevant to those who attempt to construct a global contract theory, since those whose ambitions are limited to local or political contractarianism have recourse to additional lines of argument. In particular, the local contractarian may use external moral argument to construct the required Archimedean point, or appeal to factual necessity in claiming that a particular specification of the *status quo ante* is required even though it is neither justified or justifiable.

In contrast, the global-contract theorist has only one line of argument available. He must argue that the particular specification of the initial circumstances of agreement adopted is justified precisely because it would be accepted and agreed as appropriate by relevantly rational individuals. The *status quo ante* itself must be subject to the formal test of agreement. This formulation seems to raise the spectre of an infinite regress with a search for the point from which to agree the point from which to agree the point from which . . . However, this concern is not warranted. It is conceptually possible to break the regress at the level of agreement on the *status quo ante*.[8]

A simple analogy will serve to illustrate this point. If we are planning a journey across unknown terrain, our agreement on an intended route will depend upon the perspective we gain from our starting point in exactly the way that the contractarian outcome depends on the *status quo ante*. But the possibility of asking ourselves the question 'From which point would it be best to plan the route?' is fully coherent, and the answer to the question may be expected to be independent of our current position. Of course, in this case we may presume that the notion of the *best* vantage point is defined independently of our agreement,[9] but in the contractarian case the fact that we agree that a particular vantage point is appropriate for the purpose of inquiring into ethical principles and their political implications does not commit us to any particular substantive position not already entailed by the adoption of the contractarian method, and provides the only justification admissible within that method. Of course, this argument does not show that an Archimedean point exists, still less that a unique Archimedean point exists, but it does at least establish that the search for such a point is coherent.

In the next section I shall be concerned with one aspect of this search concerning the relationship between contractarianism and rights. In the meantime we may conclude that, subject to some satisfactory specification of the circumstances of agreement, the contractarian strategy characterized by its commitments to the principle of individual relevance, mutuality of advantage, rationality and proceduralism does seem to provide a promising vehicle for the explication of the liberal theory of the state.

III Individual rights and contract

Substantive individual rights are a defining characteristic of any liberal state. Before addressing the question of whether a liberal theory of the state entails a liberal state, it is useful to address the preliminary question of whether the liberal theory can possibly support the liberal state, and, in particular, whether the contractarian strategy can ground rights.[10]

This preliminary question is not trivial, since the relationship between rights and contractarianism is complex, particularly in the case of the compromise interpretation of contractarianism that will be my major concern in this section. Of course, as I have already noted, only a global contractarian must hold that moral rights are dependent on the contract process rather than a morally prior input into that process (see, for example, Rawls 1971, p. 28). In contrast, a local or political contractarian may be willing to specify rights in one form or another as an independent input into the contract process. So we may expect that only a global-contractarian argument will be able to ground rights and so support the liberal state in a manner that is itself entirely liberal.

The consensual–global approach to contractarianism seeks to ground rights in the defining characteristics of the representative individual and, in particular, in the rational choices of such an individual. A central question here concerns the stability of the principles agreed in the social contract and the rationality of choosing a disposition that ensures or promotes compliance (see, for example, Rawls 1971, pp. 567–77; 1987). Essentially the issue is whether it is rational for the individual to commit herself to the internalization of the rights and other principles chosen at the contract stage. Individual strategies of pre-commitment of this general type are well within the bounds of possibility, so that there is at least the possibility that the consensual–global account of contractarianism can support substantive rights and, therefore, a liberal state.

The relationship between contractarianism and rights becomes more contentious when we consider compromise- or bargaining-based versions of contractarianism. Bargaining models require a specification of the initial endowments of each bargainer in order to be coherent, and these initial endowments are often identified as rights. Buchanan's view of contractarianism is bargaining-based and local in range. Buchanan holds that the appropriate starting point for a political contract is the 'natural' equilibrium of an anarchic society in which no rules or rights are recognized – the Hobbesian state of nature. This equilibrium identifies each individual's 'holdings', and it is these holdings that they bring to the bargaining table as a matter of factual necessity, even though the holdings are in no way justified or justifiable. Buchanan's local contract is, then, a means of realizing mutual advantage relative to an amoral starting point via social interaction regulated by agreed rules, but it does not offer any particular moral approval to the end-states that arise as a result of the operation of the agreed rules. In this setting it is not easy to find a place for moral rights of any sort. The local contract may certainly create and define a range of institutional or legal rights, but, even though the contract process accepts the initial 'holdings' as the appropriate – indeed, the only possible – starting point for bargaining, these holdings are never legitimized into moral rights (Buchanan 1975, pp. 21–3).

In explicit contrast with Buchanan, Gauthier (1986, pp. 193–9) argues that the acceptance of the arbitrary, 'natural' equilibrium as a starting point will undermine the normative force of the contract. In stating the relationship between his conception of contractarianism and rights Gauthier writes (p. 222) that 'Rights provide the starting point for, and not the outcome of, agreement. They are what each person brings to the bargaining table, not what she takes from it.' This seems to imply that the bargaining approach to contractarianism is restricted to the local level where moral rights may enter as a part of the specification of the appropriate circumstances of agreement. But Gauthier is a global contractarian and so must argue that the rights contained in his specification of the *status quo ante* are not logically or morally prior to the contractarian conception.

In outline, Gauthier's argument on this point begins from the proposition that it is only rational to enter into agreement with others if it will be rational to comply with that agreement once made. Under these circumstances, what can be said about rationally acceptable starting points? Gauthier contends that it would be irrational for any individual to accept an initial situation in which she suffered uncompensated costs, since this would bias the outcome of the bargain against her and so make it irrational for her to comply with the outcome. In this way it is suggested that the rationally acceptable starting position must be one which is neutral as between individuals in the sense that it embodies no prior coercion or predation. In short, it is rational for individuals intent on bargaining to insist on a starting point that respects Gauthier's interpretation (1986, p. 205) of the Lockean proviso.

This argument depends crucially on the precise specification of rational compliance. Gauthier argues that it is uniquely rational for individuals to comply only with agreements that are fair. This is termed 'narrow compliance' in contrast to any broader theory of compliance that would argue that it is rational to comply with an agreement even if it is not fair, so long as it satisfies some less restrictive criterion (clearly, the least restrictive criterion that could be adopted is that of simple advantage, whereby it is rational to comply with any bargain that makes you better off). But, as Kraus and Coleman (1987) have argued, this argument is problematic. On the one hand, if it were true that narrow compliance is uniquely rational, then Gauthier's argument is too complicated, since, if narrow compliance is uniquely rational, the *status quo ante* problem is trivial. If, on the other hand, it is rational to comply more broadly, Gauthier's argument does not fully resolve the *status quo ante* problem.

To see this, first accept that narrow compliance is uniquely rational. If agents will only comply with fair bargains, then the only bargains that it will be rational to make will be fair bargains, regardless of the initial circumstances of bargaining. So the fairness of the outcome is cut free from any need to specify the *status quo ante*. This would provide a fully self-contained global contractarianism, but would deny that 'rights are what each person brings to the bargaining table'. Rights would be simply a part of what is agreed. We could think of the overall bargain in two stages: a first stage to move from an arbitrary set of initial holdings which may have arisen from all manner of uncompensated or coercive actions to a rationally acceptable (i.e. agreed) allocation of rights; and a second stage to move from these rights to a fair and therefore rational outcome. The first stage of the contract reforms and moralizes the *status quo* whilst the second stage builds on the provided Archimedean point. Note that this conclusion runs counter to Gauthier's own criticism of Buchanan. If narrow compliance is uniquely rational, Buchanan's 'natural' equilibrium will provide a suitable starting point for bargaining, although the outcome of the bargain will be *as if* the starting point had been a suitably reformed and moralized version of the 'natural' equilibrium.

Now consider the case in which the claim that narrow compliance is uniquely rational is in error. If it is rational to comply with bargains that are less than fair (whilst still offering mutual advantage), then it will be equally rational to accept initial conditions for the bargaining process that are less than fair. So, although the argument from compliance may rule out some allocations of initial holdings as 'irrational', there seems to be no guarantee that it will reform the initial, arbitrary *status quo* sufficiently to moralize it.

In the absence of a convincing argument in favour of narrow compliance, and Gauthier's argument on this point is certainly flawed (see Kraus and Coleman)

1987, pp. 732–45), it seems that we are left with a fundamental indeterminacy in the relationship between the compromise–global approach to contractarianism and rights. But I would argue that this indeterminacy is not substantially different from that associated with the consensual–global approach to contractarianism, and furthermore that such indeterminacy is not fatal to a contractarian theory of rights.

As was indicated above, a defining characteristic of all contractarian approaches is the use of a fundamentally procedural criterion, so that there is naturally a degree of indeterminacy surrounding the substantive outcome of the contractarian process. It is for this reason that the contractarian test of any social arrangement or institution is best expressed in such a way that the arrangement passes the test if no one can reasonably object to it (Scanlon 1982). Of course, all the work here is being done by the requirement of 'reasonableness', which must include a view on rationality as well as a specification of the *status quo ante*, but the formulation does point out that it is not a particularly damaging criticism of contractarianism to claim that it does not identify the uniquely best social arrangement or institution. The contractarian strategy is not well suited to making claims of this type, but it can nevertheless partition the set of possible social arrangements into those that could be the result of 'reasonable' agreement and those that could not.

In the case of the consensual–global approach, the indeterminacy on rights is embedded within this general indeterminacy of outcomes, so that a detailed specification of the basic character of the representative individual and her decision-making process is required to narrow down the range of possible outcomes. Even then, of course, there is no guarantee of a unique outcome. In the case of the compromise–global approach, it seems that the indeterminacy occurs both at the level of the *status quo ante* and at the level of outcomes. But this appearance is misleading. As I have suggested, it is possible to recast the bargaining argument as a two-stage bargain in which rights are first established and then bargained over. Once this is recognized, it is a short step to the conclusion that rights are merely one part of the overall outcome of the bargaining process and that the indeterminacy regarding the agreement on rights parallels the general indeterminacy regarding outcomes.

Indeed, the separation of rights from other aspects of the general outcome of agreement is somewhat arbitrary and derives from the fact that writers in the compromise tradition tend to overemphasize the interpretation of agreement as exchange. The model of bargaining that is implicit (and often explicit) in Gauthier is one in which pre-existing rights are exchanged so as to maximize the gains from trade in a manner familiar from the economic analysis of market behaviour (see, for example, Gauthier 1986, pp. 227–32). However, as we have noted before, a social contract is not perfectly analogous to a market contract, and agreement – even in its compromise interpretation – is not restricted to exchange. Of course, compromise involves each person giving something up in response to similar sacrifice by others, and this trade-off can be thought of as generalized exchange, but the generalization is at least as important as the exchange in this formulation since there is no implication that the objects of 'generalized exchange' are pre-existing rights.

I began this section by noting that, whilst it is possible for a local or political contractarian to incorporate any view of rights into a normative analysis of political institutions, or indeed to construct an analysis which has no place for moral rights at all, a global contractarian must present a distinctively contractarian account of moral rights that grounds those rights in an appropriate concept of agreement. I have suggested that both the consensual–global and the compromise–global approaches to contractarianism can provide such a grounding, although the rights that result from the contractarian process are subject to a degree of indeterminacy. Indeed, although the apparent structures of the consensual and compromise approaches to global contractarianism seem to imply rather different views of rights, I have argued that there is no great distinction to be drawn. In each case it is ultimately an appeal to a particular notion of individual rationality, and, in particular, a notion of rational and voluntary compliance, that grounds rights.

Contractarian rights can therefore be thought of as those rights that can be reasonably agreed and which have the property of being self-enforcing in a community of reasonable individuals. Again, this formulation loads all of the work onto the requirement of 'reasonableness', but this is precisely the intent of any contractarian. Given a particular notion of what is individually reasonable, the contractarian method is the means of building from that notion into principles to govern social intereaction.

IV Liberal theory and the liberal state

We may now return to the substantive question of whether the liberal theory of the state entails a liberal state. The discussion so far has argued for the interpretation of the liberal theory of the state as the application of the contractarian strategy, and for the possibility of a distinctively contractarian grounding for rights. So it is at least possible that the liberal theory of the state will imply a strong commitment to individual rights and hence a liberal state. But in this final section I wish to argue that this possibility is not generally realized, so that a commitment to the contractarian strategy does not entail a commitment to substantive liberalism.

The basic point here should be clear enough from the earlier discussion. Contractarianism involves a commitment to liberty in the sense of the procedural criterion of voluntary agreement, but the liberty involved in this commitment is a generalized or formal freedom of choice which includes, *inter alia*, the freedom to choose the structure of rights in society and the weight to place upon rights-related considerations in determining social choices. It is not the substantive liberty associated with, and protected by, rights themselves. This second variety of liberty may be an outcome of the contract process, but it is by no means a necessary outcome.

Of course, this argument applies only to global contractarianism. In the case of local contractarianism, as we have already seen, it is possible to build in any particular view of rights as a background condition against which the contractarian logic operates. Clearly, if a theory of rights is chosen which defines particular individual rights and insists that they be viewed as constraints on social action, this choice will so constrain the political contract as to ensure a liberal state.[11] But the conclusion directly reflects the premise and does not reveal anything inherent in the contractarian logic.

Whether a globally contractarian argument results in a liberal conclusion or not clearly depends on the particular and detailed specification of the individuals who are party to the hypothetical contract, and the particular interpretation of reasonableness employed. But, even once these more detailed aspects of a particular contractarian argument are fixed, we have seen that we may still expect a degree of indeterminacy in the outcome of the contract. It may be that on some specifications of the contract model all feasible outcomes qualify as liberal states. For other specifications the feasible outcomes may share the characteristic of being aliberal (if not illiberal), whilst on still other specifications the feasible set of outcomes may include some that are substantively liberal and others that are not.

In approaching the normative analysis of the state, liberty may be interpreted in many different ways and at two distinct levels. I have argued that the more compelling of the two levels is that which focuses on the liberal theory of the state, rather than the theory of the liberal state, and that this can be interpreted as the adoption of the generally contractarian strategy. I have then argued that, whilst this strategy can serve to ground substantive individual rights, at least within certain limits, it does not entail the liberal state. The liberal theory of the state has a place for individual rights but is not pre-committed to their protection as the major or sole function of the state.

A hallmark of the contract process is its indeterminacy. Some may see this as a fatal weakness, but, if the contractarian strategy is seen primarily as a means of examining alternative normative claims, this flexibility is a major strength. The contractarian strategy does not provide a simple test for the ideal polity, but it can provide a fundamentally liberal method for distinguishing the good polity from the bad.

Notes

A distant ancestor of this essay was presented at the Research School of Social Sciences of the Australian National University and benefited from the comments of the late Stanley Benn,

Geoffrey Brennan and Gerald Gaus. This version of the essay owes much to discussion at a Liberty Fund colloquium on 'The Limits of Liberty' held at Chatham, Massachusetts, in June 1987, and particularly the contributions by James Buchanan, Joshua Cohen, Jules Coleman, David Gauthier, John Rawls and Thomas Scanlon. Philip Pettit provided useful comments at each stage.

1   The collections of essays in Frey (1984) and Paul, Miller and Paul (1984) offer a good point of entry to recent debate on rights.

2   Other aspects of contractarianism are emphasized in Scanlon (1977, 1982) and Hamlin (1986a).

3   Alternative views on rationality are canvassed in Elster (1979, 1983, 1986c). Hamlin (1986a) discusses contractarian applications of a variety of concepts of rationality.

4   This distinction between the global and the local is separate from the distinction between the foundational use of contract and the heuristic use of contract deployed by Scanlon (1982). Scanlon's distinction will be applicable at both the global and the local level.

5   Part 3 of Nozick (1974) contains an apparently contractarian defence of the liberal state (see note 11 below), but it is the invisible-hand theory of the first two parts of that book that I take as characteristically Nozickian.

6   I do not imply that Nozick's argument on this point is unchallengeable, only that I am not challenging it here.

7   On this see the distinction between the market and the meta-market in Hamlin (1984).

8   Despite the argument in Harsanyi (1987) that one cannot ground the practice of keeping to agreements in agreement, which is one version of the infinite regress. In fact it is possible to ground such a practice in this way if it is possible to argue that the agreement at the most basic level is self-enforcing, or the object of rational voluntary compliance. For more on the role of compliance see below.

9   So agreement is playing a purely heuristic role in the route-planning example, whereas it may be playing a foundational role in the identification of the appropriate *status quo ante*.

10 See Hamlin (forthcoming) for a critical discussion of recent attempts to ground substantive individual rights in indirect utilitarianism.

11 This is essentially the case in part 3 of Nozick (1974), where a constrained consensual–local contract formulation of the liberal state is presented.

7

Political Obligation

Russell Hardin

Theories of political obligation address what is perhaps the most bothersome issue in political philosophy: the justification of certain classes of coercion of individuals by government. In recent times, the notion of political obligation has been subjected to severe and telling attack. The principal focus of the attack has been on the element of voluntarism or consent on which obligation is often supposed to be based. If there is no consent, it is supposed that there can be no obligation. This is often little more than a definitional move. By definition, one can have an obligation only if one voluntarily assumes or consents to it.[1] As has long been argued, it is implausible to assert of many people that they have voluntarily assumed the obligation of political obedience. It follows that they cannot be politically obligated.

The argument against the factuality of consent was well put more than two centuries ago by Hume (1748). Yet, the notion of political obligation has continued to motivate many writers who seemingly accept the brunt of Hume's argument. On the definitional criticism, one might suppose these writers have simply missed the point in practice even while accepting it in theory. Alternatively, one may suppose that the definitional criticism misses a fundamentally important point. The function of a notion of political obligation is *to put the onus for governmental coercion on those who may be coerced*. Hume's dismissal of consent theory merely means that this function is not served if obligation depends on consent. One may well suppose that it can be based on something other than consent. Most political theories – perhaps all, except extreme anarchism, among those that are taken seriously by contemporary political philosophers – include justifications for coercion in certain circumstances.[2] Unless these theories are flawed at base, as genuine consent theories effectively are, they can present us with serious candidate theories of obligation.

The attack on the notion of political obligation may largely have been directed against Lockean contract thinking in political philosophy. It is an attack on a particular kind of justification for governmental coercion of individuals in certain contexts in which the individuals may be supposed to be obedient. If obedience cannot be grounded, coercion cannot be grounded. Because the general import of the criticism of Lockean contract thinking was well established long ago, the contemporary criticisms of political obligation would be of little more than marginal interest if their purpose were merely to refine the arguments of Hume and others. In the most compelling contemporary political theories, consent plays a role, if any, only at a rationalist level of derivation or justification, not at the level of practice or of actual citizens. Are the critics merely kicking a dead horse or tidying up our vocabulary? Evidently not. Some of the contemporary critics of political obligation seem to have a further purpose, which is to show that government and law can be given *no* privileged position in the binding determination of right conduct by individuals. For the Lockean contract tradition, this readily follows from the absence of real consent.[3] For theories not based on consent, however, their argument seems inconclusive. These theories may also fail to justify coercion, but they do not fail merely by definition.

Among theories under wide contemporary discussion, there are at least three general classes of political theory that are to some degree compelling but that are not subject to the standard criticism of political obligation. These are utilitarian, mutual-advantage and fairness theories. Within each of these, one can ground a principle of obligation in something other than consent. The role of obligation in fairness theories, especially that (or those) of Rawls, has been widely discussed,[4] and I shall only briefly address it here. Rawls, who is one of the definitional critics of political obligation, asserts (1971, pp. 113–14) that the notion of obligation does not apply to citizens because citizens cannot plausibly be supposed generally to have consented. However, he also speaks of the need for coercion and continues to speak of 'duties and obligations' (pp. 240–1, 333–91), so that one might suppose a coherent Rawlsian theory of political obligation could be constructed.

The extent to which a political theory can motivate a principle of obligation or of justified coercion is a measure of its credibility. A theory that cannot motivate a principle of obligation to abide by its results cannot finally be compelling. I wish here to focus on utilitarian and mutual-advantage theories, which have in common that they derive institutional arrangements and, hence, political obligation from interest or welfare. I wish to investigate the coherence of a principle of political obligation that may be derived from each of these theories. It should become clear that, while a utilitarian theory straightforwardly implies a justification for coercion in its own terms, a mutual-advantage theory faces inherent difficulties in justifying coercion to abide by its tenets. I shall briefly outline each of these classes of theory before constructing the form of their defence of political obligation – which is to say, the form of their justification of coercion by government.

On a utilitarian theory an individual may be obligated or may have a duty to obey a government if that government produces more good on the whole than any alternative. The good that an alternative might produce must include the (likely) costs of its coming to replace the extant government. It is generally supposed that act utilitarianism reduces this conclusion to the following very weak one: I should obey this government at this moment if that act of obedience has better effects than non-obedience. This is a weak conclusion because it is no more than the usual act-utilitarian principle, so that the law has no privileged role in my obligation to perform one or another action. This characterization, however, misses the point of utilitarian political theory, which is inherently about problems that individuals cannot expect to handle well without institutions, often powerful institutions. *An institutional utilitarian can justify the creation of institutions that will be coercive if these will bring about better results than non-coercive institutions would.* If this contingent condition is met, we can sensibly speak of a utilitarian theory of political obligation that is based in considerations of the general welfare.

Now consider mutual-advantage theories of politics. These do not generally require consent. Rather, they stipulate that one arrangement, *A*, is better than another, *B*, if in *A* everyone is better off than in *B*. Hence, we move from *B* to *A* because it is to our mutual advantage to do so. Of course, such a theory would be of no interest if there were never any possibility of universal improvement. Commitment to mutual-advantage theories requires belief that some governmental arrangement could be mutually advantageous as compared to some alternative, especially a *status quo* of weak or no government. Again, if this contingent condition is met, we can sensibly speak of a mutual-advantage theory of political obligation that is based in considerations of mutual benefit.

One might characterize mutual-advantage theories as a blend of elements of utilitarian and contract theories. They are, like utilitarianism, concerned with enhancing welfare. And, assuming people would voluntarily choose to be better off, they are, like contractarianism, concerned with universal voluntarism, of a kind, however, that can only be theoretically assumed rather than actually, tacitly or implicitly revealed. The principal difference between mutual-advantage and utilitarian theories of politics is that utilitarian theories readily allow trade-offs between individual welfares, whereas mutual-advantage theories do not. Rawls's theory is partly a mutual-advantage theory, although its more important element is concern for fairness in distribution (see Barry forthcoming). David Gauthier's theory of 'morals by agreement' (Gauthier 1986) is a full-fledged mutual-advantage theory. Many contemporary contractarian accounts have a strong concern for mutual advantage and, indeed, given the implausibility of any consensual basis, they may generally be more accurately characterized as mutual-advantage than as contractarian theories.

I The role of institutions in welfarist theories

How can a utilitarian or mutual-advantage theory ground obligation? Essentially through recognition of the necessity for institutions designed to achieve the ends the theory prescribes. At the political level, utilitarian and mutual-advantage theories do not focus on individual actions or choices. Rather they focus on general means for achieving relevantly determined outcomes for all concerned. Because individuals suffer from such liabilities as limited cognitive capacity, limited information, poor theories of cause and effect, and perverse incentives from interaction with others, they can generally expect to achieve better outcomes according to either the utilitarian or the mutual-advantage criterion if there are institutions to help get them to those outcomes.

Rawls argues, in 'Two Concepts of Rules' (1955), that utilitarianism is not subject to the traditional, even trite, complaint that it must violate justice in the following sense: if it were evidently true that the execution of an innocent after a contrived trial would prevent more deaths than it would entail, then a utilitarian would evidently have to recommend the unjust execution. Rawls objects to this argument that, in essence, it is set blandly somewhere out in the ether; it is not grounded in an institution that could actually carry out its recommendation. An actual institution of criminal justice is apt to work best in a utilitarian sense if it is designed to punish only those who are shown to be guilty. If so, it is such an institution that utilitarianism recommends, not the ethereal abuse of innocents to motivate others.

Suppose that we design utilitarian institutions. It is plausible that their workings would require actions of particular kinds by those who fill offices in them. These officers might decide, however, to act from direct, act-utilitarian calculations in violation of their offices. If such actions disabled the institutions, they would be wrong on a utilitarian account. Hence, the officers of our utilitarian institutions should follow the rules of the institutions, not the apparent dictates of act utilitarianism. This is a utilitarian conclusion. (See, further, Hardin 1988, esp. section 21.)

As already noted, the reason we need institutions, such as those for justice, for maintaining public works, and for collecting taxes to pay for the costs of government and its actions, is that institutions may be organized to do the job better than it could be done by the spontaneous efforts of individuals, even well-meaning utilitarian individuals. This is true in many ways. Consider two. First, institutions can help to co-ordinate actions for mutual and general benefit. Those who doubt their safety in the airspace over Chicago these days might ponder what it would be like without a coercive agency to regulate movements in that airspace. Thomas Nagel characterizes such coercions as unproblematic in that we can all be presumed to consent to the achievement of the relevant benefit and, hence, to the coercion that might be necessary to compel us in various moments, just as we must all consent to having traffic controls. As Nagel (1987, p. 224) says, such coercion 'is not really forcing people to do what they don't want to do, but rather enabling them to do what they want to do by forcing them to do it'. There may be complications of fact to muddy our account of any such coercion, but in principle this is not likely to be a contested view.

Second, one of the great values of government is to reap benefits from a division of labour in organizing ourselves beneficially. This consideration may cut much deeper into our concern with coercion. For example, a government specialist may decide on behalf of almost all of us that a certain drug or food or technology is unsafe for us and may ban its commercial development or sale. Most of us may consider this a benefit because we would be incompetent to judge for ourselves without massive wasted time on unwanted research, so that the government specialist either saves us that effort or protects us from the relevant harm. The government agent is not unlike our auto mechanics or dentists in specializing in ways that we do not. But the agent differs from these in acting, for better or for worse, without the incentives of market competition, so that no individual in the society may be able to seek alternative authoritative direction in using the putatively harmful drug or whatever. Because of this consideration, there may be real disagreement over government regulatory coercion, although there might not be.

Now note what we have done when we have put an institution in place to regulate our conduct for our own collective benefit, somehow defined. We have grounded any notion of individual political obligation *in that collective benefit*. The concept of political obligation generally is invoked to address conflicts between individual interests and the larger interests or will of a polity. In those political theories in which the larger interests of the polity are supposed to be grounded in individual interests, the notion of political obligation is inherently subject to a fallacy in reasoning about collective interests. If it is, then for these theories we may find that the notion of political obligation is incoherent for contingent reasons just as consent theories are incoherent for the contingent reason that too few of us can seriously be thought to have consented to any government. I wish to address this fallacy and to determine whether it must undercut any principle of political obligation for utilitarian and mutual-advantage theories.

The fallacy that threatens these interest- or welfare-based theories may be illustrated for certain theories based in mutual advantage. These theories are often couched in contractarian language as though individuals have somehow consented to the rule of their government and as though their consent creates an obligation. The presumption that people have consented is often itself apparently read off directly from the nature of the benefits that would flow to them from their political order. It is in this move that a fallacy potentially vitiates any claim of obligation. The fallacy is inherent in the assumption that you and I must consent to the rule of government because we must consent to what would be in our mutual interest. Unfortunately, what would be in *our mutual or collective interest* in our political organization is likely to be too ill defined to justify any particular government.

The form of the contractarian argument is that we consent to what is in our interest; the fallacy is that 'what is in our interest' is not uniquely defined, as I shall spell out below.

One way around problems inherent in supposing that we consent to government is to speak of a duty rather than an obligation to obey the law and to support a government. Hence, we might argue that there is no obligation for citizens *per se*, that there is mostly only a natural duty to abide by the laws of the state if the state or its laws satisfy some criterion. For example, Ràwls (1971, pp. 113–14) argues that there is a natural duty of citizens to abide by the laws of a state that is just. A utilitarian can argue in similar fashion that, although they may have no political obligations based in consent, individuals have a duty to abide by laws that conduce to the general benefit. Unfortunately our fallacy can afflict this argument as well: what conduces to the general benefit may not be well defined. This conclusion generally applies to utilitarian theories in which the possibility of precise addition of benefits and costs across individuals is ruled out. If our assessment of overall distributions is based on limited interpersonal comparisons, especially on only ordinal comparisons, of welfare, we cannot determine which of many optimal states is best and we are left with a fundamental conflict of evaluations that may undercut the logic of adopting one state rather than another.

For interest- or welfare-based theories, I wish to consider how certain claims for political obligation may make strategic sense, and then to consider complications that prevent them from being generally compelling. The discussion of political obligation often implicitly assumes that the structure of the problems we wish to regulate is that of certain 'easy' cases. What we wish to regulate, however, is, in principle, a much broader and more complex panoply of problems of varied structures. It is in its generalization from certain easy cases to more complex and yet commonplace problems that the notion of political obligation may lose its supposed mooring in individual interests.

It will be useful to break the discussion into parts by separately considering the kinds of political relationship we might wish to regulate with claims of obligation or duty. We may classify these political relationships in three general strategic categories of social interaction: those of essentially pure conflict, those of pure co-ordination, and those that involve a mixture of these two. In the mixed category, I shall especially be concerned with the centrally important class of interactions that we may call *co-operation* or *exchange*. I shall also be concerned with two very difficult classes of interaction that may be pervasive in political order: classes that we may call *unequal co-ordination* and *biased co-operation*. These classes of interaction will be defined later as variants of the modal classes defined immediately below.

Pure conflict interactions are represented by game 1, in which the pay-offs are strictly ordinal. The Row player can choose her strategy I or her strategy II. She ranks the outcomes, considered from her own interests alone, in the order represented by the first pay-off in each of the two cells, with the pay-off of 1 as her best outcome and 2 as her second-best outcome. Column ranks the outcomes in the reverse order. Hence, the interaction is one of pure conflict, because what makes Column better off makes Row worse off. We can, of course, vastly expand the matrix of choices for Row and Column while keeping their interaction one of pure conflict. If Row ranks the outcomes of a large matrix from 1 to 30, Column must rank them in reverse order, from 30 to 1, if the interaction is pure conflict.

Game 1   Pure conflict

		Column
	I	1, 2
Row		
	II	2, 1

A two-person interaction is pure co-ordination if, as in game 2, both players rank the outcomes in identical order. A pure co-ordination game may pose no problems of choice if both players are well informed of each other's interests and if there are not two or more outcomes tied for first choice in the two players' rankings. If there is a tie for first choice, there may be a genuine problem of co-ordinating our choices of strategies to ensure that we end up with one of the preferred outcomes. If we can communicate before choosing, we should have no problem co-ordinating. Alternatively, even if we cannot communicate easily but our interaction is iterated many times, then we may generally expect to achieve successful co-ordination by trial and error. Once we succeed, we simply continue with the successful strategy choice as a *convention* (see Lewis 1969).

Game 2   Pure co-ordination

		Column	
		I	II
	I	1, 1	2, 2
Row			
	II	3, 3	1, 1

Game 3   Prisoner's dilemma or exchange

		Column	
		Yield x	Keep x
Row	Yield y	2, 2	4, 1
	Keep y	1, 4	3, 3

While these two pure types of interaction are not without great interest, much of what is interesting in social life seems to involve interactions that combine elements of co-ordination with elements of conflict, as in what are infelicitously called mixed-motive games. The variety of such games is large even for two persons, and it increases geometrically as the number of persons involved increases. On the evidence of how much has been written about it and of how many experiments have been run on it, the prisoner's dilemma, as represented in game 3, is by far the most interesting of all such mixed-motive games. It is partly a game of co-ordination because both players prefer the upper-left outcome to the lower-right outcome. It is partly a game of conflict because the Column player prefers the upper-right to the lower-left outcome and the Row player has the opposite preference. The chief reason why the prisoner's dilemma has received such great attention is arguably that it seems to fit a vast array of actual interactions that interest us. It fits them because they are exchange interactions and the prisoner's dilemma is the game-theoretical model of exchange (Hardin 1982).

All of these strategic structures can be generalized in some meaningful way to interactions among large numbers of people, as in a legal system or a social order. Any one of these strategic categories may seem to play a larger role in the grounding of some theories of politics than in the grounding of others. For example, contractarian theories typically seem to be especially concerned with mixed interactions of exchange and co-operation to the neglect of pure conflict and co-ordination interactions. Indeed, in an extraordinary move, Gauthier (1986) goes so far as to say that, if morals are the result of (hypothetical) agreement among rational persons, they can only govern interactions with the structure of interests represented in the prisoner's dilemma. Given the entensive role of government in essentially conflict and co-ordination interactions and in mixed interactions other than the prisoner's dilemma, we must want a theory of political obligation to accommodate such interactions or to justify their exclusion. Without a sophisticated argument to say why resolution of the much broader class of interactions cannot be seen to yield mutual advantage, as resolution of prisoner's dilemma interactions generally does, we want more in our political theory than Gauthier allows in his moral theory.

Suppose we wish to achieve regulation of a particular form of social interaction. How we should best regulate it, either on a consent theory or on a utilitarian theory, may depend on which category it fits into – conflict, co-ordination or mixed motive. Political obligation and legitimacy typically are at issue in any justification of the use of coercion to motivate compliance or to correct disobedience. How we regulate an interaction and how we achieve coercion may be strongly related in that the latter may imply the former. But they may be partly unrelated in that regulation may largely be achieved without coercion. Moreover, the possibility of coercion may even be parasitic on or determined by the success of non-coercive regulation of other interactions. Our subjective sense of the legitimacy of a particular coercive move may depend on which of these relationships holds for the relevant interaction and the coercive device used.

II The hardest case: pure conflict

Pure conflict interactions do not generalize to larger numbers of players for the simple reason that three or more players cannot all have exactly opposing preferences over a set of outcomes, as two players can. They might therefore seem to be irrelevant for social analysis. Against this conclusion, note that we may often simplify large-number interactions into effectively two-party interactions if we may sensibly suppose that the large numbers are actually assignable to two conflicting groups. This is essentially the move Rawls makes in his difference principle: he evaluates or ranks outcomes according to how they benefit the worst-off class in the relevant society, as though all others were in another, more or less opposing, class. The worst-off class should be made to benefit at the expense of the residual class of all others if that is possible without making some other group the new worst-off class and making them even worse off than the original worst-off class was.

Such pure conflict interactions are inherently problematic for any theory of political obligation or duty. They can be dealt with under utilitarian theories if sufficiently strong interpersonal comparisons of welfare can be assumed to justify a claim that transfers from one class to another yield net benefits. Any such assumption is rejected by many, including contemporary economists who object to interpersonal comparisons of welfare, although modest comparisons are commonly assumed by political theorists, even if often only implicitly.

Pure conflict interactions may be dealt with on traditional contractarian theories only if we can presume that all would agree to bear the relevant costs. *Prima facie*, this sounds like a dubious presumption. On my reading, this troubling issue is not addressed in an articulate way by anyone in the contractarian tradition before Rawls. Rawls deals with it by supposing that, *ex ante*, we choose a set of institutions that would maximize the worst-off state we might find ourselves in. This move involves a normative imposition on our choices. One might also read some of Rawls's argument as supposing that we trick up the problem of such a pure conflict in distributive results as a problem of the mutual advantage to be got from our prior joint organization of society (see Hardin 1988, ch. 4). If we succeed in the latter move, there is then no problem of pure conflict but only one of mixed-motive or exchange. That is to say, we do not simply face the task of distributing what we have produced; rather, we co-operate for mutual advantage to create a particular political order. A full definition of that order includes what we produce as well as how we distribute it. Ideally, the problem we now face is an easy case of simple co-operation, as discussed below. Hence, we might suppose it possible to obtain genuine agreement *ex ante* to the resolution of certain classes of (*ex post*) pure conflict interactions so that we could then assert a political obligation to abide by the relevant resolution from a claim of consent or mutual advantage.

III The easy cases, 1: pure co-ordination

Suppose you and I are in an interaction of pure co-ordination, as represented in game 2. We are both indifferent between the two outcomes with pay-offs (1, 1) but we both clearly prefer either of those outcomes to the other outcomes. If it is clear to me that you have already chosen your strategy I or that you probably will, then I prefer to choose my strategy I. If you have chosen or are likely to choose your strategy II, then I also prefer to choose my strategy II. Now suppose there are many of us involved in an interaction that is a straightforward generalization for many persons of game 2. Also suppose we choose strategies more or less independently in the sense that we do not directly communicate and we do not receive direct signals from some co-ordinating authority. If it appears to me that virtually everyone is choosing strategy I, then I shall wish to choose strategy I.

If we generalise this interaction to a large number of actors in a relevant way, I shall seem to have even less choice in the determination of which outcome we co-ordinate on than I should in a two-person case. If most others have chosen or seem likely to choose strategy I, then I should do so as well. If we iterate the interaction several times, we can generally expect all of us to reach the same solution even without extensive communication or co-ordination by an active agent. It would be pointless for me to try to get everyone to co-ordinate on strategy II if they are virtually all co-ordinated on strategy I. It would be pointless, first, merely because I should gain nothing from the change. But it would also be pointless because it would be difficult for me to give the others any incentive to switch strategy choices. In a two-person co-ordination, the fact that I choose strategy II would be incentive for you to choose it as well.

In one important sense it would be odd to speak of political obligation to go along with a large-scale co-ordination. The sense is this: that it would be odd in general to speak of my obligation to do what is in my interest. The obligation seems otiose. What moral force there is in the obligation comes from the fact that it is in my interest. Why would it be immoral and hence contrary to duty to violate the co-ordination? Because it would violate my interest.

There may still be some sense, however, to the claim that I am obligated to go along with a co-ordination: namely, that my not going along might harm others. For example, if I choose to drive on the right in Australia or on the left in North America, I run the risk of harming someone else in addition to harming myself. One may suppose that I have a natural duty not to harm others where there is no off-setting beneficial reason, and that this duty comes into play once certain co-ordinations are achieved or once certain conventions are established. Hence, I may have a duty to go along with an established co-ordination; and for relevantly political co-ordinations, such as those to achieve beneficial order, I may have a specifically political duty to go along. In general, however, it would be odd to have to invoke such a duty, because failure to observe it would be directly contrary to anyone's own interest.

Here the duty is not conceptually otiose because the duty or obligation derives from the interest of others and is not merely the circular moralization of one's own interest. But still the duty need not affect anyone's motivation. Suppose that the point of speaking of political obligation is largely to justify the use of coercion to motivate compliance with some aspect of political order. The point of coercion typically is to give people different incentives, to make some action be in their interest rather than contrary to their interest. Using coercion to get someone to conform to a co-ordination that is already in her interest merely makes it more in her interest. If coercion affects behaviour in such a case, we must wonder whether it really is *such* a case.

IV The easy cases, 2: simple co-operation

Simple co-operation has the structure of the prisoner's dilemma, game 3, which is the structure of ordinary exchange. You have what I want; I have what you want; we would both prefer to swap than to keep what we have. We may generalize this in an appropriate way from two to *n* persons, in which case it becomes a problem of collective action. Once our co-operation involves many more than two persons, however, it may begin to be true that there are no relevant incentives to co-operate. In the two-person case, I have incentive to co-operate if that is the only way for me to get what you have. In the *n*-person case, I may still benefit from the co-operative actions of everyone else even if I do not act co-operatively. If the cost to me of my own co-operation is less than the additional benefit to me from my own co-operation, I have an incentive not to co-operate or an incentive to free-ride.

In a multi-person co-ordination, the incentive for me to choose one strategy rather than another typically increases as the number of others in the co-ordination increases. In a multi-person co-operation, the incentive to me to choose the co-operative strategy typically decreases as the number of others in the co-operation increases. My own interest and the interests of others are likely to be in clear conflict in such a co-operative interaction. Hence, the potential force of a notion of obligation or duty to co-operate may be much greater than that of an obligation or duty to co-ordinate. Moreover, the role of coercion seems clear in this context. We might suppose that, if we put to a vote the question whether all co-operate or none co-operate, there would be a unanimous preference for having all co-operate. Hence, we might think it justified to coerce anyone benefiting from the co-operation of others to co-operate as well. This is a position that Hart (1955, p. 183) and Rawls (1971, p. 112) have supported and that, of course, others have disputed (see Hardin 1985, esp. pp. 412–16). I think the issue is one that depends in part on the problem raised below (under 'Biased co-operation'): whether I should be coerced to co-operate to our mutual advantage may turn on whether I can reasonably claim to think there would be a better alternative. As a rule, it would be odd to suppose that there would be *no* alternative that any particular one of us would prefer. The rare exception to this possibility would presumably be an extraordinarily important instance of mutually beneficial action in circumstances that made for a virtually unique recommendation for individual action toward the collective benefit.

V Unequal co-ordination

Suppose we are involved in a co-ordination problem analogous to that in game 4. I prefer the outcome (1, 2); you prefer the outcome (2, 1). Both of us would strongly prefer either of these to the other outcomes. Suppose further that there is no way for either of us to compensate the other or to bind ourselves to compensate the other for acquiescing in our preferred outcome. Hence our successful co-ordination must put one of us at a disadvantage relative to the other in that one of us must receive only a second preference while the other receives a first preference. We are in an unequal co-ordination.

Game 4   Unequal co-ordination

		Column	
		I	II
Row	I	3, 3	2, 1
	II	1, 2	4, 4

Now let us generalize game 4 from two to n persons in the following way. Some of us, m persons, prefer one outcome over all others, and the remainder of us, $n - m$ persons, prefer a different outcome over all others, and all of us prefer either of these two outcomes over all others. As in the n-person simple co-ordination game discussed above, we may now find ourselves *individually* unable to affect the outcome that is selected. We may simply find ourselves individually best off if we go along with the nearly unanimous co-ordination that has been achieved.

For some of us, this co-ordination will yield the best of all outcomes; for others it will yield only a second-best outcome. The difference may be substantial. Consider two examples that are commonplace in our lives. In order to achieve productive co-ordination of our efforts, the best arrangement for us may be to have a strong organizational hierarchy or to have a clear division of labour even without organizational hierarchy. Either the hierarchy or the division of labour may imply great inequality of benefits. In the hierarchical organization of our production it may not matter very much for our productivity who is on the top and who is on the bottom. But it may matter very much to any individual whether she is on the top or on the bottom. Similarly, division of labour may be very efficient for total production, but the division may put some in activities or occupations that are far less desirable than others. Even in the mini-society of a family, efficient production may imply unequal roles.

In the general class of interactions represented by game 4, the acquiescence of those who are at a disadvantage in the unequal co-ordination is merely a matter of necessity or interest. Suppose it ceased to be in the interest of some of them to acquiesce – for example, because they could co-ordinate among themselves on forcing an alternative co-ordination on the larger society. There might then be no obvious argument that it would be wrong for them to cease to acquiesce. Any claim that we are obligated to go along with a generally beneficial co-ordination is ill defined for this interaction, because more than one 'generally beneficial' co-ordination is possible. Hence, a claim of political obligation to maintain a generally beneficial co-ordination cannot stop someone with a revolutionary intent to reco-ordinate. There might be claims for political obligation that would have force here – for example, one might urge against the revolutionary that revolution cannot succeed or that it will be woefully harmful to virtually everyone – but such claims would not derive directly from the co-ordination structure of the interaction.

The more a sense of political obligation is needed to make things work in such an unequal context, the less it is likely to be justifiable. Why? Because the more it is needed to override individual interest the less it can be justified on the ground of its serving individual interests.[5] Hence, the notion of political obligation becomes not merely otiose but spurious in the context of unequal co-ordination.

VI Biased co-operation

As usual, let us address the problem of biased co-operation by first considering a two-person case in order to make the issues clearer. Suppose you and I each have two goods. You have x and y; I have u and v. Your two goods are near-substitutes for each other, mine are near-substitutes for each other, but either of yours would be a good complement for either of mine in the following senses. Two goods are substitutes if they can each perform roughly the same function for us, as, say, pasta and potatoes might substitute for each other as starches in a meal. Two goods are complements if each of them adds to the value or enjoyment of the other, as, say, pasta and sauce complement each other.

Suppose further that we have slightly different preferences over various possible outcomes involving trades between us. In general, however, we would both rather make a trade of one of our goods for one of the goods of the other. I would most prefer one trade, for example, v for x; you would most prefer a different trade, for example y for u. But neither of us would prefer to have both of the other's goods to both of our own. My preferences over all possible pairs are in the order ux, vx, uy, vy, uv (my original holdings) and xy (your original holdings). Your preferences are identical except for reversing the final two pairs in the list. Our problem, then, is that we could engage in several exchanges of one of my goods for one of yours, but we would not wish to trade both for both. That is, we face a choice among several (four) mutually exclusive bilateral exchanges, any one of which would be desirable to both of us if there were no alternatives. But, if you get your most desired trade, I do not get my most desired trade.

Whatever trade we now make may be unequal in the sense that, out of all possible outcomes, you will rank the result of our trade higher in the list than I will or *vice versa*. For example, suppose our trade leaves you with y and v, and me with x and u. I now have my most preferred pairing, while you have your fourth preferred pairing. If you get your most preferred pairing, u and x, I may get only my fourth preference, and so forth. If the differences in our absolute valuations over our rankings are large, we may find our resulting trade quite conflictual, even though it benefits both of us as compared to the *status quo*. An argument merely from mutual advantage cannot settle which of various trades we should make.

Such problems may not generally be grievous in actual trades between individuals, because, outside families, we do not generally engage in such commodity-for-commodity trades. Rather, we trade goods (or time and effort) for money and money for goods without any need to match what I trade away and what I receive in trade with the counterparts of any particular other person. In political decisions over collective provisions of group goods, however, we may necessarily have to choose between a good that one group prefers and an alternative, largely substitute good that another group prefers. For example, we may give subsidies to those who seek private education or we may directly subsidize public education. To the extent that we trade off one of these kinds of programme for the other, we differentially benefit one group over another. Yet it may genuinely be believed by all that more education of anyone tends to benefit the whole society. That is to say, if one of these policies were impossible, we might all opt for the alternative. But, if both are possible, if they offer differential benefits, and if the two are largely mutually exclusive or are largely substitutes for each other, then we face a conflictual choice. If we make one collective provision, the other may cease to be a beneficial prospect because its cost will now outweigh the incremental additional benefit it might bring beyond what has already been brought by the first collective provision.

The problem here is accurately described as one of biased co-operation rather than merely as an instance of the unequal co-ordination discussed above. Note one important difference. In a case of unequal co-ordination, the result of the co-ordination is essentially self-enforcing against anyone who wishes to change the result to a more favorable outcome. In a problem of biased co-operation, we may all still prefer to be free riders on the collective provision, which may be achieved only through sanctioning all of us to generate relevant contributions, such as tax payments. There might be little or no hope of successful, voluntary collective provision of either of two (or more) outcomes that, although each is unanimously preferred to some *status quo* of no provision at all, are conflictingly ranked by various groups.

It is here, of course, that the problem of political legitimacy, obligation or duty enters. Am I obligated to contribute to our collective provision if I strongly prefer a different collective provision? One cannot simply answer this query with a claim that I am better off with the provision we have than with none. One must be able to say why I should be bound by a provision that is for me, and perhaps a very large group of others, inferior to what we could achieve with an alternative provision that *similarly* would make everyone better off than they would be with no provision. This question need not be bothersome if we seldom face such conflictual collective actions or provisions. Unfortunately, in a complex society with varied tastes and needs, we can arguably expect such conflicts over virtually all significant collective provisions. Hence, the static comparison between a particular collective provision and the *status quo* cannot settle the question of political legitimacy for that provision. The easy case of simple co-operation discussed above cannot generally fit the problem of political obligation or duty. Hence, mutual-advantage theories cannot motivate a principle of political obligation because the notion of 'mutual advantage' is too ambiguously defined in general.

VII Conclusion

For the last two classes of problems, unequal co-ordination and biased co-operation, it is inherent in political order that we often must choose one or the other mutually exclusive provision or regime in such hard cases. While the one or the other choice or even both choices might readily pass the test of utilitarianism, it is unclear how either can be said to pass the test of mutual advantage, which is inherently ill defined in the face of such choices. Mutual-advantage theories may be a contemporary effort to resuscitate some core part of contractarianism in moral and political theory. (This seems clearly to be true for the theories of Rawls and Gauthier.) Hence, they are framed *ex ante*, as though the problem is to compare possible regimes to some *status quo* of very limited or no government. In this move they are grievously afflicted by our fallacy. Alternatively, they could be useful in an effort to argue that it is in our mutual advantage to abide by an extant regime. In such an argument, the additional costs of making a serious change may typically mean that it would not be to our mutual advantage to move to any very different alternative regime. This, however, would be a very dispiriting use of mutual-advantage theory. Of course, in so far as mutual-advantage arguments are used in ideal theory, as they are by Rawls and Gauthier, this alternative use would be of little or no interest.

There are various ways in which we might deal with the problems of biased co-operation and unequal co-ordination in political life. Rather than try to judge the merits of a particular, perhaps fundamentally important, result of such interactions, we might judge the fit of that result with prior notions of how to resolve them. For example, Brennan and Buchanan (1985) wish to avoid conflicts of choices over actual goods and policies by reaching agreement on the structure of the institutions for making such choices. Alternatively, we might suppose that some particular institutional arrangement, such as majoritarian democracy, for making such choices is special or morally privileged (see, for example, B. Barry 1979). A major objection to first selecting an institutional arrangement and then letting it make the conflictual choices is that we may already face the conflictual choices at the level of choosing among institutional arrangements. As Brian Barry (1979) notes, in other words, of majoritarian democracy, if the majority population is green and the minority is orange and if their interests differ systematically, we may wonder how we could consensually agree on majoritarianism even *ex ante* from behind a more or less opaque veil of ignorance. Buchanan often notes that, in constitutional and social choice more generally, we start from here and now. Most of us will agree with this as a pragmatic judgement, although many may disagree with it as a judgement of ideal moral or political theory. In either case, we will have to recognize that, practically, Buchanan's dictum implies that the choice of institutional arrangements does not cut the knot of conflicts over specific interests.

We might suppose that we could still find a society in which interests on political issues were so congruent that its members would not face such conflicts as those in interactions of unequal co-ordination or of biased co-operation. In such a society it would be hard to give much force to a notion of political obligation just because there would be no conflict of interest over political decisions. In less simple societies, however, 'collective interest' may be too conflicted a notion for political obligation to be grounded in it.

Notes

This essay was written while I was a Visiting Fellow in the Research School of the Social Sciences of the Australian National University. The idyllic conditions of intellectual life at ANU, with the glorious, not to say improbable, background of Australian flora and fauna, were a splendid stimulus to writing. I wish to thank Philip Pettit, Frank Jackson and Jane Marceau for their sponsorship of my time at ANU. I also wish to thank Philip Pettit, Reynolds B. Schultz and participants in the faculty seminar of the Center for Ethics, Rationality and Society at the University of Chicago for extended comments on an earlier draft of the paper.

1 Hart (1955), pp. 175–91; Rawls (1971), p. 113; Simmons (1979), pp. 14–16. Simmons gives useful citations to much of the extant literature on political obligation.
2 Simmons seems to be a fairly extreme anarchist. See Simmons (1987), esp. n. 9.
3 Walzer (1970, esp. pp. 99–119) gives an articulate account of Lockean consent and its difficulties.
4 Simmons (1979, ch. 5) argues that a fairness theory cannot yield a principle of political obligation, but his argument turns on defining obligation as based in consent. See also Klosko (1987a, 1987b).
5 Hume (1739–40, III. ii. 9; 1978 edn, p. 553) argues that the obligation to obedience to government ceases when 'interest ceases, in any great degree, and in a considerable number of instances', to be served by government.

Part III

The Responsibility of the State

8

The State as a Moral Agent

Robert E. Goodin

Individuals find all sorts of excuses for not doing the right thing. What follows is a story about how two such excuses cut across one another in some rather surprising ways. The failure of isolated individuals to do the right thing is excused, but only at the price of permitting (or perhaps even requiring) co-ordinated collective action wherein individuals may be rightly required to play their respective parts.

The analytic key to this argument is simply the proposition that the state is a moral agent, too. It has responsibilities of its own (or, if you prefer, we have responsibilities through it) even where – indeed, especially where – we as individuals are excused from any responsibility for undertaking isolated, independent action. Hence the basic finding of this essay: arguments for letting individual moral agents off the hook have the effect of putting collective moral agents such as the state on it, in their stead.

I Two excuses

How exactly we are to determine what is the 'right thing' to do is problematic. Happily, that whole set of issues can be safely left to one side for the purposes of this essay. My story here begins after that one is finished. Even after it has been agreed what the right thing to do would be – however that has been decided – there is still a variety of excuses that can be given for not doing what it is agreed that, in some sense, ideally we ought to do.

Two such excuses concern me here. One can be called the 'libertarian' excuse: it is right that something be done, but wrong to force people to do it. The other can be called the 'no individual responsibility' (or, more colloquially, the 'not my job') excuse: it is right that something be done, but it is not my job to do it; I have no individual responsibility in the matter.

Each of these excuses is plausible in its way. Take the libertarian excuse, for example. There genuinely are many things that we think it right that people should do, but wrong that they should be forced to do.

One reason has to do with the crucial role of people's intentions among the right-making characteristics of the act. Sometimes it is thought not to be enough that the right thing be done; it must also be done for the right reasons, if it is to count as morally worthy. Locke gives one indisputable example in his *Letter Concerning Toleration* (1689), when he points out that pious acts performed by non-believers merely to avoid social sanctions will not suffice to procure their salvation. Kantians would place most acts in the same category. Where the right act must be performed for the right reason, if it is to be right at all, forcing people to perform it would be futile. If their reason for performing the act were merely to avoid social sanction, then they would be acting from the wrong reason in a way that undermines the rightness of the act itself. It is strictly impossible, in such circumstances, to force people to act rightly.

Another argument tending towards the same practical conclusion has to do with the value of liberty. In the above argument, right acts lose their rightness when performed merely to avoid social sanction. In this next argument, right acts retain their rightness even when forced; but force constitutes a moral cost all its own, to be set off against any moral gains achieved by securing superior performances. This story can be fleshed out in various ways. We might say that liberty is a moral end in itself, and that its being infringed is in itself a moral cost. Or (or 'and': these are nowise incompatible options) we might take a 'developmental' line, emphasizing the importance of letting people learn from their own mistakes, so that they make fewer of them in the future. Here, liberty would not be an end in itself, but rather a means of producing better outcomes at less cost in future.

The 'not my job' excuse, similarly, often has a good deal of surface plausibility about it. There may be something paradoxical about admitting that it would be good for something to be done and yet, at one and the same time, denying that it would be good for you to do it. But the paradox is more apparent than real. In truth, there are various plausible reasons for admitting that it would be good for something to be done (by someone) and yet denying that it should be morally mandatory for you, in particular, to do it.

One reason might be that the good to be done is something that you yourself simply cannot do. Sometimes the impossibility is strictly logical. It may be good that parents care for their own children; but, not being one of this child's parents, that particular good is not one that can be attained by your caring for the child. Other times, the impossibility might be merely contingent. As it happens, you are incapable (or much less capable than someone else) of doing what is required to promote the particular good in view. Yet other times, the impossibility might be of a psychological sort. Given your own deep commitments (to people, projects, and so on), and given your own psychological make-up, you simply cannot bring yourself to do what might be required of you to promote the good wherever and whenever you could. There are some things that you might do that truly are above and beyond the call of moral duty; some of them are such that it is all right for you to omit performing them (Pettit and Goodin 1986, pp. 651–9; Urmson 1958).

This last proposition, in particular, relies on something like the 'bottomless pit' objection. At root, the protest there is that, if you were morally required to do all the things of this sort that would be morally good to be done, then too much of a sacrifice would be demanded of you. This might be due either to the depth or to the scope of those demands. Doing the right thing on any one occasion might be just too costly reasonably to demand it of a person; or, while doing the right thing on any one occasion would not be so very costly, there might be just too many occasions that are identical in all morally relevant respects for us reasonably to expect you to do the right thing in all of them (Fishkin 1982).

That latter thought is much of what motivates the standard distinction between 'perfect' and 'imperfect' duties. The former are strong demands – obligations to be discharged every time the situation arises. The latter are weak demands, in comparison. You must discharge such obligations on at least some occasions, but you need not discharge them on all occasions when they arise. Contractual obligations are a standard example of the former, 'duties of charity' of the latter. This distinction between perfect and imperfect duties has implications for the enforceability of such duties, in turn. Since we ought always discharge each perfect duty, it is morally proper to enforce such duties whenever they arise, in a way that it would not be appropriate to enforce each instance of an imperfect duty which we need not discharge every time it arises.[1]

II Exculpating individuals, inculpating states

Those are very standard perspectives on a pair of very standard excuses. My aim here is neither to challenge nor to elaborate on them. It is instead to show how those two excuses can cut across one another. The first step in this argument lies in showing how the second ('no individual responsibility') excuse, while exculpating individuals, inculpates collectivities. The next step, in section III below, is to show how that in turn undermines the 'libertarian excuse', justifying collective enforcement of moral demands upon individuals.

So let us consider, then, the excuse that something is 'not my job' or 'not my responsibility'. Certainly there are good reasons (of a pragmatic, and perhaps even deeper, sort) for a moral division of labour. There are good reasons for assigning particular, morally important tasks to some particular moral agents as their exclusive realm of responsibility. Once that assignment has been made, there are good reasons (pragmatic, certainly, and perhaps even deeper) for not trespassing upon someone else's moral preserve. If that is what we mean by saying, 'It's not my job' or 'It's not my responsibility', then the force of that proposition is plain for all to see.

The form of the phrase 'It's not my job' may well serve to suggest that that is what the excuse standardly means. Saying, emphatically, 'It's not *my* job', might seem to carry with it the unspoken message that it *is* someone else's. But, of course, there is no reason for supposing that that will always be true. If responsibility has been assigned to no one, then it is true of each in turn that it is 'not my job'.

In that case, much of the former force of the excusing proposition is lost. If it is neither your job nor anyone else's, then the objection to doing something that it is 'not your job' cannot be that you will be meddling in someone else's moral business. It cannot be that you will be undermining the moral division of labour. And, while it is still perfectly possible, it is much less likely under those circumstances that you will be cutting across someone else who is trying to do the job himself. Thus, it is much less clear why you should be excused from doing something, just because you have not been assigned responsibility for it, when no one else has been, either.

As Austin says (1956–7, p. 3), excuses characteristically get us out of the fire into the frying pan. Getting off the hook in one way puts you on the hook in another.[2] Or getting someone off the hook puts someone or something else there, in his place. That is as much the case as ever with the 'no individual responsibility' excuse. It gets individuals off the hook, but succeeds only in putting the group there in their place.

What is no one's responsibility is everyone's. If it is right that something be done, and no one in particular has been assigned responsibility for doing it, then we are all responsible for seeing to it that it be done.

To say that all are responsible is not necessarily to say that each is responsible, though. Still less is it to say that each is necessarily responsible for attempting to do whatever must be done himself. The act in question may be such that it is either unnecessary or even counterproductive for everyone to perform it. It may be the cast that, once any one of them performe dit, none of the others would need to; or it may be the cast that, once any of them commenced performing it, others' attempting simultaneously to do so would constitute counterproductive interference. Or the 'bottomless pit' problem, canvassed above, might arise: asking everyone to perform all morally desirable actions might impose an unreasonable sacrifice on each of them. For such reasons, we typically – and rightly – suppose that, when responsibilities have not been allocated to anyone in particular within a group, the most that can be said is that each of them has an imperfect duty to perform at least some (but not necessarily all) of the acts that we might ideally wish be performed.

The same general principle gives rise to much stronger implications at the level of the group as a whole, however. When no one in particular bears responsibility for performing some morally desirable actions, everyone collectively has a strong, perfect duty to see to it that those things are done, within the limits of the capacities of the group as a whole to do so without undue sacrifice (Goodin 1985, pp. 134–44).[3]

(Of course, the 'bottomless pit' objection might serve to exculpate groups as well as individuals. If moral duties far outstrip the resources of the group as a whole to discharge them, then the group as well as the individuals should be excused from at least some of those duties. Poverty-stricken Somalia was at least arguably in that position during the drought. But often pits that seem bottomless from the perspective of the individual are perfectly manageable from a collective perspective. If we can merely ensure that everyone contributes his fair share, we can manage the burden perfectly happily; the only reason the pit looked bottomless from the individual's perspective was that he was contemplating having, at least potentially, to do his bit and everyone else's as well. In this essay, I shall be concerned only with burdens of this latter sort – i.e. where the 'bottomless pit' argument excuses individuals but not groups as a whole.)

The argument for strong collective responsibility in such cases proceeds by two steps. First, notice that the problems posed above for individual action in the circumstances envisaged are all, in essence, co-ordination problems (Lewis 1969; Goodin 1976, chs 4, 5). Where two or more people try to do the same good deed, their efforts might prove counterproductive; or one's good deed might render the other's superfluous. Either way, there is a need for co-ordination. Similarly, the danger of bottomless pits arises principally because, in the absence of co-ordinating mechanisms, the conscientious rightly dread that the unconscientious will shirk their duties, leaving the former with much more than their share of the moral chores to do. Running through all the rationales for the 'not my job' excuse, then, is this one common feature: they all point to co-ordination problems, of one sort or another.

The second step is this argument is to show that the solution to such co-ordination problems is, of necessity, a responsibility peculiar to the group as a whole. To some extent, this follows from the very nature of co-ordination. By its very nature, co-ordination is not something that can be performed by one actor in isolation. By its nature, 'co-ordination' refers to the relations between things: between muscles, in a graceful dancer's body; between departments, in a smoothly functioning state; or, in the case of social co-ordination, between your actions and others'. Co-ordination simply cannot be an attribute of your action alone, or of others' actions alone. Rather, it can only be an attribute of yours *together with* theirs. And that, in turn, is the essence of a 'group action' (Jackson 1988).

All that that argument strictly shows, of course, is that it is only in groups that behaviour can be socially co-ordinated. That does not yet establish that it is the job of groups to co-ordinate behaviour. Co-ordination, by its nature, is a collective enterprise. But it remains possible for the co-ordination to be accomplished *by* individual action *in* groups. The collective nature of the enterprise is respected by stipulating 'in groups'. But that does not strictly imply that the only way to co-ordinate behaviour is through some heavy-handed, formal, collective action 'by groups'.

Casual reflection on the co-ordination process clearly reveals that neither formal organization nor collective participation of the group as a whole is always strictly necessary for co-ordination to succeed. Quite the contrary. Co-ordination is sometimes best achieved by delegating responsibility for co-ordination to some particular member or members of the group. Other times it is best accomplished by assigning the task to someone outside the group altogether. Still other times, co-ordination might best be left to emerge naturally, through group interactions or through a shared perception of certain 'obvious' points as the foci for concerted action. Any of these solutions might, in principle, produce the desired co-ordination (Goodin 1976, ch. 5).

Having said all that, however, there remain certain roles which groups necessarily have to play in co-ordinating behaviour. First, where co-ordination does not emerge naturally, co-ordination schemes can function as co-ordination schemes at all only if they are embraced by the group whose behaviour is to be co-ordinated by them. This, in turn, means two things: someone must intentionally have engineered the co-ordination scheme; and everyone must intentionally act in compliance with it.[4] That is to say, co-ordination requires everyone to 'track' everyone else's behaviour: when one person's behaviour changes, everyone else must take note of that fact, and be prepared to make the necessary changes in their own in response (Nozick 1981, pp. 317–26). Where this does not happen 'naturally' (for instance, through the market), it can only happen intentionally, either directly (through the actor's own intentions) or at one remove (through the actor's intentional response to the system engineer's intentional designs).

Secondly, even where there is no need to organize a co-ordination scheme formally, the group as a whole still has a residual supervisory function. This entails, in the first instance, a responsibility to undertake regular monitoring. It entails, in the second place, a responsibility to be prepared to organize a more formal co-ordination scheme should less formal ones fail to perform satisfactorily.

Thus, groups must be at least *ultimately* responsible for co-ordination. The reason is the same as the reason why I must be responsible for my own sins, or why the sole onlooker must be responsible for rescuing the drowning swimmer: no one else can, or will. Co-ordination is, by its nature, *our* collective enterprise. No other agent, individual or group, can do it for us. If the behaviour is ours, then any co-ordination it manifests must necessarily be ours – at least in the sense of being an attribute of our, rather than anyone else's, behaviour.

If it is good that we should co-ordinate our behaviour in these ways, as *ex hypothesi* it is in the cases here in view, then we must ultimately be prepared to do so through our own collective efforts. If individuals are rightly to be excused from achieving the good through their own isolated actions, pleading 'It's not my job', then the collectivity must be empowered and enjoined to do whatever is necessary to eliminate those barriers that block morally efficacious individual behaviour. The collectivity must be empowered to *make it* someone's job, if anyone is to be allowed to plead, 'It's not my job.'

What it might mean to hold responsible a group as a whole, where the group is in no way formally organized, is perhaps unclear. Responsibility implies agency, and agency implies some capacity for intentional action. Unorganized groups lack that. Random collections of people (for instance, that group of people occupying the third carriage of the 17.27 train from London to Clacton) are incapable of forming any 'collective intention' until they first form themselves into a properly constituted 'collectivity'; so, too, are members of an unruly mob in the street (Held 1970, 1972; French 1979, 1984). People might be held individually responsible for joining in the mob's rioting; or they might be held individually responsible for not doing whatever was required to constitute themselves into a proper collectivity, capable of rescuing others who are trapped in the carriage when the train crashes off the rails (Goodin 1985, pp. 134–44; Pettit and Goodin 1986, pp. 673–6).[5] But the group, as such, cannot bear any responsibilities until it is properly constituted.

Where there is some collective agency in existence, though, there is no problem in ascribing group responsibilities of this sort directly to it. The state is pre-eminent among such organized collectivities. Our paradigm of moral agency is essentially individualistic, to be sure. The natural person is our model. Only those things that are sufficiently like natural individuals – only those things that are possessed of clear values, goals and ends, and capable of deliberation upon and intentional implementation of action plans in pursuit of them – can count as agents at all, for moral purposes. It is only to them that moral injunctions can be addressed. The limits of their capacity for effective action mark the limits of our moralizing.

But artifically created agencies are agents, too. Most especially, the state is a moral agent, in all the respects that morally matter. It, like the natural individual, is capable of embodying values, goals and ends; it, too, is capable (through its legislative and executive organs) of deliberative action in pursuit of them. The state is possessed of an internal decision mechanism (a constitution, and the processes that it prescribes) that mimics perfectly, for these purposes, that which is taken as the defining feature of moral agency in the natural individual. Without such mechanisms, the state would not be a state at all. It would lack the minimal organizational content required for that description to fit. With such mechanisms, the state is indisputably a moral agent, much like any other (French 1979, 1984; Held 1970, 1972).

None of this is necessarily to suggest that collectivities – even organized ones – have responsibilities which are not reducible to the responsibilities of individuals comprising them. It can, of course, be argued that they do. Indeed, that interpretation seems to follow naturally from ascribing some independent moral agency to the organization as such (Held 1970, 1972; Jackson 1988). But it is also at least arguable that all the responsibilities of the organization are, in the final analysis, responsibilities of individuals – both individuals in positions of responsibility within the organization, and individuals on whose behalf the organization acts.

Nothing in the present argument requires me to take sides in this dispute. My claim could, in line with the latter position, be read as simply maintaining that individuals are excused from doing the right thing under one set of circumstances but not another. Specifically, where doing the right thing requires co-ordinated social action, they are excused in the absence of mechanisms to provide that co-ordination. They are not excused in the presence of mechanisms to provide it. Nor are they excused from a duty to create and maintain those mechanisms to provide such co-ordination.

Neither is any of this to suggest that the state is the only collective agent capable of providing social co-ordination. Corporations, clubs, churches, and so on, are all, in principle, capable of helping to co-ordinate individual behaviour in much the same ways. All of them are, by reason of their internal decision apparatus, capable of being held responsible for doing so, in much the same way as the state. And so on.

Still, the state must be ultimately responsible, because the state is the pre-eminent organization among them in any given territory. Other organizations exist by leave of – and at least in one (legalistic) sense, only under a charter from – the state. Any sanctions that those other organizations want to impose upon their members in order to enforce a co-ordination scheme can ultimately only be imposed by leave of – and, often, only with the assistance of – the state, through its monopoly on legitimate violence. If co-ordination is required, other organizations might be responsible in the first instance for providing it. But, by its nature, the state must be the collective agency ultimately responsible.

Lest the basic structure of my argument get lost among the finer details, let me now summarize the argument so far. The key moves in the argument have been: first, to show that the validity of the 'no individual responsibility' excuse follows from the impossibility of efficacious individual action, which in turn follows from the existence of a co-ordination problem of some sort or another;

and, second, to show that, at least in the presence of formally organized collectivities, the existence of a co-ordination problem implies that the collectivity (and, among collectivities, ultimately the state) must bear ultimate responsibility for providing the co-ordination that is required in order for people to be able to do the right thing. In short, the same thing as makes it valid for individuals to offer the excuse of 'no individual responsibility' implies that there must, in such situations, be a collective responsibility.

III Take no liberties with shared responsibilities

The next step in my argument builds on the results of the last. Once it is established that we have some shared, collective responsibilities to do something or to see to it that something is done, libertarian excuses can be shown to lose much of their force. The libertarian excuse is principally an excuse for not forcing people to discharge their *own* isolated, individual moral responsibilities. It does not work nearly as well (typically, it does not work at all) as an excuse for allowing individuals to refuse to play their part in discharging shared, collective responsibilities, and thereby to prevent us from discharging *our* moral responsibilities.

At root, the libertarian principle is one enjoining us to mind our own moral business. If a moral agent fails to discharge his own duties, that is his problem, not ours. It is wrong of him not to do what he should do, of course. But it is his wrong, not ours. It would we wrong of us to interfere in what is not, ultimately, any of our moral business by attempting to force him to do his duty.

Indeed, in the paradigmatic application of this libertarian principle it is doubly 'his own business', for the duty which we are excused from enforcing upon him is one of a peculiarly self-regarding kind. Not only would it do no good for a person to be forced to worship a god in which he does not believe, but he alone would suffer from his delict.

Not all applications of the libertarian principle point to duties that are quite so narrowly self-regarding, of course. Other people often will suffer as a result of the agent's moral delicts, being harmed in one way or another. The point of the libertarian principle is not to deny that this ever happens; it is instead to emphasize that, when it does, the blame falls squarely upon the individual whose duty it was to do those things. It was his job to do them, not ours to make him do them. If he has wronged others through his delicts, the wrongs are wholly chargeable to his moral account. It is nothing to do with any of the rest of us. Any writs that are issued in consequence of the delict should be addressed to him, not us. In that sense, at least, even other-regarding acts are his business, not ours.

All that is meant merely by way of explicating, not of defending, the libertarian principle. Whether or not it is ultimately defensible, even as applied to isolated, individual moral responsibilities, I propose to leave here as an open question.[6] My aim here is merely to show that, whatever you might think of that principle as applied to isolated, individual moral responsibilities, it is clearly inapplicable to shared, collective moral responsibilities.

Where shared, collective responsibilities are concerned, it *is* – by definition – everyone's business what everyone else does. And this tautology is far from an empty one. It is everyone's business, first and most simply, because it is a responsibility that everyone shares with everyone else. It is everyone's business, secondly and more importantly, because, for anyone else's contribution to be efficacious, each agent must usually play his part under the scheme that has been collectively instituted for discharging that shared responsibility.

When isolated, individual moral responsibilities are not discharged, various other people might be harmed. But at least no one else will (necessarily, or even usually) thereby be prevented from discharging his *own* moral responsibilities. When an individual fails to discharge responsibilities assigned to him pursuant to some scheme for discharging shared, collective responsibilities, this is not the case. The success of others' acts pursuant to such schemes will indeed typically be predicated upon the success of his own.

The need for co-ordination of this sort was what excused isolated individuals from acting on their own, and what in turn gave rise to the collective responsibilities in the first place. The failure of any one party to abide by the co-ordination scheme will typically undermine, to some greater or lesser extent, the success of the scheme as a whole, thereby preventing other moral agents from successfully discharging their assigned duties. It is for that reason that we may rightly force people to do their duties pursuant to schemes for discharging shared, collective responsibilities – even if we may not so enforce isolated, individual responsibilities.

The rather more grand way of phrasing the point here might be couched in terms of undermining moral agency. Failure to discharge isolated, individual responsibilities may well result in other people's being harmed. That is wrong. But it is, at least in principle, a remediable wrong. People can, at least in principle, always be compensated for harms to their interests (or so the libertarian would claim, anyway). Failure to discharge shared, collective responsibilities has more grievous consequences, undermining in certain crucial respects other people's moral agency itself. For that, compensation is in principle impossible: there must be a moral agent to be compensated, and it is that very moral agency that is being undermined.[7]

A less grandiose, and more satisfactory, way of putting the point would be this. It may well be possible to compensate people, in *some* sense or another, for preventing them from doing their moral duty. Certainly there must be some sum of money large enough to make it up to them, in the sense that the people concerned would think themselves globally better off being very rich delinquents than they would have been as very poor saints. But global well-being is not the right standard here. Moral delinquents are *worse people*, not just worse-*off* people.[8] Morally conscientious people keep separate accounting categories, entering moral credits and material pay-offs in completely distinct columns. To say that they might be compensated, in the sense of being made globally better off by some transfer of money, is not to say that the surplus in the material-reward column can wipe out the deficit in the moral-virtue column. They may be better off with compensation, but they are differently off. Morality cannot be traded off for anything but morality. That is what explains the impossibility of compensating other people for the wrong done to them when they are prevented from discharging their collective moral responsibilities. That is what justifies us, *pace* libertarian principles, in forcing people to play their part in collective moral enterprises – so that others may play their part in them, too.

All that is then left to underwrite the libertarian argument for not forcing people to do what they should do is the 'value of liberty'. In the circumstances here envisaged, though, the value of liberty weighs on both sides of the scale. We infringe a person's liberty by forcing him to do his moral duty, to be sure. But we also allow him to infringe others' liberty (i.e. their liberty to play an effective part in some collective scheme for discharging their shared moral obligations) if we allow him to default on his own obligations under that scheme. In such circumstances, we should not be surprised if the liberty of the many is characteristically taken to outweigh the liberty of the one.[9]

All of this is simply to say that, where there is a collective responsibility to co-ordinate individual behaviour in pursuit of some morally important goal, it is legitimate for the collectivity to impose sanctions upon individuals in pursuit of that goal. Of course, it is perfectly true that not all co-ordination schemes require such enforcement. As I have acknowledged in the previous section, people are sometimes prepared to play their assigned roles without any external sanctions whatsoever. So my argument here is not that we should necessarily always enforce co-ordination schemes. It is, rather, that we should always be prepared to enforce them as necessary.

Neither is it necessarily the case, even where enforcement is required, that it is always essential to the success of a co-ordination scheme that everyone's compliance be secured. Often, we can afford a few defectors without any serious loss to the overall success of the project; indeed, in so far as possible, it is only sensible to engineer back-ups and redundant systems into co-ordination schemes so as to guarantee that this is the case. But, even where we could afford a few defectors, we none the less ought to impose the same sanctions against all of them alike. On this conclusion, considerations of fairness and prudence converge. If we were to set a differential tariff, depending on the actual harm that any particular defection caused, then everyone would be jockeying to be among the 'affordable' defectors. There is, then, a grievous risk that too many would end up defecting, and that the success of the co-ordination scheme would be compromised in consequence (Taylor and Ward 1982; Pettit 1986a).

None of these arguments in defence of collective enforcement of co-ordination schemes to discharge collective responsibilities applies peculiarly to the state. All collectivities have a similar right to sanction their members for non-compliance with co-ordination schemes. States can fine and imprison, seize and sequester. So too can clubs fine their members, corporations demote or dismiss their officers, and so on. All such sanctioning might be legitimized in precisely the same terms.

Still, as argued in the previous section, all of that private sanctioning behaviour is conducted within the framework provided by state authority. It is that which ultimately stands behind all sanctions levied by lesser organizations. So, in that sense, the state has to be the ultimate source of sanctions. In that sense, it is towards the state's sanctioning powers that these arguments in justification are principally addressed.

Neither do any of the arguments offered so far specify the limits to the sorts of sanctions that may legitimately be imposed in pursuit of social co-ordination. After all, some sorts of co-ordination matter more to us than others; and, logically, we should surely be able to levy larger sanctions in support of more important goals. By the same token, surely it cannot be legitimate to levy any sanction, however large, in pursuit of any collective enterprise, however trivial.

Some purchase on the problem of specifying appropriate limits to sanctions might be obtained through the self-same notion of a co-ordination problem that legitimates the sanction in the first place. Inherent in the notion of a scheme is the idea that it makes everyone better off than he would be in the absence of co-ordination. ('Better off' here should of course be read as embracing 'discharging one's moral duties' as well as merely 'maximizing one's wealth, status and power'.) From this, it would seem to follow that the maximum sanction that may legitimately be levied as a penalty for non-compliance is the amount that the individual profits from others' co-ordination in circumstances wherein he fails to co-operate – i.e. the difference between what he gets when he defects from a co-ordination scheme to which others adhere, and what he would have obtained in the absence of such a scheme altogether (Goodin 1976, ch. 4).

That solution is not without problems, of course. The counterfactual – how well he would have done in the absence of the scheme – is hard to specify with any confidence or precision. So, too, is the individuation of co-ordination schemes problematic. Should we regard every act of social co-operation organized through the same agency as being part of a single big scheme? In that case, people who defected in one minor respect from any part of the scheme could legitimately be deprived of the benfits of all aspects of the scheme taken together. Alternatively, we might suppose that there are lots of little, self-contained co-ordination schemes, from which one might defect without compromising one's entitlements to the fruits of the other schemes organized by the same entity. Despite such non-trivial problems, of both practicality and principle, this none the less seems to provide a useful framework for thinking about such matters.

Again, let me summarize the basic logic of my argument lest the detail obscure the basic structure. The argument of the previous section established that the same thing that makes the 'no individual responsibility' excuse work to exculpate individuals from responsibility also works to inculpate collectivities, imposing upon them responsibilities to act so as to provide the needed co-ordination of individuals' behaviour. The argument of this section has established that, whereas compelling people to do their individual moral duties might be impermissible, it is perfectly permissible to compel people to play their necessary parts in discharging collective responsibilities. That permissibility of compulsion arises from the fact that delinquents actually hinder others from discharging their own responsibilities under a co-ordination scheme. That is what makes it others' business what the delinquents do or fail to do; that is what justifies others in compelling the delinquent to play his necessary part in the co-ordination scheme. In short, the 'no individual responsibility' excuse undercuts the libertarian plea of 'no legitimate compulsion'. You cannot have it both ways. Where one claim has force, the other is for the same reason deprived of its.

IV Applications

For some indication of the practical import of this argument, consider two applications. One has to do with the state's responsibility for its citizens' physical security, and its right to employ coercive sanctions pursuant to the exercise of that responsibility. The other has to do with the state's responsibility for its citizens' economic security, and its right to employ coercive sanctions in pursuit of that.

This pair of applications is nowise unique. Various other examples could have been offered instead. But the pair I have chosen is particularly significant. Between them, 'providing for the common defence' and 'promoting the general welfare' represent two of the most central spheres of state activity. More to the strategic point of the present essay is the fact that one of these activities (promoting physical security) is broadly embraced by libertarians, whereas the other (promoting economic security) is stoutly resisted as a legitimate area of state responsibility. Showing that state respon-sibility – backed, indeed, by compulsion as necessary – can be justified in precisely the same manner in each of these cases will incidentally serve to undercut the libertarian case against compulsory state measures directed at promoting economic security.[10] That, too, is illustrative of the range and significance of the argument I have here been mounting.

Take first the case of physical security. Each individual is, of course, morally bound to refrain from attacking anyone else; and it is hard to see how the excuses here in view could ever release him from that duty. But each individual is also obliged to help protect others from attack. This, typically, is a duty that does call forth the sorts of excuses discussed here under the 'no individual responsibility' heading. Sometimes the cost of protecting another's life or property would be the grave endangering of your own – especially if you are the only one to come to the other's aid. Sometimes it is clear that someone should help, but it is unclear who among several equally eligible candidates should render the assistance. Sometimes the desired protection can be accomplished only through a complex series of tasks that must be performed by different people, and your contribution would be useless (or worse) unless you could be sure that others would play their parts (cf. Held 1972, pp. 114–15). And so on.

Because of the need for co-ordination in all these respects between people's efforts at protecting one another against physical assault, we typically excuse people from any individual responsibility in such matters. At most, 'Good Samaritan' laws might impose a 'duty of easy rescue' upon people, when it is clear what they could do to help and when rendering such assistance would be virtually costless for them (Weinrib 1980; Kleinig 1976).

But for the same reason that we ordinarily excuse individuals from responsibility for protecting one another's physical security, we typically (and rightly) deem it a collective responsibility. It is a duty of the group as a whole to create and sustain some scheme for co-ordinating its members' efforts at protecting each other's physical security; and, once some such collective scheme has been organized, the group has the right to use such force as necessary for compelling compliance with that co-ordination scheme, within the limits set by its nature as a co-ordination scheme. (That is merely to say that it must not exercise such force against anyone as to leave that person worse off than he would have been in a 'state of nature', where there was no such scheme in operation at all and everyone was free to attack him.) As regards questions of physical security, all this is fairly well accepted, even by libertarians of Nozick's ilk (Nozick 1974).

The same sort of argument can also be made, however, as regards economic security. There, too, the 'no individual responsibility' excuses are commonly invoked. Charity may be a moral duty, but it is an imperfect one. There are simply so many people in need that I would impoverish myself trying to cure poverty single-handedly. Besides, it is a complex issue, and there is no way for isolated individuals to be sure that their well-intentioned acts of private charity are not counterproductive (McKinsey 1981). And so on.

This, too, points to the need for co-ordination between people's duty-bound efforts at protecting one another's economic security. On account of that, we typically excuse people from individual responsibility in such matters. But, again for the self-same reason, we ought to impose collective responsibility in these matters.

Here, again, if we take seriously the proposition that individuals have a moral duty (albeit only an imperfect one) to protect others' economic security, then it is their duty to create and sustain some scheme for co-ordinating aid-giving efforts within their group. Once some such collective scheme has been organized, the group has the right to use such force as necessary for compelling compliance with that co-ordination scheme, again within the limits set by its nature as a co-ordination scheme. Here that merely means that it must not exercise such force against anyone as to leave him less able to discharge his aid-giving duties than he would have been in the absence of such a co-ordination scheme in the first place.

This is a conclusion that libertarians would resist strongly, of course. They maintain that it is right to give, but wrong to be forced to give, charitable relief to those less fortunate (Nozick 1974, pp. ix–x; Waldron 1986, p. 466). But the argument here is perfectly parallel to that developed above for enforceable collective protection of physical security. In that form, it is an argument which they regularly welcome.

V Conclusion

The upshot of this argument is thus powerfully anti-libertarian. The conclusion is that the state has the duty to organize – and the power to enforce, as necessary – various sorts of co-ordination schemes to aid its citizens in discharging their individual (albeit imperfect) moral duties.

The larger target is moral shirkers more generally, though. People regularly try to find excuses for not doing the right thing. Some of the excuses they offer do indeed seem compelling. The argument of this essay, however, is that, in their frenzy to excuse their delicts, these moral shirkers tend to trip over their own excuses.

Excuses rarely excuse completely. Some of them cut across one another in surprising ways. As I have shown here, we can sustain shirkers' claims that people have 'no individual responsibility' in certain matters only by admitting that collectivities (such as the state) do have responsibility in those matters, and indeed that they have powers of compulsion as necessary to discharge those responsibilities. Dedicated moral shirkers will, of course, derive little comfort from such findings. But that is all to the good.

Notes

I am grateful to Alan Hamlin and Philip Pettit for comments on an earlier draft of this essay.

1   While it may be inappropriate to force you to do x on each of the n occasions when it would be possible for you to do x, it would none the less be appropriate to require you to discharge your imperfect duty of doing x on at least some of those n occasions. The barrier to enforcement of such a duty is presumably purely administrative: it is simply harder to enforce a rule that you should sometimes do x than it is to enforce one that you should never do x or that you should always do x.

2   Consider the case of impossibility by reason of avoidable ignorance or incapacity. Then impossibility excuses your failure to do the right thing in the present instance. But it does so at the cost of blaming you for not doing in the past what you needed to do to avoid being incapacitated now, and of obliging you to do now whatever is required to make sure that you are not similarly incapacitated when next you are required to act. See, on this, Goodin (1982), ch. 7; and Zimmerman (1987).

3   For applications to professional morality, see Wasserstrom (1975, p. 9; 1983, p. 30); and for applications to international ethics, see Goodin (1988).

4   That is not necessarily the same as everyone's intentionally abiding by the co-ordination scheme. People might just intend, for example, to avoid sanctions designed to enforce compliance. But so long as the scheme has been intentionally engineered in such a way as to guarantee that that is extensionally equivalent, that is enough. The condition as stated would, of course, be perfectly consistent with everyone's intentionally abiding by the scheme or with everyone's having a hand in intentionally engineering the sanction that, at a later stage, is their focus in deciding to comply with it.

5   In so far as social co-ordination is required to generate a solution to a co-ordination problem, there is a danger of infinite regress here. But usually there will be enough obvious co-ordination points, or political entrepreneurs, or super-conscientious individuals to break out of that vicious circle.

6   Myself, I would just as soon see duties not to murder and rape socially enforced; but that is an argument we need not enter into here.

7   Some such principle might be at work in cases such as murder and grievous bodily harm, too. What justifies us in prohibiting those acts *ex ante*, rather than merely requiring compensation *ex post*, may well be that there compensation is in principle impossible. In the case of murder, clearly – and of gross physical harm, only slightly less so – that impossibility of compensation can be traced to the (total or partial) destruction of the moral agent who would have to have been compensated.

8   True, when someone is prevented from doing his duty, it is not his fault in the same way as it would be if he had merely failed to do it, all of his own accord. But a person who is relieved, rather than resentful, that others have prevented him from doing his duty would hardly count as a morally conscientious agent.

9   It is of course easy to justify infringement of your liberty where you have explicitly consented to a co-ordination scheme with the enforcement provisions that are now

being used against you. But even where you have not consented, such infringement of your liberty may be none the less justifiable. If you have a moral duty that can only be discharged through co-ordinated action, and that co-ordination can only be achieved through a scheme with enforcement provisions of that sort, then you have a duty to consent to such a scheme and such enforcement provisions, whether or not you have actually done so. That duty, rather than your consent, is what would really justify the levying of sanctions.

10 The same strategy is deployed with great success by Shue (1980), chs 1, 2.

9

The Freedom of the City: A Republican Ideal

Philip Pettit

Normative theories of the state can be distinguished in a variety of ways: by their assumptions in argument; by their methods of argument from those different assumptions; by the sorts of state which the argument leads them to recommend; and so on. But perhaps the most common way of taxonomizing such theories is by reference to the different personal goods which they propose for the enjoyment of the members of a polity. It is this taxonomy which is usually in play, for example, when we distinguish liberal, utilitarian and egalitarian philosophies: these are associated respectively with the liberty, the utility and equality which they propose for the enjoyment of citizens.

In this essay I wish to put forward a political philosophy that is distinguished by the sort of personal good which it recommends for the polity's concern. For reasons that are discussed later, I describe the philosophy as a republican theory of the state. The personal good which the theory focuses on·is the franchise enjoyed by a person when, as we say, he has the freedom of the city: he is a full citizen, with all the rights and responsibilities that that status entails.[1]

The essay has six sections. In section I, I introduce the ideal of franchise more fully. And then in sections II–V I show that a political philosophy of promoting franchise promises to be attractive in a number of ways. Section II shows that the ideal invoked is inherently plausible. And the following three sections give grounds for thinking that a philosophy of promoting franchise should pass the most important tests associated with the requirement of reflective equilibrium. This is the requirement that the theory should support the bulk of our considered judgements on more particular matters; it should lead to results that are more or less palatable, at least after some retraining of the taste buds.[2] The tests that I associate with the requirement are that the theory should lead the state to take rights seriously, to try to moderate the effects of asymmetries of power, and to concern itself with the satisfaction of basic needs. Section III deals with rights, section IV with powers and section V with needs. In section VI I explain my reasons for describing the philosophy as republican.

I The ideal of franchise

Although the term 'franchise' is now mostly used in reference to voting, its original meaning is much broader. Deriving from the ethnic term 'Frank', it connotes the full freedom or citizenship which members of that nation enjoyed in Frankish Gaul. It is connected with the adjective 'frank', since full membership of a community goes with openness and lack of fear.

C. S. Lewis (1967, p. 125) offers a nice way of introducing the term. Speaking of 'freedom' and 'franchise', as distinct from the Latin *libertas* and the Greek *eleutheria*, he writes,

> The mediaeval words nearly always refer . . . to the guaranteed freedoms or immunities (from royal or baronial interference) of a corporate entity which cuts across states, like the Church, or which exists within the state, like a city or guild. . . . This led to a development unparalleled, I believe, in the ancient languages. By becoming a member of any corporation which enjoys such *freedom* or *franchise* you of course come to share that *freedom* or *franchise*. You become a *freeman* of, or receive the *freedom* of, that city. . . . These are familiar. But a further development along this line is more startling. *Freedom* can mean simply 'citizenship'. . . . This meaning is fossilised in the surviving English use of *franchise* to mean the power of voting, conceived as the essential mark of full citizenship.[3]

Using the word with something like its original meaning, I shall define 'franchise' in three clauses. Although the definition is stipulative, it should be clear that the clauses are motivated by an intuitive notion of what full citizenship involves. Further motivation is provided in the next section.

A person enjoys full franchise if and only if

1   he enjoys no less a prospect of negative liberty than is available to other citizens;

2   he enjoys no less a prospect than the best that is compatible with the same prospect for all;

3   it is common knowledge among citizens that the first two clauses obtain,
     so that he knows that they do, knows that others generally know this,
     knows that others generally know that he knows, and so on.

This account of franchise will not be self-explanatory, although the motivation
should be clear enough. Two concepts in particular require further
explication: that of negative liberty and that of a prospect of negative liberty.
But before pursuing that explication there are three general observations that I
should like to make.

First, franchise is defined so that a person can enjoy it less than fully, though
there are a number of ways, corresponding to the three clauses in the
definition, in which his enjoyment may fall short of that ideal. Secondly,
'franchise' is defined so that, once the lower limits of the first two clauses are
passed, and the third clause is satisfied,[4] a person has it in full measure: no
increase beyond those limits increases franchise, strictly speaking, though it
will increase the prospect of liberty. And, thirdly, the definition presupposes
that we know who the citizens of a society are. I shall assume that they include
all current adult residents. I do not speculate on when adulthood begins and,
although I shall speak in what follows only of the treatment of citizens, I
assume that non-adults ought to be accorded franchise in whatever degree is
thought to be compatible with their status.

The notion of a prospect is fairly straightforward. The prospect of x which
someone enjoys is fixed, I shall take it, by two factors: the quantity of x on offer
and the person's chance, objectively assessed,[5] of getting that amount. Thus, if
a person has a one-in-ten chance of getting ten units of liberty, then he enjoys
the same prospect as someone who has a one-in-five chance of getting five
units.

Our use of the notion of a prospect may cause anxiety on two counts. First, it
allows different levels of liberty, so long as they are balanced by different levels
of chance or assurance, to count for equality of prospects. And, secondly, it
allows low levels of liberty, so long as they are balanced by high levels of
assurance, to constitute maximum prospects. But neither worry is serious. The
first should be allayed by the observation that the surest way to equalize
prospects across people will be by equalizing both liberties and levels of
assurance; the sorts of calculations otherwise required do not inspire
confidence. The second worry should be reduced by the observation that in
maximizing prospects it is all too likely that we shall find a ceiling on the levels
of assurance available, in which case further enhancement of prospects will
require the extension of liberties.[6]

The notion of a negative liberty is more familiar than that of a prospect of it,
but its explication is a matter of some controversy. Rather than get embroiled
in analytical debates, however, I shall be breif and stipulative. I have defended
the definition with some reference to those debates in another place (See Pettit
forthcoming b).

A person is negatively free to ϕ, I suggest, if and only if three conditions are fulfilled.

1   In normal conditions the normal agent can ϕ without the special collaboration of circumstances or colleagues.
2   Were the agent to try to ϕ, then no one would prevent or frustrate the choice, or contribute to its prevention or frustration, while being in a position to know that that was what he was likely to be doing.
3   No one coerces the agent not to ϕ by credibly threatening such prevention or frustration.

The definition requires some elucidation. The first clause is designed to identify the types of options which are suitable candidates for the domain of personal liberty: notice that the concern is personal liberty, not the liberty of agents in the sense in which groups and institutions count as agents. It means that the following options, for example, are unsuitable candidates, since they require the sort of special collaboration ruled out: building the largest house in town, changing job, communicating a particular set of ideas, associating with others. But, in case these exclusions seem excessive, notice that ϕ-ing may stand for counterpart activities such as building a house, availing yourself of an opportunity to change job, expressing certain ideas, and associating with any others who like your company. Those activities are possible only in certain congenial contexts: the physical milieu must provide oxygen, for example, and the social milieu must not be actively hostile. But there is an intuitive sense in which they do not require the special collaboration of circumstances or colleagues.

The second clause is unclear in so far as prevention and frustration require further definition. To prevent someone from ϕ-ing is to make it physically impossible for him to do so, removing that option from his feasible choice set; it may involve locking him up, tying him down or depriving him of resources necessary for the choice. To frustrate the agent's choice of ϕ will not be to interfere so directly but it is to intervene in his life in a distinctively damaging way. If an agent chooses to ϕ, then he presumably does so because of the prospects he associates with that option. To frustrate his choice will be to worsen those prospects in such a manner that a normal agent who foresaw that intervention would not have chosen to ϕ, at least in normal circumstances: that is, absent an emergency or the like. The frustration may be brought about by imposing an appropriately heavy punishment on the agent or by ensuring that the prospects which made the choice attractive are appropriately unlikely to be realized.

The third clause is necessary because the threat of prevention or frustration might block someone ϕ-ing, even though the threat is not capable of being carried out and the second clause is satisfied. Our definition identifies that sort of obstacle as a block to freedom, even though there is a sense in which the obstacle may be imaginary. But, though the obstacle may be imaginary, it must not be fanciful. This is because the threat that poses it must be credible: roughly, it must be a threat which in the agent's situation a normal person would have had reason to believe, and to believe with sufficient confidence for the prospective prevention or frustration to go proxy for the real thing.

So much, then, for the definition of franchise. We have seen enough to make it clear what franchise involves and enough to make it clear, moreover, that franchise is a good of persons. But, if the ideal is to be used to identify a political philosophy, then some further explication is required. We need to say what the state should be expected to do about the franchise of citizens, if it is to be appropriately responsive to the ideal. I assume that the cause of franchise requires the existence of some kind of state; the question is, exactly what sort?

Should the state simply respect or honour franchise, exemplifying the sort of respect for liberties which it expects others also to evince? In its behaviour towards citizens, should it impose on itself all those constraints which it expects citizens to satisfy in their behaviour towards one another? Hardly, since then it could not prosecute or punish those who do not themselves honour the franchise of others. But should it perhaps go only one step further and, apart from the intervention involved in coping with offenders or invaders, stick to the rule of honouring franchise?

The alternative to honouring franchise in this punctilious way is for the state to do all it can to maximize the franchise enjoyed among its citizens. Doing all it can will often require it to honour franchise, but equally it may require sorts of treatment which count in some tallies as invasions: for example, levies imposed for purposes of redistribution within the society. This maximizing alternative we may describe as promoting franchise.[7]

It may be that a philosophy of promoting franchise will have consequences which ought to lead us to reject it. If so, that should become clear in later sections. But for the moment it seems more straightforward to take the promotional alternative. Franchise is something that comes into existence via the institutions of the polity; it is not a property of people which pre-exists those arrangements. Thus it is natural to say that the polity should so organize itself and so operate in practice that franchise is maximized. To require the state to honour franchise even when that means less franchise overall looks like an arbitrary prescription.

Some devotees of the minimal state may feel that they ought to baulk at the notion that the state should be in the business of promoting as distinct from honouring franchise. But the following observation may allay their anxiety. This is that rules of property, which are generally dear to minimalists, look likely to be required if the state is to promote franchise, whereas this is not clearly so if there are no rules to begin with and the state is supposed just to honour franchise. The project of promoting franchise might well require establishing and supporting rules of property, for such rules would expand the domain of liberty, ensuring that there are a greater range of activities that normal agents can perform without the special collaboration of others: specifically, those activities which require material resources that would be in dispute without property rules. Prior to the rules people are not free to perform the activities in question, though they are not unfree either: they are, as we might say, non-free. After the rules have been introduced, many people are free in the relevant respects, even if some are rendered unfree by theft and the like.

The republican philosophy which I am proposing, then, requires the state to promote the franchise of its citizens. In the sections that follow I shall be looking at questions of how attractive such a philosophy is. But, before going on to those matters, there is a preliminary line of objection to discuss.

The objection is of a sort that is often made against utilitarianism. The utilitarian proposes that the state should maximize utility as our republican philosophy proposes that it should maximize franchise. But it is often observed that utility may be maximized by a very unequal arrangement under which the privileged enjoy such a high degree of utility that this more than compensates for the lower degrees available to others. And that observation is readily turned into an objection, because such unequal treatment offends against the considered judgements that most of us share and gives the philosophy little chance of attaining reflective equilibrium. The question, then, is whether a similar objection can be made to the philosophy of maximizing franchise.

Happily, it cannot. Franchise is defined in such a way that, while it requires the attainment of certain lower limits on the prospect of liberty – those mentioned in the first two clauses – it does not increase as those limits are transcended. Thus, assuming that satisfaction of the third clause does not come in degrees, there is no parallel to the utilitarian predicament of having to choose between enormous utility for a few and considerably less utility for all. At any point where only some individuals have attained the limits required for franchise, the state will have to improve the comparative lot of the less well-off if it is to increase the franchise enjoyed in the society. In very harsh circumstances there may be a hard choice between leaving a given number below the limits and raising some by reducing others; but that sort of problem is far from the endemic predicament of utilitarianism and related philosophies.

II The plausibility of the ideal

So much for the definition of our ideal. In this section I want to show that the promotion of franchise offers a plausible criterion for evaluating the polity and indeed a plausible objective for the polity to pursue. Perhaps the first thing to say is that in one respect franchise represents, by contemporary standards, a rather novel sort of value. It is possible to taxonomize personal goods along two dimensions, and the surprising thing is that, so far as common-or-garden values go, the box where franchise naturally fits is otherwise empty.

The first dimension of the taxonomy divides welfare values and values of agency: that is, values that have us judge people primarily for what they have or enjoy and values that have us judge them primarily for what they are allowed or enabled to do.[8] The second dimension distinguishes asocial and social values: that is, values that can logically be realized for an individual in the absence of community and values that do not permit this. The two dimensions cross to form this matrix:

	Asocial	Social
Welfare	1	2
Agency	3	4

It should be clear how currently fashionable values fit within the boxes of this matrix. Utility belongs in box 1, since it casts the bearer as a possessor of goods and since on most construals it can logically be enjoyed by the totally isolated individual.[9] Equality, in the natural sense of material equality or equality of resources, belongs in box 2; while it also casts the bearer as the possessor of goods, it requires the presence of the people with whom he achieves equality.[10] And liberty, understood as exemption from the constraints mentioned earlier, fits in box 3; it takes the bearer in the role of agent but it can be realized for an agent in the absence of other people. What holds of liberty holds also of common variants on the notion. These all involve liberty plus some further capacitating factor and they belong in box 3, so far as the capacitating factor does not introduce the presence of other people as a logical requirement. Variants on liberty such as autonomy, sovereignty and effective liberty are clearly in box 3. And so is positive liberty, except when it is understood, untypically, as the liberty to participate in public decision-making.[11]

We may conclude that, so far as fashionable simple values are concerned, box 4 remains open.[12] The interesting thing, however, is that franchise clearly belongs in box 4. It takes the agent in the role of agent rather than in the part of a possessor of goods. And it is a value whose realization is logically impossible outside a community of other people. Thus the value of franchise serves nicely to complement the usual simple values that are considered in political philosophy.

But, granted that franchise is a distinctive value, the question we must address is whether the promotion of franchise represents a reasonably plausible ideal. Leaving aside the promotional aspect of things, the best way to establish the plausibility of the ideal is to show that franchise relates closely and convincingly to some of our currently recognized values. I wish to show that it is the sort of value you will be led to countenance if you make the rquirements of freedom explicit and if you interpret them in a certain, persuasive light.

Franchise, as our definition makes clear, involves the commonly recognized value of negative liberty but imposes three sorts of further requirement. First, it stresses the importance of comparisons with others in the community: for full franchise, a person must enjoy at least the same prospect of liberty as others. Secondly, it emphasizes the significance for franchise not just of happening to enjoy certain liberties, but also of having the assurance of enjoying them. And, thirdly, it requires that the enfranchised person know, in common with other citizens in his community, that he enjoys the appropriate prospect of liberty. We shall do a lot to make franchise look like a plausible ideal if we can provide a unified motivation for those extra requirements. I believe that such a motivation is available.

Assuming that we can iron out indeterminacies in the notion of negative liberty, let us ask what sort of condition would ensure perfect liberty. The answer that you give to this question will depend in good part on whether you are an atomist or a holist in your view of the relationships between people. It will turn on whether you think that the notion of the totally isolated individual is logically coherent or not: the atomist believes in the coherence of the notion; the holist denies it. The difference between the atomist and holist views of society is a matter of great importance, not just in the present debate, but also more generally. Unfortunately it has not always been given the attention it deserves, for this 'horizontal' question about how, essentially, people relate to one another has been continually confused with the 'vertical' question of how far the institutional forces in a society preclude or pre-empt individual initiative (see Pettit forthcoming a).

If you take an atomist view of society, then there will be at least some temptation to provide a quick and easy answer to the question of what would ensure perfect liberty. The quick and easy answer is: the condition of the solitary individual. You will be tempted to say that someone perfectly enjoys liberty if and only if there are no other people around to get in his way: no other people to obstruct or vitiate or punish his choices; no other people to threaten such interference. You will be tempted in other words to take perfect freedom as an asocial condition that is always compromised, no matter how trivially, by the presence of other people. If you do take that line, of course, then you will have most modern political philosophy on your side. That may be because the atomism which legitimates your account of perfect liberty is an important part of the modern philosophical tradition.

But suppose that, instead of taking an atomist view of society, you adopt the holist perspective; or suppose that you decide for other reasons that the conceit of the solitary individual is not appropriate in this context. In that case the quick and easy answer to our question will no longer be available, for you will have to define the condition of perfect liberty in such a way that it is available to someone in society. You will have to think of it not as an asocial condition compromised in any political arrangement, but as a certain sort of social status.

I wish to show that, if you view the condition of perfect liberty as a social status, then reflection is quite likely to persuade you that it must involve requirements of the kind involved in the definition of 'franchise'. If I can show this, then I hope that I will have done all that is necessary to make franchise look like a plausible ideal. Even someone who accepts atomism is bound to allow that it may not be an appropriate framework for thinking about questions of political philosophy; the solitary individual may be logically possible but it remains that people are always born into society. Thus even someone of the atomist persuasion must be impressed if the holistic explication of the condition required for perfect liberty gives us a derivation of franchise. As it happens, I reject atomism and so I have extra reason for endorsing the result of explicating that condition holistically (see Pettit forthcoming a).[13]

Three things naturally follow if the condition is a social status.[14] The first thing is that whether someone perfectly enjoys liberty will depend not just on how he fares in himself but on how he fares comparatively with others in his society. No one can perfectly enjoy liberty under a given culture, for example – no one can perfectly enjoy an exemption from suitable constraints – if he is subject to more constraints than others or is more likely to be subject to them. Perfect liberty is no longer to be defined on an intrinsic basis, as the absence of any sort of prevention, frustration or coercion; it is to be defined comparatively.

The second thing that follows if perfect liberty is a social status is that it must require for the person in question not just as much exemption as anyone else from relevant constraints, but also an assurance, and indeed as much assurance as for anyone else, of that exemption. If perfect liberty is defined as the condition of the solitary person, then not only are the constraints absent; their absence is also assured. This is not so, however, if the condition required for perfect liberty is assumed to be a social status. A person might just have the good luck not to suffer any more invasion than anyone else in the society, but we should hardly say that he therefore enjoyed liberty to the same extent as others. Certainly we should not say this if the others had the advantage over him of enjoying a guarantee against invasion. If perfect liberty is cast as a social status, then it must be made explicit that it requires a suitable assurance of the absence of constraint as well as the absence itself.

Finally, the third thing that follows if perfect liberty is a social status is that it must require not just the assured absence of constraint, but a knowledge of that assured absence. Under the atomist explication a person could not enjoy liberty perfectly without being in a position to know that he enjoyed it; all that he would have to observe is that there is no one around to get in his way. Under the holist explication a person could enjoy the absence of invasion involved in perfect liberty without being in such a position; he might, for example, think that he was subject to more constraints than others, when in fact he was not. Thus the enjoyment of perfect freedom requires not just the assured absence of invasin, but also an extra factor: the awareness of that assured absence.

But, more than that, under the holistic explication the perfect enjoyment of liberty would also seem to require that the awareness in question be shared by a person with others in the community, so that it is common knowledge that he enjoys the assured absence of constraint. This is because the assurance of exemption from constraint will be increased if everyone knows that the person is provided with such assurance, knows that he is provided with it, and so on. Common knowledge would give a booster to the assurance required for perfect liberty.

The upshot of these three implications is that, if it is understood holistically, then perfect liberty, like dignity or authority, is going to be a condition that a person can enjoy only so far as he has a certain standing relative to others. It is going to be tantamount to freedom in the sense of franchise or freedom of the city. The freedom of the city stands in nice contrast to the freedom of the heath, and it is hardly unfair to say that, where the holist inevitably construes freedom as the former value, the atomist is easily led into taking it for the latter.[15]

This is sufficient, I hope, to show that the ideal of promoting franchise is a plausible one to invoke in the normative theory of the state. It is nothing more or less than the ideal of promoting negative liberty, with the requirements of that negative liberty explicitly spelled out: specifically, with the requirements spelled out in a non-atomistic fashion. Franchise is not a value conjured out of the air for analytical purposes; it has a respectable pedigree.

III   Franchise and rights

If a political philosophy is to satisfy the requirement of reflective equilibrium, if it is to yield results that are not in incorrigible conflict with our considered judgements on particular matters, then so far as most of us are concerned it must support a dispensation of rights. The idea of people's having rights, rights against the state as well as against one another, is deeply embedded in the Western tradition of political thinking. A theory which meant that no one could have such rights, or even that no one could have such rights over substantive matters, would stand little chance of winning widespread allegiance. In this section I shall show that the philosophy of promoting franchise offers reason for the state to give certain negative liberties the status of rights. In later sections I shall show, though only in passing, that the argument extends further and that the state is also given reason to establish rights of other kinds.

A person enjoys a right to x, I maintain, only if he can make a personalized, privileged and precise claim to x against relevant others. The claim will be personalized if and only if those against whom it is invoked cannot ignore the right on the grounds that such a violation means less violation by others of the right to x on the part of others. The claim will be privileged if and only if those against whom it is invoked cannot ignore the right on the grounds that thereby one of an open-ended list of objectives is better promoted; there must be at least some objectives which it trumps. The claim will be precise if and only if it, and the circumstances which trigger it, are well-enough defined for anyone to be clear about when the claim is satisfied, and when it is not.

I do not mean to argue here for this construal of rights as personalized, privileged and precise claims; I have already done so elsewhere (Pettit 1987a, 1988). It is sufficient for me to observe in defence of the construal that it makes rights into more robust assets than most rival interpretations. Thus I cannot be accused of facilitating the task of this section, which is to show that if the state is to promote franchise then it must guarantee certain rights of choice.

On the face of it there seems to be no difficulty with such rights. If the state is to promote franchise, then the first thing required is that it should protect it against the interference of others, and this means that it should protect a certain set of negative liberties for each person. To protect negative liberties is to recognize them as legal claims – perhaps even as constitutional claims – which citizens can effectively invoke. More importantly, it is to recognize them as claims that they can invoke in the manner of rights. A person's liberty to do something will be legally protected only if in at least some circumstances the fact of infringement is enough on its own to trigger his claim: enough, that is, regardless of whether goals such as the minimization of overall violation of that claim, or the promotion of certain social objectives, are the better achieved thereby.

This line of argument shows that a state which promotes franchise – in particular, a state which tries to protect certain negative liberties – will give people legal and perhaps constitutional rights against other people, including agents of the state; it will ensure that violations of those liberties are subject to legal sanction. Unfortunately, however, it does not take us out of the woods. The trouble is that the argument does not mean that the state itself will take such rights seriously, regarding them as having any more weight than the legal sanction attaching to their infringement confers. Even if the state decrees it illegal for the state itself to invade such liberties, the goal of protecting the liberties overall will often offer a reason for the state to break its own law and invade the liberty of a particular person. Suppose that framing and convicting someone known to be innocent of a crime will have an important deterrent effect on crime and will block the possibility of a riot. Why shouldn't the state retain the extra-legal discretion to victimize such a person, given that that invasion of his legal right will produce more enjoyment of the right overall?

It may be said that no state could get away with systematically retaining such discretion. But there is still trouble in store. Even if the state cannot get away with systematically retaining the discretion to invade anyone's legal rights, still the zealous agent of the state will often find himself in a position where there is a good chance that he will get away with such invasion. If the original suggestion is well motivated, therefore, then it means that that type of agent is given reason to invade in any situation where a particular invasion promises to minimize invasion overall. The protection of certain negative liberties may motivate the legal establishment of corresponding rights but it will not provide zealous agents of the state with a reason to take the rights seriously; so far as those agents are concerned, it will not give the rights any moral as distinct from legal force (see Lyons 1984). On the contrary, there are circumstances where the goal of maximally protecting the liberties, thereby promoting franchise, will counsel such agents to try to get away with invading some individual's legal liberty rights. Or so at least it appears.

What we need to show, then, is that the promotion of franchise cannot itself motivate the state or agents of the state to contemplate invading the liberties involved in a particular person's having that franchise. We have to establish that there is something self-defeating about the state's espousing that goal and allowing itself to consider such invasion. More directly, we have to show that, if the agents of the state are to promote franchise, then they are required not just to protect certain liberties by making them into legal rights, but also to give those liberties the status of rights which make a claim independently of their legal recognition. Happily, this can be demonstrated.

Suppose that the political authorities do not collectively or at least individually give moral importance to the liberty rights which they establish in law. That means that on some occasions they will be prepared illegally to invade an individual's rights, albeit for the best of reasons. That means in turn that they will run a certain risk: the risk that it will come to be generally known or suspected that they do not take liberty rights seriously. In itself the running of the risk will fit with the general project of promoting franchise. It will do so at least if the magnitude of the risk is sufficiently small and the evil risked is sufficiently unimportant for the potential gain of the invasion to outweigh it (see Pettit and Brennan 1986). But the question which I wish to raise is whether the evil risked can really be sufficiently unimportant in the calculus of political authorities, if their prime concern is to maximize franchise.

The evil risked from their point of view is that people generally come to realize that they are not after all assured in the degree they had imagined against infringement of their liberties and indeed that they are not assured in the same degree as agents of the state. That evil must assume enormous proportions for any authorities who are concerned with maximizing franchise in our sense. The reason is that, if people generally come to recognize this, then their franchise is jeopardized by that very fact. They will fail to satisfy the third clause in our definition of franchise, not to mention the corresponding failure to satisfy the first. Franchise requires the subjective dimension involved in people's knowing, and indeed sharing in the common knowledge, that they enjoy a suitable prospect of liberty. For any agent or agency which is concerned with promoting franchise, therefore, the risk of undermining that subjective factor must be a risk to be avoided at almost all costs.

The lesson is clear. If the state or the agents of the state are genuinely concerned with the promotion of franchise, then they cannot sensibly retain for themselves the moral discretion to invade the liberty rights which they legally protect. It would be self-defeating of them to do so, for there is no protection against a threat from the protector and retaining that sort of prerogative would run the risk of a uniquely damaging subversion of franchise. In order to promote franchise, the state and its agents must bind themselves to honouring the liberties to which they give legal recognition. They must commit themselves to adopting an attitude of rigorous respect.

The argument just given turns on the fact that the promotion of franchise is a goal that is undermined by its direct pursuit; it is essentially a by-product of a different mode of decision-making (see Elster 1983, ch. 2). An agent of the state who wishes to promote franchise among a given constituency cannot alow consideration of how that goal is best served to figure in all his decision-making, for, if he does, then those on whom his actions bear are likely to recognize that they are susceptible to his interference: he will interfere whenever that is how the overall promotion of franchise is best served. The agent can only hope to promote franchise indirectly, by publicly adopting appropriate constraints on how he makes his decisions and by letting the evidence of those constraints have the desired effect. His beneficiaries will enjoy franchise in relation to him through knowing that the constraints bind him and that in appropriate circumstances no goal, not even the promotion of franchise itself, can motivate a breach.

While the criterion of promoting franchise is a consequentialist yardstick for judging the state, the consequentialism involved in adopting it here is of a restrictive variety (see Pettit and Brennan 1986). The restrictive consequentialist evaluates action by reference to a certain consequence or package of consequences, but, because the consequence may be a self-defeating one to pursue directly, he does not expect the agents on whom his evaluation bears to select their actions by deliberative consideration of how best to promote it. He expects that they may have to tie their hands and restrict the compass of their deliberation in order better to promote the desired result. I am a consequentialist in requiring the state to promote franchise; but I am a restrictive consequentialist so far as I recognize that the way for the state and its agents to do this is not by directly pursuing that goal. If franchise is to be politically promoted, then the state and its agents must tie their hands; in particular, they must take seriously the liberty rights to which they give legal recognition.[16]

It appears, then, that our philosophy of having the state promote franchise is at least going to satisfy the first of the three tests that we associated with taking certain rights seriously: specifically, the rights which give expression to certain negative liberties. This is a significant and satisfying result, for it marks a contrast between our philosophy and most other consequentialist theories of the state: most theories which assess the state by its promotion of a goal. Even a theory which set for the state the goal of minimizing the violation of negative liberties – even a consequentialist version of libertarianism – would not do so well by liberty rights. It would be unable to show that the political authorities ought to give moral as well as legal force to those rights, taking them seriously enough to be inhibited about the type of violation which promises to decrease violation overall. This is because it would be unable to give sufficient importance to the evil of jeopardizing people's awareness of having a suitable prospect of liberty. Undermining this awareness would be an offence against franchise, as our definition makes clear, but it would not be a violation of liberty.[17]

IV   Franchise and powers

If a political philosophy is to stand a chance of attaining reflective equilibrium with most people's considered judgements, then not only must it leave room for the state to take rights seriously; it must also provide the state with a reason for trying to moderate differences in the powers that accrue to different members of the society. The state should not be rendered insensitive to such asymmetries; on the contrary, it should be motivated to guard against their effects.

Differences of power arise with the political organization of a society. Once there is an allocation of the rights of coercion implicit in such organiza- tion – the rights of legislation, adjudication and administration – then there is already a hierarchy of power. That hierarchy creates a problem, for it introduces new possibilities of corruption, usurpation and all the melancholy ills of the political world.[18]

The question before us in this section is whether the philosophy of promoting franchise would sensitize the state to that problem. And clearly the answer is that it would. The requirement that people know that they enjoy a prospect of liberty no less than that available to others places severe restrictions on how power can be distributed. It puts constraints on the procedure for the distribution of power and constraints on the pattern of power's distribution.

Suppose that a state was organized on lines of hereditary rule, whether in monarchical or oligarchical style. Suppose further that everyone had the legal liberty rights required for franchise and that the rulers took those rights seriously, being concerned and clear-headed about the promotion of franchise. Even in such a near-utopian situation, the distribution of power would militate against the promotion of franchise. Those outside the political elite would not be in a position to know that they enjoyed the same prospect of liberty, even if they did enjoy it. They would naturally suspect that the elite were in a better position to guard themselves against obstruction, frustration, coercion and the like. After all, the elite would certainly seem to be in a better position to guard themselves against any invasion of franchise by the state itself.

If franchise is to be maximized in a society, then it is clearly necessary that power be distributed by a procedure, and in a pattern, which sustains the awareness among the general population that they enjoy equal assurance with the power-holders of having suitable negative liberties. This line of thought argues for a variety of restrictions on the distribution of power; the restrictions are institutional safeguards of franchise.

The safeguards in prospect will certainly include many familiar constraints, though they may also extend to constraints currently unimposed in most societies. Among the familiar constraints, we may expect to find the separation of legislative/administrative and judicial powers; election to the legislature/administration; universal suffrage; universal eligibility for office; strict procedures for appointments to the judiciary; the possibility of legislative debate on administrative decisions; the possibility of appeal against judicial decisions; the possibility of impeachment of public officials; the right in certain cases to trial by jury; a procedure of administrative review; freedom of information legislation; anti-trust legislation; and the like.

To put safeguards of this kind in place, the state will have to confer certain rights other than liberty rights on its citizens. It will have to give them immunity rights which mean that they are guaranteed against certain sorts of treatment by those who are given rights of coercion: by the powers that be. It will have to give citizens immunity rights against being denied their vote, against being denied their right to stand for election, against being denied access to the courts, and so on. But not only will the state have to give legal force to these rights. If the argument of the last section is sound, then the state and its agents will have to take those rights seriously and make it clear that they are doing so; they will have to give the rights moral as well as legal force.

These considerations are enough to show that, if a state is oriented by the philosophy of promoting franchise, then it will be suitably sensitized about the problem created by differences of power. We may note in concluding this section that the sensitization of the state may lead it to impose novel sorts of constraints on the distribution of power as well as those mentioned above. There is a need to reflect on what constraints are currently required for the maximization of franchise. I cannot say where that reflection would lead, for I haven't done the necessary work. But there is certainly every reason to think that it would generate a case for novel restrictions; it would be very surprising if the *status quo* turned out to be the optimal way of arranging things.

V Franchise and needs

If a political philosophy is to enjoy widespread reflective equilibrium, then it must satisfy at least one further condition apart from those associated with rights and powers. It must be a philosophy which would make the state responsive to the basic needs of its citizens. It must generate a political concern for the frustration of people's needs for shelter, sustenance, health care, education, and the like.

The question for this section is how far our republican theory does sensitize the state to people's needs. The most common complaint against any theory which gives negative liberty the sort of importance we do is that it must neglect or underrate issues of need. The question here is whether our theory does any better.

My answer is that it does substantially better and indeed that it does as well as we ought to want. There are three main categories in which people require security against frustration of their needs if they are to have the franchise of their society. Roughly, they require security against ignorance, against poverty and against ailment and handicap. Otherwise put, they need epistemic security (i.e. education), they need social security and they need medical security.

There are at least two reasons for having the state guarantee the education of citizens; I abstract here from the question of precisely what level of education ought to be guaranteed. The first is that, unless someone has certain intellectual skills – those required will vary between cultures – he will not be able to participate fully in the local institutions and he will not therefore enjoy the same assurance as others, let alone knowledge of having the same assurance as others, in the possession of his liberties. The second consideration is that, if a person is intellectually under-equipped in this way, then he will be more susceptible than others, and may recognize that he is more susceptible than others, to certain infringements of his liberty rights: for example, to certain sorts of deception, manipulation and discrimination. The first consideration is one of incapacity, the second one of vulnerability.

The same considerations provide reasons why a state concerned with maximizing franchise should guarantee a certain level of protection against poverty: a certain social security. It is obviously the case that the resources sufficient to provide against poverty in one society may be far from sufficient in another, but, apart from taking note of the fact, I shall not say anything more on precisely what resources are required.[19] The first consideration is that, if someone suffers poverty, then his assurance, and his awareness of the assurance, of enjoying appropriate liberties is put in jeopardy. Like ignorance, poverty means the inability to participate in the apparatus of assurance, for it undermines someone's capacity to keep abreast of what is happening in his society, to maintain access to political and legal institutions, to command the attention of those who are meant to protect him, and so on. The second consideration, which is probably more important in this context, is that like ignorance poverty involves a distinctive vulnerability to the invasions of others; it renders someone less resistant to invasions such as assault, theft and coercion, even if it sometimes makes him a less likely target.

Apart from these two considerations in favour of a social-security system, there is also a subsidiary argument that may be invoked for why the state should provide against poverty. The argument is that poverty, as our folklore has it, breeds crime – for our purposes, the invasion of others' liberty rights – and that the best way of coping with such crime may be to deal with its source. Any state concerned with promoting franchise is bound to try to minimize the invasion of liberty-rights and this may give it a reason to establish a social-security system.

The argument for having a medical-security system is that ailment and handicap are distinctive sources of poverty. They are distinctive, so far as the provision of social security may not be enough to guard against them. The handicap may be too severe, the ailment too sudden, for even a moderately well-off citizen to be able to cope without falling below the poverty line. Thus the considerations marshalled in favour of having a social-security system argue in addition for providing a separate system of medical security. The state may provide such security by requiring everyone to take out appropriate insurance, by offering such insurance itself, by making available the services that insurance would buy, or whatever. Such variations do not matter for our purposes. The point to emphasize is that it may not be enough for a state concerned with promoting franchise just to provide against poverty, say by a negative tax system, a dole, or an income supplement. It may have to provide specifically against the sort of poverty consequent on illness or handicap.[20]

These arguments for state provision of epistemic, social and medical security might be outweighed if the costs to the franchise of those paying for the services were too great. They might be too great if, for example, the state were to tax at its whim, selecting individuals or amounts more or less arbitrarily. In that case the net taxpayers would be subjected to an uncertainty which would radically undermine their franchise. But clearly there is no need for the state to tax in such a Robin Hood fashion. And, assuming that taxation follows more regular procedures, any cost to the net taxpayers will be more than compensated for by the benefit to those who are helped by the redistribution. After all, there need be no cost whatsoever in terms of strict franchise; there will be no cost so long as the net taxpayers know that they retain the prospect of liberty at or above the lower limits specified in our definition.

Where providing against differences of power involves establishing institutional safeguards of franchise, providing against the frustration of need involves establishing safeguards of a more personal kind. We saw in the last section that putting institutional safeguards in place means that the state has got to give legal recognition to certain immunity rights and that by the argument of the previous section it will then be obliged also to take those rights seriously: to give them moral as well as legal force. What we may add by way of concluding the present section is that putting personal safeguards of franchise in place means a similar commitment by the state to the recognition of certain other rights.

If the state is concerned to promote franchise, then, while this concern will require a response to the frustration of basic needs, it ought also to ensure that that response is of a rights-centred kind. Our comments on how net taxpayers should be treated suggest that everyone ought to have immunity rights against the sort of arbitrary taxation which would jeopardize franchise. And fairly obvious considerations about the effects of different security systems suggest that equally everyone ought to have security-rights to whatever levels of provision are thought to be necessary for franchise. The person who is dependent on the state for the satisfaction of certain basic needs ought to be given the sort of assurance of satisfaction which only security rights can provide; otherwise he cannot enjoy the equality with others which is necessary for franchise. But not only should such immunity rights and security rights be given legal recognition by the state. As the argument in section III makes clear, the political authorities ought also to find reason in the promotion of franchise for investing such rights with moral as well as legal force. They ought to be motivated to take the rights seriously.

VI   A republican theory

Among the traditions of thinking about the state within which freedom has been hailed as the supreme political value, two are particularly salient.[21] The one is the relatively recent tradition of liberal thought, the other the rather more ancient tradition of republican thinking. Liberalism has been the more dominant strand in Western philosophy over the past 200 years.[22] Republicanism had been in the ascendant, at least if recent commentators are to be believed, for about three centuries before that. This republican tradition, derived from the civic humanism of the ancient Romans, is well charted in J. G. A. Pocock's now classic study *The Machiavellian Moment: Florentine political thought and the Atlantic republican tradition* (1975).[23]

There are at least two respects in which the philosophy described here breaks with common liberal assumptions, and it turns out that in these respects it is of a piece with the republican tradition. Although the philosophy may be aligned in other ways more with liberal than republican thinking, I have chosen to focus on these two facets and to present it as a republican theory. The choice is not unmotivated, for the facets in question are probably the most distinctive aspects of the theory.

The first respect in which the theory breaks with the liberal tradition has already received some emphasis. It is that the theory interprets freedom not as the bare having of certain negative liberties, but as the being assured in a suitable measure of having them – particularly in a measure commensurate with others – where it is also common knowledge that this condition is fulfilled. The theory construes freedom as franchise: as the condition of citizenship in a suitable legal order.

There have been some figures within the broad liberal tradition who have espoused the notion that liberty essentially involves a socio-legal condition of this kind.[24] But on the whole liberals have taken freedom to involve social and legal arrangements only instrumentally: only so far as circumstances mean that there is no way for liberty to be promoted other than by the instrumentality of such institutions. They have construed it as the freedom of the heath rather than the freedom of the city. Thus Benn and Peters (1959, p. 213) write,

> There is much to be said . . . for the classical tradition of English political theory, which interprets 'freedom' negatively, as the absence of restraints imposed by the power of other men. . . . Law may be a necessary condition for liberty, since one man's freedom depends on the law's restraints on others. But if the law must restrain some to protect the liberty of others, liberty cannot mean submission to law.

The second respect in which the theory departs from liberal ways of thinking is closely related to this first break. It has to do not with the sort of value that freedom is taken to be, but rather with the sort of institutions that are thought to be most desirable under a dispensation of freedom. There are three broadly different types of institution for producing a public benefit from agents who are not individually motivated by a desire to produce that benefit: from individuals who may each wish for the realization of that benefit but who are directed in the first place to more self-serving ends. I shall describe these as the *formative*, the *supervisory* and the *aggregative* institutional types. While my theory joins liberal approaches in endorsing the aggregative kind and in rejecting the supervisory, it is distinctive in adopting an unambivalently positive attitude to the formative.

Consider any circumstance where there is a public benefit to be wrung from individuals who are primarily directed to more private concerns. The situation may be the classic free-rider problem, where all are better off if some benefit is brought about rather than not but where each reasons that he is best not contributing himself: if sufficient other people contribute, then his contribution is superfluous; if sufficient other people fail to contribute, then his contribution is in vain; and it is practically certain that he will not be the one to make the number of contributors just sufficient (see Pettit 1986a). The formative, supervisory and aggregative institutions correspond respectively to three factors which are always present in such a circumstance.

The three factors are the actions of the individuals involved, the aggregate result of those actions, and the mechanism whereby the actions are geared into the aggregate result. The formative institution puts such obstacles, penalties and rewards in place that individuals are motivated to act as if they were concerned with the public benefit: that is, to act in a distinctively virtuous way. The supervisory institution has some agency of the state monitor the aggregate outcome and interfere with it whenever this is necessary for the public benefit. And the aggregative institution puts a mechanism of aggregation in place which means that individual actions, even if they are not distinctively virtuous in character, will combine to promote the public benefit.

Any theory which gives importance to the value of freedom, at least freedom in the sense in which this involves negative liberty, is bound to take a hostile attitude to the use of a supervisory institution.[25] Equally, any freedom-centred theory is bound to be well disposed to the use of an aggregative institution, where there is one available. Thus any such theory is certain to favour the use of the competitive market where it can be shown, as neoclassical economists claim, that this produces a social optimum with minimal formative or supervisory constraints. With regard to the formative institution, however, there is an interesting difference between the sort of theory put forward here and standard liberal approaches.

The standard liberal approach is to say that any formative institution means removing or at least endangering someone's liberty, since it involves applying the apparatus of the law to affect negatively the choices that people make.[26] It may mean removing an option, as when individuals are simply blocked from doing something; it may mean imposing a penalty on the choice of an option, as when that choice is made illegal; or it may mean interfering in some way with natural outcomes so that a reward is offered for the choice of some other option. But in every case the formative institution appears to damage people's liberty and so to earn the hostility of the liberal. He sticks by the view, in Isaiah Berlin's words, that 'all coercion is, in so far as it frustrates human desires, bad as such' (Berlin 1969, p. 00).[27] Or, as J. S. Mill puts it, 'all restraint, qua restraint, is an evil' (1861, ch. 5).

Of course the liberal will have to tolerate the use of the formative institution, since there is no hope of organizing a society in which people enjoy liberty without recourse to coercive law; even to get a competitive market running smoothly, it may be necessary to surround it with legal bans against misrepresentation, against the formation of cartels, against failure to honour contracts, and the like. But the point is that the liberal will only have recourse to the formative institution reluctantly. He cannot endorse it wholeheartedly. Thus Berlin (1969, p. 00) can write, ' "A free man", said Hobbes, "is he that . . . is not hindered to do what he hath the will to do." Law is always a "fetter", even if it protects you from being bound in chains that are heavier than those of the law, say, arbitrary despotism or chaos. Bentham says much the same.'[28] Indeed he does. 'As against the coercion applicable by individual to individual,' he says, 'no liberty can be given to one man but in proportion as it is taken away from another. All coercive laws, therefore, and in particular all laws creative of liberty, are as far as they go abrogative of liberty' (Bentham 1843).

The theory defended in this essay suggests a different attitude. When freedom is construed as franchise, it is understood in such a way that there is no freedom without the creation of a system of mutual assurance of noninterference among the members of a society. Whatever is necessary to set up such a system of mutual assurance cannot be seen, then, as an invasion of people's freedom; it can scarcely be an invasion of something which does not pre-exist it. And so, when freedom is construed as franchise, we are forced to take a different view of the formative institutions involved in creating a suitable system of mutual assurance. We are forced to see them in a positive light. Ironically, since he is one of the heroes invoked in later liberal thinking, Locke (1690, *Second Treatise*, section 57) gives nice expression to the sentiment we must espouse: 'that ill deserves the name of confinement which hedges us in only from bogs and precipices. . . . For in all the states of created beings capable of laws, where there is no law, there is no freedom.'[29]

This positive attitude to formative institutions need not be an incautious one. We can adopt it while recognizing that, even when formative institutions promote franchise, they still negatively affect people's liberties; that such institutions may easily pass the point of promoting overall franchise and actually reduce it; that, if the institutions lead to the punishment of an offender, then that punishment certainly reduces his franchise; and that, if the state proposes to introduce or intensify any formative institutions, then it incurs an obligation to justify doing so: the onus of proof is on its side. The important point is that the attitude is bound to generate an interest in exploring the full realm of possible formative institutions, whereas the negative attitude of the liberal is likely to kill any such interest.

The realm of possible formative institutions includes the legal checks and sanctions which are required for establishing people's rights of liberty, immunity and security. But it also includes rather less invasive initiatives. First, it will include the organizing of things in such a way that public pressure should force agents to take a certain line. Thus the arrangement whereby the members of a jury or judicial bench can be challenged to defend their vote before other members puts pressure on them to vote on the basis of publicly avowable considerations. And, secondly, it will include the devising of schemes for the reward of those agents or actions which further the public interest in some distinctive way. This latter category may not seem to affect people's liberty at all, but it should be remembered that, even if the reward does not cost the taxpayer anything, the rewarding of some will mean the punishing of others: it will mean imposing on them a positional or comparative cost.

We have identified two respects in which our theory differs from standard liberal approaches: first, that it introduces a social as distinct from an asocial conception of the freedom ideal; and, secondly, that it involves an unambivalently positive attitude towards formative as well as aggregative institutions. It remains to show that in these respects the theory is of a piece with traditional republicanism.

The source of republican theory in modern Europe is by all accounts Niccolò

Machiavelli. Not being a Machiavelli scholar, I am loath to present an exposition of his views; in any case, any exposition I might offer would naturally be suspected of being driven by my theory. Happily, however, there is a way around both problems. In some recent articles on Machiavelli, Quentin Skinner presents his theory as displaying precisely the two features that mark off the approach taken here (Skinner 1983, 1984; for background, see Skinner 1978, vol. I).

Skinner (1983, pp. 12–13) is explicit that whereas contemporary liberals view freedom as an asocial condition, Machiavelli saw it as something realized only in society, and that whereas contemporaries espouse formative institutions with reluctance, Machiavelli saw them as part of what freedom entails:

> Among contemporary theorists, the coercive apparatus of the law is generally pictured as an obvious affront to individual freedom. The power of the law to constrain us is only held to be justified if, in diminishing the extent of our natural liberty, it serves at the same time to assure more effectively our capacity to exercise the freedom that remains to us. . . . For Machiavelli, by contrast, the law is in part justified because it ensures a degree of personal freedom which, in its absence, would although collapse. If the coercive apparatus of the law were withdrawn, there would not be a greater degree of personal liberty with a diminished capacity to enjoy it without risk; due to our self-destructive natures, there would rather be a diminution of personal liberty, a rapid slide towards a condition of complete servitude.

One of the most distinctive themes in the republican tradition of Machiavelli is the necessity of virtue among the citizens, and it may seem that in this regard, if not in others, the theory defended here represents a very different approach. But I do not see it that way. On the contrary, the republican emphasis on the need for virtue becomes in most authors an emphasis on the need for institutions that will encourage virtuous behaviour among the citizens, and such institutions are precisely the formative institutions discussed above. Machiavelli put as much emphasis on virtue as any other republicans, but he did so with a view to identifying the means of encouraging virtuous behaviour, for he saw people as unlikely to be spontaneously good. As Skinner (1984, p. 219) says, in expressing Machiavelli's point of view, 'unless the generality of evil men can be given selfish reasons for behaving virtuously, it is unlikely that any of them will perform any virtuous actions at all'.

The republican emphasis on the need for virtue is simply a different way of giving expression to a sentiment of approval for formative institutions. The republican line is that virtue, or at least virtuous behaviour, must predominate among the citizenry if they are to enjoy liberty and that formative institutions are a way of ensuring that that requirement is met.

Thus Skinner (1983, p. 10) can write as follows of Machiavelli:

> When he contends . . . that the indispensable means of preventing corruption is to invoke the coercive powers of the law, he is not merely endorsing the familiar observation that the law can be used to make us respect each other's liberty. He is also suggesting that the law can act to free us from our natural but self-destructive tendency to pursue our selfish interests, forcing us instead to promote the public interest in a genuinely *virtuoso* style, and thereby enabling us to preserve our own individual liberty instead of undermining it. He is claiming, in effect, that the law can – and must – be used to force us to be free.

Alan Ryan (1983, p. 219) gives expression to the same understanding of republicanism when he writes,

> This line of thought denies that there is a sacrifice of liberty if some sorts of economic activity are forbidden for the sake of republican virtue. We cannot infer from the fact that something is a man's property that he is therefore at liberty to do what he likes with it, and read arguments about stopping him doing what he likes as arguments about the terms on which his liberty is to be traded against other values. That is certainly the standard modern view, but is not the republican view.

It seems fair to conclude that the two respects in which the theory presented here departs from most liberal approaches are respects in which it rejoins the republican tradition which liberalism superseded. I describe the theory therefore, with some licence, as a republican theory of the state. In doing so I hope that I shall not offend historical sensibilities too grossly.

I do not think that I should, for the two respects in question relate to features that were probably very important in the emergence of the liberal tradition. That tradition appeared in the wake of a habit which earlier republicans would have found extremely foreign: the habit, as we might describe it, of state-of-nature thinking, in which the legitimacy and desirability of the polity is considered against the foil of an imaginary pre-social condition. Although the connection is not inevitable, it is obvious that state-of-nature thinking readily generates the notion that freedom should be seen as an asocial status, not as something akin to citizenship. I believe that this connection was made in the early days of the tradition which came to be identified as liberalism and that the first respect in which our theory is non-liberal is of some historical significance.

The same holds, I suggest, of the second respect in which it breaks with liberal assumptions: namely, in its complacency about formative institutions. Just as state-of-nature thinking was associated with the period when the liberal tradition emerged, so was an even more important event: the discovery, as we might call it, of the aggregative institution, specifically of the invisible hand. When Bernard Mandeville and Adam Smith identified this institution in their rather different ways, they called attention to a possibility which had scarcely been remarked before: the possibility that certain spheres of social life can thrive if, and indeed only if, the state severely restricts its formative or supervisory interference in those spheres (see Goldsmith 1987). I believe that enthusiasm for the aggregative institution, and an associated suspicion about the alternatives, has characterized the liberal tradition and may even be part of its founding source.[30] This enthusiasm may explain for example why the evil of corruption, an evil which the formative institution is meant to solve, ceased to be the main social problem for liberals. It gave way to the evil of state interference – the assumption being perhaps that there is no guarding against state corruption – where such interference is characterized as whatever hinders the operation of the aggregative market mechanism. The enthusiasm may also explain why the liberal tradition has tended towards libertarian extremes in which aggregative institutions are given a more and more exclusive role in the organization of social life: this, to the extent even of replacing democratic structures.[31]

This is enough by way of explaining why I describe my approach as a republican theory of the state. In conclusion I would just note that the definition of republicanism assumed here gives it a broader cast than is ascribed either by those who think it is sufficient for republicanism to reject a monarchy or by those who think it is sufficient to believe in the value of participatory democracy. Republicans in my sense will be anti-monarchical, for no ordinary citizen enjoys franchise fully if there is a monarch – or, at least, a more-than-token monarch – with whom to compare him. Equally, republicans in my sense will be enthusiasts for the public forum, since publicity is a crucial institutional safeguard of franchise. But these are corollaries of the proper definition of republicanism; they do not belong to its core.

VII   Conclusion

I hope that I have done enough to show that a political philosophy of promoting franchise ought to have great contemporary appeal. The ideal hailed has the attraction of turning on the notion of individual liberty, and it has the twin virtues of answering to the concerns of those on the liberal side of politics who worry about individual rights and those on the radical who worry about differences of power and the frustration of needs.[32] Besides, as we have just seen, it connects with a significant and well-tested tradition of political thought; it is a theory of a distinctively republican stripe. In conclusion I shall mention one further strength of the theory and also a feature that may be counted as a weakness.

The weakness is that the theory may not legitimate some interventions of the state that are currently justified on more-or-less utilitarian grounds. Thus it may not justify the state in acting to provide any old public good or, more generally, in acting so as to solve the prisoner's dilemmas in which people find themselves. Such interventions will be justified if they are necessary for moderating differences of power or for satisfying some people's basic needs. Thus the theory would not block the state from providing a weather-forecasting service or a system of health inspection, since these sorts of things serve to guard against dangers of impoverishment or disease. Again, certain state interventions will be justified, we may presume, if they are required to safeguard the prospects of future citizens. Thus the theory would not stop the state from assuming responsibility for the protection of the environment or even the protection of certain intellectual and cultural traditions. Finally, it is worth noting that the theory would seem to allow the state to intervene, say, to build a road network, provided that those who use that network pay for it, whether by means of a toll or a fuel tax. But, for all these considerations, the theory is still more limited than a utilitarian philosophy and the limitation is worth noting; it may yet cause problems.

The further strength of the theory is that it is comparatively resistant to the communitarian line of criticism which has recently been addressed with some passion to political philosophies such as Rawls's.[33] There are a number of strands to this line of criticism, but perhaps the main one is a charge that the sort of political philosophy in the dock is atomistic in character, failing to take account of the communal nature of human beings. This charge does not carry against our theory, since franchise is something like a holistic version of liberty: it embodies the requirements of perfect liberty, once they are construed under the assumption that the notion of the solitary individual is incoherent or at least inappropriate. Franchise is freedom in a sense in which communitarians can be concerned about it. I don't see what more they could ask for.

Notes

I was greatly helped by written comments on an earlier version of this essay from John Braithwaite, Geoffrey Brennan, Alan Hamlin, Chandran Kukathas, David Miller, David Neal, Wojciech Sadurski and Hugh Stretton. I also benefited from conversations with John Braithwaite, Geoffrey Brennan and Knud Haakonssen and from stimulating discussions when I gave talks on the material covered in the essay at the University of Western Australia and University College, Dublin.

1 Although I shall always refer to the citizen in the masculine, I do not mean the mode of reference to connote any sexist presumptions.
2 See Rawls (1971). See also the discussion and references in Pettit (1980), ch. 4.
3 Cf. Taylor (1984), p. 100: 'A notion of freedom quite common in the ancient world saw it as consisting in the status of the citizen. . . . Freedom, on this view, consisted in a certain place within society.'

4   I shall assume that satisfaction of the third clause does not come in degrees, though that is something of an idealization.

5   On the different senses in which probability may be objectively assessed, see Horwich (1982), ch. 2.

6   Cf. Rawls (1971), p. 244. It is worth remarking in this context that I ignore the difficulties often raised in discussions of Rawls as to how liberties should be weighted in estimating maxima. Such difficulties are the common inheritance of most contemporary political philosophies.

7   I assume that the rational way to promote is to maximize rather than to satisfice; this is plausible, I believe, once it is seen that maximization may require satisficing procedures. See Pettit (1984, 1986b).

8   This distinction is drawn in Sen (1985b).

9   It won't satisfy this condition, for example, if it involves the actual satisfaction of a person's preferences, given that those preferences range over what others do and how they fare. But, even among preference utilitarians, most will see nothing better in the actual satisfaction of preferences than in their as-if satisfaction.

10   On the construal of equality of resources, see Dworkin (1981).

11   Although it is true that positive liberty involves negative liberty plus some capacitating factor, there may also be a further requirement involved: a requirement that the agent achieve a distinctive sort of moral perfection. See Baldwin (1984).

12   The proposition does not hold of compound values. Equal liberty belongs in box 4. Among relatively unfashionable simple values there are of course examples which belong in box 4. For a family of cases, see Elster (1986b).

13   For background material, see Pettit and McDowell (1986). I may say that, while I reject atomism, I take an individualist view on the 'vertical' question. See Macdonald and Pettit (1981), ch. 3.

14   The following few paragraphs borrow but also depart in some measure from Pettit (1987c).

15   On the contrasted images of city and heath, see Ignatieff (1984).

16   Notice, however, that it is an open question whether the promotion of franchise requires all the liberties which are commonly defended. It might be, for example, that franchise is best promoted in some circumstances if the police have the right, though perhaps under only very strict conditions, to tap the phones of criminal suspects.

17   Weinstein (1965, pp. 156–7) writes, 'The difference between being free and feeling free is clear enough, but not always noted. . . . The notion of feeling free has an importance place in political theory, even though hitherto its place has often been unacknowledged or unclarified by thinkers who have implicitly attached importance to it.' See, too, Berlin (1969, p. 158): 'it is not with liberty, in either the "negative" or the "positive" senses of the word, that this desire for status and recognition can easily be identified'.

18   In my discussion I try to avoid the difficulty of defining power analytically. For an overview of some of the complexities involved, see the editor's introduction in Lukes (1986).

19   I am sympathetic to the line run by Sen (1983).

20   Compare the specific egalitarianism proposed by Tobin (1972). Tobin's line is developed in Walzer (1982) and Weale (1983).

21 I ignore the natural-law tradition, and more broadly the tradition of natural liberty, which stood as the main opposition to republicanism or civic humanism in the few centuries prior to 1800. For a brief survey, see Tully (1984). For further background, see Tuck (1979).

22 See Gray (1986a), for a short account of the tradition. See also Arblaster (1984); and Dunn (1979), ch. 2. I think of liberalism as a nineteenth- and twentieth-century tradition and I do not mean my characterization to encompass forebears such as Locke, Hume and Smith.

23 For earlier studies, which emphasize the influence of Machiavelli in England prior to the eighteenth century, see Fink (1945) and Raab (1964). Pocock shows the continuity into the eighteenth century, and indeed into the American revolution, of the Machiavellian ideas. For a recent essay on civic humanism in eighteenth-century Britain see Goldsmith (1987).

24 See, for example, Green (1889). Another exception would seem to be de Tocqueville; see Boesche (1987). Perhaps both of these thinkers are better cast as republicans, in the sense defined here. Some would cite as a more recent exception F. A. Hayek. Thus John Gray (1986b, p. 61) writes, 'In Hayek's conception of it, individual liberty is a creature of the law and cannot exist outside any civil society.' But on the other side Norman Barry (1979, p. 101) says, 'I emphasise that Hayek thinks there is a causal connection between laws as general rules and liberty rather than a logical connection.' I leave the final judgement to others.

25 And not just for the obvious reason that in its operation it involves interference with people. As Geoffrey Brennan reminded me, the liberal may also object on the ground that to give any agent or agency the power of supervision is to presuppose that the supervisors will act for the public good. It will be rational to accord the power of supervision only if a formative institution can be found to ensure that the supervisors do act in that way.

26 This approach is implicit in the common assumption that any form of coercion – in a broad sense of 'coercion' – is a violation of a person's freedom, whether or not the coercion is part of the rule of law. See Feinberg (1972), pp. 23–4. See, too, MacCallum (1972), p. 189. An exception to this line of thinking may be Robert Nozick. See Nozick (1974), p. 262; and, for an interpretation, Cohen (1978).

27 Berlin has a broad concept of coercion. 'Coercion implies the deliberate interference of other human beings with the area in which I wish to act' (1969, p. 00).

28 Berlin describes this as the understanding of the 'classical English political philosophers'. It should be mentioned, however, that there is typically a much less hostile attitude among liberal theorists to law which restricts the power of the state, albeit this is coercive too. See, for example, Cranston (1967), p. 49; and Arblaster (1984).

29 On Locke and liberalism see Dunn (1979), p.38ff. See also Tully (1984). Locke is difficult to categorize in terms of our contrast between republicanism and liberalism, as his remarks often give expression to the natural-law approach which we are ignoring: see note 21 above. For my own part, I think of liberalism as roughly a post-1800 philosophy.

30 But I also think that the enthusiasm is misdescribed as an enthusiasm for the

self-regulating order. It is striking that the successful formative institution is also self-regulating: it is self-sustaining, even if it is not self-starting.

31   It may also explain the general preference among liberals for pluralist as distinct from corporatist structures in the politics of interests. The pluralist structure is aggregative, since the idea is that, if different lobby groups each push their own interest with the government, there ought to be a tendency to have the different interests satisfied as well as possible. The corporatist structure is formative, since the groups are coopted by government into a single body and pressure is thereby put on them to adopt a common point of view.

32   I see the piece as a successor to Pettit (1987b); although it shifts perspective, it picks up most of the themes emphasized in that paper.

33   See, for example, the critical papers in Sandel (1984).

10

Power and Control in the Good Polity

Partha Dasgupta

The comparative merits of different forms of social organization have continually been at the centre of debate in economics and political philosophy. They will remain there. For here one faces the grandest of human concerns, embracing as it does issues bearing on liberty and welfare, people's aspirations, their potential and realized capabilities and the fulfillment of their needs. It enables us to see individuals in a social context, to ask about the possible features of a civil society, the obligations that people may have to themselves, to one another and to agencies created by the polity. We are also able to inquire into the obligations that such agencies have to people and to one another, the extent to which responsibility needs to be delegated among offices and persons, the role that dispersed information may play in answers to these, and so on. The debate is central to any discussion of the kind of society we ought to aspire to be members of; or, to put the matter in a different way, as Bernard Williams does in one of his recent books (1985, p. 1), 'It is not a trivial question, Socrates said: What we are talking about is how one should live.'

In this essay I shall discuss a few central issues which emanate from these questions, those which have been much explored by economists and political philosophers in recent years. And I shall approach matters in the spirit of an economist. By this I mean that I shall study social organizations in terms of the resource-allocation mechanisms they promote and sustain. Now, at first blush this may appear too restrictive, for there must surely be more to social organizations than that. In fact, of course, it depends upon how we choose to define 'resources'. We can think of them in a wide sense or we can think of them in a narrow sense. We can always define resources in so wide a way that we are able to incorporate any feature of a social organization we care to think of as an aspect of resource allocation. As elsewhere, what we gain in terms of generality, in terms of coverage of issues in political philosophy, we lose in terms of the sharpness of what we are able to *say* about them.

Economists have traditionally restricted their analyses to resources viewed in a narrow sense. Two of the stellar showpieces of economics, the two fundamental theorems of welfare economics, identify the precise sense in which market transactions among anonymous buyers and sellers can lead to a 'welfare-efficient' allocation of resources. (See sections II and III below.) These are sharp results, among the sharpest in the social sciences. But they are purchased at a price. Resources are viewed in a somewhat narrow sense; more tellingly, the concept of the goodness of a state of affairs is too restrictive. The importance of these theorems – especially the second of them (see section III) – lies in the fact that they outline the nature of the good polity when goodness is seen in a particular light. They extol the virtues of a particular type of markets – the competitive type – acting in harness with certain kinds of government intervention. So, then, if we seek to defend social organizations that are not the kinds specified in these theorems, it may be because our notion of the goodness of states of affairs is richer than what the theorems envisage. In fact this is the route I shall wish to take. The purpose of this essay will be to study the relative merits of different forms of social organization in the light of different conceptions of individual and the social good. Sections II–V will contain discussions of certain distinguished social organizations which suggest themselves when we seek the fulfillment of needs, welfare, rights and certain kinds of freedom in our conception of the good. But, in order to do this, we need first of all an account of the polity which is to form the subject of discourse. I go into this briefly in section I.

I Government as an agency

In what follows I shall be thinking of society as a co-operative venture for mutual advantage. The government is thus an agent, but empowered with just the right kind of authority to be able to perform as an *effective* agent.

This conception is not new. It dates back at least to Aristotle. In his *Politics*, Aristotle saw the state as the perfect community, in fact a partnership, 'having the full limit of self-sufficiency, which came into existence for the sake of living, but which exists for the sake of living well'. Thus, in particular, the state is a product of reason. Its political authority is concerned primarily with the resolution of conflicts that arise as people pursue their own particular interests, or more generally, their conception of the good. To be sure, this is not the only conception of the state that one can have. There are others, most notably Marxist conceptions, which differ considerably from this. But it is a convenient one for me to adopt, because it enables me to discuss the possible *design* of social organizations, or, in other words, the relative merits of alternative social organizations in terms of the goodness of the states of affairs they promote.

There is a particular task which the state in this conception must perform, one which is at the centre of discussion whenever economists study social organizations. It is the *co-ordination* of the different activities that persons in an interrelated world are engaged in while in pursuit of their interests. By 'co-ordination' I mean something quite different from resolution of conflicts. I mean that there needs to be some kind of balance among various activities, often production and consumption activities, so that, for example, shortages do not occur in some commodities and surpluses in others; for either would signal some form of waste, and thus a loss in terms of the goodness of a state of affairs. This role of the state also appears in Aristotle, and it is elaborated upon by his medieval followers, most notably Marsilius of Padua.

The state comprises various functional parts. They function in different ways so as to provide collectively for human needs, those whose fulfillment characterizes the life well-lived. Each part of the state is defined by its caring for a different human function; farmers for their nutrition functions, the 'mechanic artisan' for the 'sensitive' function, and so on. At a broader level of classification, Aristotle saw the state as comprising six parts, with their associated office: the agricultural, the artisan, the military, the financial, the priestly and the judicial or deliberative. It is imperative that each constituent performs its proper operation without interfering with the others. Today we call this co-ordination. Plainly, in order to achieve such co-ordination one needs some form of regulation, and this regulative function, in Aristotle's view, falls properly on the government.[1]

Exactly what the form of regulation the government ought to be allowed to impose is, of course, the nub of the matter, and more than 2000 years of discussion has not resolved it. I think it is wrong to expect it ever to be 'resolved'. It is not that sort of question. Nevertheless, there has been great progress in this inquiry in recent years. We know far more today of the ramifications of the issue of co-ordination. We understand now the intimate connection between ways of achieving co-ordination and conceptions of the life well lived. In all this discussion in recent years the market as a social organization has received a great deal of attention. And it is as well to start with conceptions of the good polity which urge us to regard markets as the type of resource-allocation mechanism that ought to be promoted.

II Markets and negative freedom

Defence, and in many instances outright advocacy, of the market mechanism, with its attendant and extensive set of private property rights, has ranged from grounds that are supremely instrumental to those that see unfettered markets as an embodiment of the good polity, as fundamental to the description of a society that nurtures lives that are well lived. At one extreme is an advocacy based on the primacy of such individual rights as those which are shown ultimately to justify a nightwatchman government, a government whose activities are limited to the provision of a few basic public services, such as the enforcement of contracts and the protection of persons or groups against force, theft and fraud; or, in other words, those services that enable persons to undertake voluntary production and exchange or, more generally, those which enable people to protect their personal property. This is not the place to evaluate the ingenious notion that the historical entitlements which people have to commodities and resources have priority over all else, an idea which lies behind the celebrated recent advocacy of the nightwatchman government or minimal state (Nozick 1974).[2] But we should note here that this advocacy is not based on instrumental grounds. Rather, it sees the unfettered and unassisted market mechanism – described in rich detail by Professor Nozick – as the only justifiable mechanism for resource allocation because it alone is consonant with the protection, even embodiment, of what Berlin (1969, Essay III) would classify as *negative freedom*; that is, an absence of coercion, an absence of 'the deliberate interference of other human beings (or human agencies) within the area in which (one) could otherwise act' (Berlin 1969, p. 112). For it is negative freedom which the protection of historical entitlements in Nozick's sense ultimately protects and promotes.

Nozick's conception of the market mechanism is a good deal broader than the competitive market mechanism to be found in the economist's treatise. The emphasis is on the ability of individuals and agencies to enter into voluntary transactions. There is no presumption that such a myriad of transactions is mediated by competitive prices. Nozick's ideal resource-allocation mechanism – if he would permit the use of such a technocratic term – is any that emerges from voluntary transactions among people who have titles to those commodities and resources to which they have historical entitlements. The competitive market mechanism would be only one among the many mechanisms that could in principle emerge.[3]

At another extreme is the advocacy of von Hayek, who claims not at all to understand the market mechanism and warns us all not to try to do so but asserts nevertheless that the mechanism is, most especially in theory, the best guarantee for *progress*. Here it will be out of place to present the various strands in Professor Hayek's political philosophy.[4] What we should note is that Hayek's advocacy of an unbridled market mechanism is based on instrumental grounds. Progress is the goal which is sought. It is thus a basic virtue of a society to generate it. Negative freedom – the protection of each person's private sphere against invasion by others – is only a means to this. It would not seem in Hayek's writings to be a primary moral good: 'if the result of individual liberty did not demonstrate that some manners of living are more *successful* than others, much of the case for it would vanish' (Hayek 1960, p. 85; emphasis added). Contrary to what is often done, it does not do to bracket Hayek's and Nozick's conceptions together.

At another extreme is the advocacy by Lord Bauer of what one could call an *assisted* market mechanism (see Bauer 1971, 1984). The role of the government in this scheme of things is more extensive than that assumed by Nozick's minimal state. The political philosophy is quite different. Much emphasis is placed upon the growth of economic well-being of those who seek it. Information about new commodities, new techniques of production and external markets is an essential commodity for the furtherance of production and trade. So are communication networks – roads, cables, and so forth – which are the means of transporting goods and services. It can be argued as a matter of fact that pre-industrial societies suffer particularly from a lack of such infrastructure. Their availability is a precondition for the growth of markets. It can also be argued that production of such infrastructure is greatly hampered if left exclusively to the private sector. Bauer's government would be vigorous in providing this class of commodities, in addition, of course, to the commodities provided by the minimal state. But that is about all. Bauer's advocacy of such an assisted market mechanism is in part based on the promotion of negative freedom in the economic domain and in part on the belief that it offers the best chance for the growth of material well-being for those who truly seek it. Partly, too, there is an underlying suggestion that government assistance diminishes and corrodes self-reliance and ultimately an individual's sense of responsibility, and thus self-respect. (I shall argue in section IV that this suggestion can be very misleading.)

Finally, there is the suggestion that such an assisted market mechanism also offers the best chance of avoiding the oppression of one group of people by another. There is, however, no claim that political democracy, in particular political freedom, is implied by well-functioning economic markets, or that it implies them.[5] Bauer's advocacy of the assisted market mechanism is based upon the demands of negative freedom of a special kind.

The argument to be found for the market mechanism in economics textbooks is, however, none of these. The advocacy there is for a particular kind of market mechanism, the *competitive price mechanism*. The idea here is that all transactions are mediated by prices. To be precise, it is assumed that each and every commodity and service has a market and thus a price and that individual agents, whether persons or firms, are sufficiently small relative to the markets for no single individual's plans to affect the magnitude of market prices. (This last explains the use of the qualifier 'competitive'.) A competitive market equilibrium is a set of prices, one for each and every distinguishable commodity and service, such that the demands made for each commodity and service by all individuals and firms at these prices equal the supplies made available at these prices. We have here a precise sense in which competitive prices provide a co-ordination for the activities of a myriad of agents in a deeply interrelated world. And the striking thing is that this co-ordination is provided with the minimum of publicly known information. At a market equilibrium each agent needs to know his own endowments (goods and services he has an initial right to), his own mind and market prices. Each firm needs to know its own production possibilities and the market prices. Market prices need be the only publicly known pieces of information.[6] (I am restricting attention to equilibrium prices. How equilibrium prices may be attained in a market economy is a difficult matter. Arrow and Hahn 1971 provide an account of these issues.)

But in fact competitive markets provide more service than co-ordination. What is called the First Fundamental Theorem of welfare economics is widely interpreted as asserting that a competitive market equilibrium allocation of commodities and services is efficient, in the special sense that there does not exist a feasible allocation at which all individuals' welfare or utility levels are at least as high as at the equilibrium allocation and at least one individual's welfare level is higher.

Efficiency in this sense is widely known as Pareto efficiency, and this is what I shall call it here, to contrast it to efficiency in other senses (see section V). The First Fundamental Theorem, of course, envisages the government as an agency of the state. It is more active than Nozick's minimal government. The point here is that there are a number of commodities which are unusually difficult to market effectively: for example, public health protection against communicable diseases. The theorem assumes that such public services as these, and others such as law enforcement, are supplied by the government, possibly via non-market channels. (In one interpretation the government pays for the costs of providing these services by imposing lump-sum taxes on members of the polity. But it supplies the goods free of charge. In another, it charges differential prices for their supply, different prices to different types of people, and pays for the cost of production from these charges.) The theorem presupposes that people's initial endowments of goods and services are sufficient to enable all members of the polity to survive (see Koopmans 1957). In section IV, I shall go more deeply into the question of commodity needs.

The literature on the ramifications of this theorem is vast. (Koopmans 1957 and Arrow 1971 present characteristically penetrating accounts of this line of argument.) For our purposes here, one point worth noting is that the theorem, *as usually described*, is based upon' the hypothesis that an individual's choice of commodities and services is guided exclusively by his conception of his own welfare.[7] This is not to say that a person may not have concern for others, merely that the satisfaction of such of concern would reflect a corresponding attainment of the person's own welfare. But all this supposes that a person's actions are directed exclusively at furthering his own welfare. This is a substantive claim about individual motivation, and a great deal of work in psychology and anthropology suggests that it is false. (For extensive discussion of this, see Leibenstein 1976; Scitovsky 1976; Hirschman 1982.) The point I am drawing attention to is not that people may be irrational. It is rather that people's motivations are richer in content than personal-utility maximization. Altruism is not the only source of being other-regarding. People are also guided by their sense of duty, obligations, and so forth. However, the theorem itself is not false. What I am arguing is that the *interpretation* it is commonly given is false. What the First Fundamental Theorem actually asserts is something else. It asserts that a competitive market equilibrium allocation sustains a kind of *choice efficiency*; that is, there does not exist a feasible allocation at which all individuals enjoy consumption bundles of commodities and services which are at least as high in the rankings based upon which these individuals actually choose, and at which at least one individual enjoys a bundle which is higher in the ranking over bundles upon which his own choice is based. Call the function which represents the ordering upon which a person's choice is actually based his *felicity function*.[8] Even leaving aside individual irrationality, it can be argued that an individual's felicity function does not necessarily coincide with his utility function, or for that matter the function which would reflect his well-being – or, more generally, his interests and advantages (see section IV). Contrary, then, to what is often thought, the First Fundamental Theorem does *not* assume that people are utility-maximizing. Nor does the theorem suggest that competitive markets guarantee persons freedom of choice; less still, equality of choice: an individual with little purchasing power would have a greatly restricted set of commodity bundles to choose from. What the theorem in fact claims is that the market mechanism provides a form of aggregate efficiency in the exercise of choice over commodity bundles. This is the precise and limited sense in which Milton Friedman (1962) is surely correct in his assertion that the market mechanism provides a social system in which people are free to choose (but see section IV).

The First Fundamental Theorem of welfare economics provides both the sharpest and bluntest justification of the (competitive) market mechanism. It is the sharpest because it makes precise an analytical feature of competitive market equilibrium allocations: there is nothing mystical about the claim, nor does the justification rely on historical evidence (for example, to the effect that the economies with the freest markets grew the fastest). And it is the bluntest because Pareto efficiency – or, more accurately, choice efficiency – yields a mere partial ordering; not all states of affairs are comparable by the criterion. Efficiency is silent on the distribution of welfare – or, more specifically, the distribution of felicity and choice. What determines the extent of choice for an individual is his initial endowments of goods and services (including his own innate abilities), and the terms at which he can convert goods and services into goods and services via production and market exchange. A person with limited endowments will have little by way of *power* – to have his interests sufficiently attained in the state of affairs which emerges under the market mechanism – and precious little in the way of *control*: to shape his life on the basis of his own choice of a sufficiently rich set of projects and plans. In short, the First Fundamental Theorem of welfare economics is non-committal about the distribution of power and control and, at a step removed, non-committal about the distribution of felicity among members of a polity. It is the Second Fundamental Theorem of welfare economics which addresses distributional issues. The next section goes into this.

III   Generalized utilitarianism and the Second Fundamental Theorem of welfare economics

For concreteness I shall continue to assume that a state of affairs is an allocation of commodities and services among members of the polity – end-states, to use Nozick's terminology (Nozick 1974). Services include activities in general. So the concept of a state of affairs is a broad one, as I suggested earlier. Call the function which represents the social ordering over states of affair the *social evaluation function*. The social evaluation function reflects public judgements concerning the relative goodness of alternative social states. (It is most often, misleadingly, called a social welfare function in the literature on welfare economics.) A much-discussed class of moral theories is the one which asserts that the goodness of a state of affairs can be judged solely in terms of the *utility* allocation resulting from it. This is often called *welfarism* (Sen 1977) or *generalized utilitarianism* (Maskin 1978).[9] It is most often assumed in such theories that the moral evaluation of end-states subsumes the Pareto partial ordering. This means that, if all persons enjoy at least as high a utility level at one end-state as at another and if at least one person enjoys a higher utility level, then the social evaluation function judges the first end-state to be superior to the second. This is not an innocuous moral assumption, even under welfarism, but little purpose will be served here by violating it.

The most celebrated example of generalized utilitarianism is, of course, utilitarianism itself. Here, the social evaluation function ranking end-states in terms of their goodness is the sum of individual utilities.[10] Now, summation is only one operation available for aggregating individual utilities. Different types of aggregation of individual utilities for constructing a social evaluation function display different public judgements regarding the distribution of utilities (see Dasgupta, Sen and Starrett 1973). The sorts of moral axioms which enable one to move from generalized utilitarianism to utilitarianism have been much explored in the social choice literature in recent years. (The vital papers here are d'Aspremont and Gevers 1977; Maskin 1978). Each type of social evaluation function presupposes a degree of feasibility in measuring individual utility; it also presupposes the feasibility of a particular type of interpersonal utility comparison. These two issues are, of course, related. For example, if the social evaluation function is utilitarian, individual utilities must be cardinally measurable – they must be unique at most up to a positive affine transformation – and, while individual utility *levels* need not be comparable, their *scales* must be.[11] To take another example, if individual utilities are wholly non-comparable, then, even if they are cardinally measurable, it would not be possible to arrive at a social evaluation function. Public judgements on states of affairs may then reflect a partial ordering; for example, the Pareto partial ordering (see Sen 1970).

The Second Fundamental Theorem of welfare economics, as noted earlier, is motivated by the need for a discussion of good social arrangements in a polity which is able to arrive at distributional judgements concerning commodity allocations. Assume for the moment that people maximize their personal utilities, that the moral theory guiding public judgements is generalized utilitarianism and that it subsumes Paretianism. The theorem asserts that, under certain conditions bearing on individual choice, values and production technology, and on the assumption that the government has full information about technology, individual utility functions and individual endowments, the best feasible state of affairs can be sustained as a competitive market equilibrium, provided the government in advance imposes a suitable lump-sum wealth redistribution. (For excellent expositions of this, see Koopmans 1957 and Meade 1976. For a full mathematical treatment of the two fundamental theorems, see Debreu 1959; and, for a recent discussion of modern price theory, see Duffie and Sonnenschein 1988.) Loosely speaking, the theorem suggests that public judgements concerning the *distribution* of goods and services ought to be implemented by (lump-sum) taxes and subsidies and that the *efficient co-ordination* of various activities ought to be left to the market mechanism. This dual system, of government regulation in the form of taxation and subsidy, on the one hand, and decentralized decision-making in the market place – mediated by the price system – on the other, has been at the centre of discussion in the literature on welfare economics and public finance. So long as the claims of individuals to have their interests taken justly in account are met, the theorem suggests a form of social organization in which persons can exercise both power and control over their lives. In such a polity, if power and control are both vastly limited it is because the economy as a whole is poor, not because the distribution is unjust.

There is, in fact, an alternative social organization which is equivalent in terms of the allocations of utilities achievable by the polity envisaged in the Second Fundamental Theorem. It is one where the government expropriates the initial endowments of goods and services held by individuals and reallocates them by command. Under this command system, members of the polity exercise power: their interests are taken into account in the social evaluation function which ranks alternative allocations of resources. But they do not exercise control, for they do not exercise direct choice over the shape of their lives (see Dasgupta 1980, 1982). To be sure, under the command system persons consume goods and services they would have chosen had the decentralized price mechanism been established. Here, then, the government is delegated responsibility with vengeance: it calculates what people would have chosen and then proceeds to choose on their behalf. In terms of the allocation of commodities attained, the two social organizations are identical. But they differ as regards the allocation of agency roles. Of course, the equivalence between these two forms of social organization rests on narrow grounds. If individual utilities themselves depend upon the extent to which choice can be exercised, the two forms of organization are not equivalent, even as regards the allocation of utilities.

The Second Fundamental Theorem describes a particular kind of social organization. It is widely interpreted as presuming, as is the First Fundamental Theorem, that individual choice is guided exclusively by a person's perception of his own welfare. This is a false interpretation. What is does assume is that the soical evaluation function is based solely on individual felicities. It does not assume that a person's felicity is identical to his utility. Having noted the point I do not propose to labour it. So for the moment I shall ignore it. I continue to assume, then, that individual choice is guided exclusively by the individual's perception of his own welfare, and that the perception is correct. What gives the theorem particular vitality is that it presents a social organization where people exercise both power and control to shape their own lives. In the process of exercising control, individuals do not need to concern themselves with the social good. Bernard Williams' criticism of utilitarianism (see Williams 1973, 1985), that it does not recognize the distinctness of persons, that it glides over their separateness and aggregates them into one whole, would have been invulnerable to criticism if it indeed required each person always to act on behalf of all. Williams sees this as a requirement of utilitarianism, and thus finds it repugnant. What the Second Fundamental Theorem does is to show that it is possible in principle to design social organizations that are guided by utilitarian public judgements, where none the less persons, *qua* persons, can be wholly self-regarding, pursuing their own sense of welfare. This is what decentralization in decision-making amounts to.

The point is that in reaching public judgements – or, in other words, in prescribing social choice – aggregation cannot be avoided. A judgement would not be a public judgement if it were otherwise. Except in the most trivial of societies, both individual interests and individuals' choices exercised in the pursuit of their sense of the good clash. It has been argued most forcefully by Williams in recent years that in matters of personal morality individual separateness must count (see also Nagel 1986, for a powerful exploration of this viewpoint, and Sen 1985b, for a classification and evaluation of these positions). Granted, it can be argued from this that public judgements ought to take this distinctiveness into account. But this only implies that in reaching public judgements the aggregation ought to be based upon individual separateness, not that aggregation should be avoided. The weakness of utilitarianism in particular, and welfarism in general, is not that they necessarily call upon individuals to forsake the claims of their separateness when choosing their courses of action. (The Second Fundamental Theorem of Welfare Economics, as we have noted, describes a social organization where individuals can maintain their separateness in the sense in which Williams urges us to think about the matter.) The weakness, rather, is that it embraces an unusually narrow view of persons. The agency aspect of persons assumes a purely instrumental role. More particularly, each individual's interests and advantages are gift-wrapped tidily in his utility or welfare function.[12]

From the perspective of arriving at public judgements, does this restriction matter? It can be argued, after all, that in most cases a person's interests and advantages point in the same direction as his welfare, so that a public judgement arrived at on the basis of generalized utilitarianism is unlikely to get things wrong – at least in practice (see Hare 1981 for this line of defence). It may then be argued that this last is the acid test for moral theories which are used for prescribing social choice. Generalized utilitarianism, it can thus be argued, may be repugnant as a basis for private morality, but it has the virtue of getting things approximately right when used for arriving at public judgements.

I think there is something in this line of argument, but not an awful lot. The problem is that, even if in general people's interests and advantages point in the same direction as their utilities, it is not enough to ensure that public judgements will be approximately right. *Quantitatively*, prescriptions may be wide of the mark. Then, of course, there is the fact that it is not unusual for interests and advantages to run counter to utility, or welfare, let alone counter to the basis upon which individual choice is exercised. In developing countries mothers in impoverished circumstances routinely sacrifice their own interests for the sake of their families. There is, for the greater part, no complaint; indeed, there is an internalization of such acts via the claim that the family's welfare is the mother's own. This identification, which, so far as one can judge, is often nearly complete, is nurtured by the sense of duty and obligation engrained in women by their societies from an early age.[13] Here, then, is a sort of situation where a person's sense of duty may direct her to take actions which are indeed welfare-enhancing for her. But they are a far cry from actions which would promote her own interests and advantages. The fact that she *gladly* offers herself to be used does not obliterate the fact that she *is* used. The rupture between utility and advantage is complete here, as is between felicity and advantage.

IV   Positive freedom, needs and commodity allocation

In section II we presented several expressions of the moral basis of the market mechanism as a form of social organization. One recurring theme was the protection of negative freedom. This is often identified with the market. In his classic essay on liberty, however, Isaiah Berlin disentangled *two* concepts of liberty which, although they had become fused in the literature and in one's thinking, had historically 'developed in divergent directions not always by logically reputable steps, until, in the end, they came into direct conflict with each other' (Berlin 1969, p. 132). In contrast with freedom from coercion, including of course freedom from state interference, Berlin spoke of *positive freedom*, the *ability* 'to be somebody, not nobody; a doer – deciding, not being decided for, self-directed . . . conceiving goals and policies of [one's] own and realizing them', and of the ability 'to be conscious of [oneself] as a thinking, willing, active being, bearing responsibility for [one's] choices and able to explain them by reference to [one's] own ideas and purposes' (p. 131).

At one level the two concepts – negative and positive freedom – amount to the same thing. Both are concerned with the extent of one's feasible set of choices. Indeed, there has been much discussion in the literature of whether they *are* distinct concepts. In what follows I want to explore the idea that they differ, and that they differ by way of the *sources* which constrain choice. More specifically, I want to distinguish constraints that are imposed upon one by others, in particular by the will of others, from constraints upon one's actions that arise because of a lack of commodities which are a means of undertaking such actions. For example, a person may be assetless and, more importantly, chronically malnourished, lacking thereby the motivation and physical capabilities he needs in order to be employable in a freely functioning labour market, his sole means of escape from the bonds of deprivation. He does not enjoy positive freedom. He is unable to be a 'thinking, willing, active being'. Such a person does not have life plans or projects, or 'own ideas and purposes'. But, if he is not prevented by others from seeking and obtaining employment in a freely functioning labour market, he is negatively free. In this example, what keeps him in wretchedness, what deprives him systematically of freedom to *do* things, is a lack of commodities.

There is, of course, a vicious circle here. It is a lack of command over commodities which has so weakened the person as to prevent him from joining the labour force, the means of enabling him to attain some command over commodities. So one may argue that the 'agency' constraining his ability to be able to function as an active and willing being is the social organization: in other words, the workings of the free play of the market. (Why did he lack commodities to begin with?) But this would miss the point. The direct reason behind the person's inability to function here is physiological: he is undernourished. If his disability is reversible, it can be reversed only by the supply of commodities, namely nutrients and medication. The social organization in which a person is so deprived is the background frame; so to speak, it is one step removed. The market mechanism is not an agency. No single *person* is responsible for his deprivation. I shall suggest below the sense in which it can be argued from this situation that the deprived person has a right to expect the *polity* to modify the resource-allocation mechanism.

Commodities do not possess intrinsic value. Their value derives exclusively from the uses to which they are put and is measured in terms of their contribution to the human good.[14] Social organizations are the medium through which this conversion occurs. Different social organizations sustain the process in different ways and to different extents. This has been the central dogma of economics and it realizes its sharpest focus in that aspect of the human good which concerns positive freedom.

One advantage of viewing positive freedom in the way I am viewing it here is that it provides a link between the ability of persons to function and the *commodity needs* this gives rise to. The idea of commodity needs has played a minor role in recent economic analysis. This has been because of the almost exclusive attention paid in welfare economics to a felicity description of states of affairs. Needs are not an independent notion here; they are seen *through* felicity. (For example, necessities are defined as commodities for which demand, based on felicity, is inelastic; that is, approximately independent of their price.)

The exception is development economics, where descriptions of states of affairs in terms of commodity availabilities and levels of well-being have been a commonplace for years. What are often called social indicators – for example, the extent to which a population has access to drinking water, basic medical facilities, adequate nourishment and primary education, and indices of life expectancy at birth, infant and child mortality, and adult literacy – provide aggregate information about these aspects of states of affairs.[15] The idea is not to see them as a reflection of aggregate felicity and utility realized in the economy, although they plainly affect both, and so should also be valued because of that. The idea rather is to see them as they are, as aspects of states of affairs, and to evaluate economies on such bases.[16]

That 'need' is a modal notion has been re-emphasized in recent writings (see in particular the wide-ranging treatment in Wiggins 1987, and Barry 1965). Unlike 'desire' or 'want', it is not an intentional verb. The idea of *basic needs*, as it appears in the literature on development economics (for pioneering work in this field, see Streeten et al. 1981), addresses commodities such as basic food and drinking water, accomodation, primary medical care and education and sanitation facilities – goods that are the means of being able to function, prerequisites of the individual's ability to pursue his conception of the good. Rawls's well-known concept of *primary goods*, while embedded in a different philosophical system, is also exemplified by such commodities. ('Primary goods . . . turn out to be those things which are generally necessary for carrying out . . . plans successfully whatever the particular nature of the plan and its final ends' – Rawls 1971, p. 411. Rawls's primary goods include liberty and self-respect. I am concentrating here on physical commodities.) Sen's focus on individual capabilities and the commodity basis of the realization of capabilities (Sen 1985a) follows from the same concern.

Commodity needs are not all or nothing. Being able to function is not a uniquely specifiable thing. There is plainly a continuous gradation – specifically, degrees of well-being. The feasible range of the distribution of human good depends upon the economy's endowment of commodities, including the state of technological knowledge. The point is not that the human good is historically specific. What is limited by endowments and technology is the extent to which the good can be achieved.

This emphasis on the ability of persons to undertake motivated activities, to exercise their realized capacities – their innate or trained abilities – and the recognition that the exercise of our natural powers is a leading human good, has strong historical antecedents, most especially Aristotle, in his *Nicomachean Ethics*. Much attention is paid by Aristotle to the connection between enjoyment and the exercise of one's capacities. Rawls (1971, p. 414), over an extended discussion, calls this link the Aristotelian Principle. There is no suggestion, though, that 'enjoyment', as conceived of in the principle, is the same as 'utility' or 'felicity', as we use the terms today. That it is not is implied by the centrality of the *agon* in Greek thinking. The point of interest is in a person engaging in and bringing to fruition the kinds of activities that, upon rational reflection, go towards making his total life well lived. A similiar emphasis on the exercise of one's faculties is to be found in classical Indian ethics, most especially that which is enunciated in the *Bhagavad Gita*. The centrality of resource allocation in all this lies in the fact that commodities are a means by which activities can be undertaken. One can curb one's desires and wants, and thus commodity requirements. Indeed, several ethical systems instruct us to do precisely that. But, if the exercise of one's natural powers is a leading human good, there is no getting away from commodity needs.

There is a link between the modern concept of basic needs and the Aristotelian Principle. The principle affirms that enjoyment is by no means the result of *returning* to a healthy or nornal state or of making up deficiencies. Many kinds of enjoyment arise only when we exercise our faculties (see in particular Rawls 1971, p 426, for further elaboration). What the Aristotelian system does is to show how such basic commodity needs are in themselves a part of what creates a right to them. A similar viewpoint is evoked in Marx's conceptionn of needs and commodity entitlements.[17].

The inability of the market mechanism to guarantee the satisfaction of basic needs in an economy which is in principle productive enough to satisfy them has not had much attention in analytical welfare economics. As noted earlier, the First Fundamental Theorem assumes in effect that individual endowments of goods and services are sufficient for survival. (The Second Fundamental Theorem addresses distributional issues directly. So survival is guaranteed by lump-sum redistribution of assets, unless the economy is so poor that not all *can* survive. In what follows I ignore this possibility. It would take us into a different range of questions.) More importantly, analytical welfare economics for the most part has not recognized that there is a wide range of levels of survival, specifically that there are various degrees of undernutrition and morbidity. Undernourishment is not the same as hunger. A central feature of it is a restricted ability on the part of the person to perform tasks, whether mental or physical.[18] With the advent of modern public medicine – elimination of smallpox, reduction in malaria, and so forth – it is possible for people to remain alive but in a sort of twilight zone of varying levels of ill-being. The headcount of deaths from starvation in a country can thus be low even with large numbers of undernourished persons.

Economists face a persistent difficulty in that they are restricted to pure analysis and historical studies. (Controlled experiments are for the most part not possible.) Now, historical evidence rarely clinches matters, most especially if we are trying to understand the structure of pure forms of social organization. For example, it does not require acute perception to note the existence of massive commodity deprivation in developing economies that combine in varying degrees markets and oligarchic and government controls. What prescription follows from this as regards changes in power and control if history is to be the sole guide? The answer is at least ambiguous, as a massive and contentious literature in development economics shows. For example, explanations of the phenomenal performance of South Korea in raising national income and fulfilling basic needs have varied from the suggestion that markets have been free to function there to the claim that they have been under significant, but judicious, government control (see, for example, Datta-Chaudhury 1979; Bhagwati 1988). It has also not gone unnoticed that both South Korea and Taiwan (another economic success story) enjoyed substantial land reform just after the Second World War, so that neither economy had to carry a sizable army of assetless people (see Adelman 1980).

Theoretical analysis cannot, to be sure, settle the matter. But without it onne cannot tell what are the limits of social organizations. A significant claim that has typically been made for the market mechanism is that even a person possessing no physical assets can join the labour force, and thereby step onn the escalator to possible future success. Equality of opportunity is something freely functioning markets are thought to sustain. The analytical basis of this claim is unfortunately incorrect, because the underlying theoretical construct which permits one to make the claim does not recognize that at systematically low levels of nutrition intake a person's capacity for work is affected adversely. There is thus a possible vicious circle here. Those who have no title to non-wage income are vulnerable in the market for labour, their sole means of generating income.[19] How precisely this linkage works – between access to non-wage income and opportunities in the labour market – has only recently been explored analytically (see Dasgupta and Ray 1986, 1987a). The moral is clear: a person requires guaranteed access to certain essential commodities – basic needs, in the sense in which the term is used in development economics – if the pure form of the market mechanism is to guarantee him productive work, and thus access to further commodities.

There are various ways in which such basic commodity needs can be guaranteed. Asset redistribution (for example, land reform), as envisaged in the Second Fundamental Theorem, is one. Direct action by the government is another. Food and medical subsidies, negative income taxes and food-for-work programmes are yet other forms of social security in operation in various countries. The founding fathers of the modern welfare state would have had little patience with theoretical arguments such as those I am discussing here. Commodity deprivation among the poor of Europe was there for all to see, and towards the end of the nineteenth century the idea – if not the actual expression – of social rights had taken sufficient hold to legitimize the basis of the modern Welfare State (see especially Marshall 1965; also Rimlinger 1983). And, yet, without a theoretical basis the conceptual background of the precise form of social organization being advocated is always suspect. In the next section, I shall look briefly at the modifications to the Second Fundamental Theorem that are required when commodity needs are brought explicitly into the discourse.

V   Commodity needs and exchange restrictions

In a celebrated passage on a hypothetical case involving Wilt Chamberlain and his fans, Robert Nozick (1974) argues that the demands of equality can clash systematically with the right which persons have over the use of those commodities to which they have historical entitlements. Nozick suggests that equality-seeking ethical systems would prohibit Chamberlain and his fans from engaging in mutually beneficial trades, where each of thousands of fans pays Chamberlain a small sum for the pleasure of watching him play basketball. (The point of the objection being that Chamberlain would become still richer by this agreement.)

We noted in section III that, in the social arrangement envisaged by the Second Fundamental Theorem, once the optimal lump-sum endowment transfers have been made such mutually beneficial trades are not prohibited. The allocation of resources sustained by such a polity satisfies choice efficiency (see section II). Considerations of the distribution of felicities are met by lump-sum transfers. There is no room for further gains from production and exchanges on the part of members of the polity once markets have cleared. In particular, Chamberlain and his fans would not be prevented from coming to an agreement such as the one Nozick envisages. Put another way, there are no exchange restrictions in the polity which arranges matters in line with the Second Fundamental Theorem.[20]

Recall that the theorem assumes that public judgements are reflected by a social evaluation function based exclusively on individual felicities, and that it subsumes the Pareto-partial ordering as applied to felicities. Now, felicities offer rather limited information about states of affairs, limited even from the moral point of view. In the previous section I argued that the notion of commodity needs does not find independent room if the moral language is restricted to felicities. In what follows I shall argue that, if, in addition to felicities, the moral theory incorporates considerations of commodity needs, some forms of trade restrictions may well be required. Put another way, considerations arising from commodity needs clash with the rights people may be thought to have to voluntary transactions. To put it in yet another way, if commodity needs have independent status in a moral theory, then Pareto efficiency in felicities will in general have to be forsaken.

To see this, a formal model will help. Consider a society of two individuals interested in two commodities, x and y. Let x_1 and y_1 be the quantities of the two goods consumed by person 1, and x_2 and y_2 the quantities consumed by person 2. We may assume that the economy has initial endowments of X and Y amounts of the two commodities. A resource allocation is a quartet of magnitudes, (x_1, y_1, x_2, y_2). It is a feasible resource allocation if $x_1 + x_2 \leq X$ and $y_1 + y_2 \leq Y$.

For simplicity of exposition, I assume that each person is entirely self-regarding. Thus, person 1's felicity is dependent solely on the pair (x_1, y_1) and person 2's felicity is dependent solely on the pair (x_2, y_2). Let f_1 and f_2 be the individuals' felicity functions. Then $f_1 = f_1(x_1, y_1)$ and $f_2 = f_2(x_2, y_2)$. Given this, we may identify a social state, or end-state, with a resource allocation. (Since we know the felicity functions we can immediately compute felicities from a knowledge of the social state.)

The Second Fundamental Theorem assumes that the social evaluation function is defined exclusively on felicities. Let E be the social evaluation function. Then the theorem assumes that $E = E(f_1, f_2)$. It follows that the social evaluation of an end-state (x_1, y_1, x_2, y_2) is $E[f_1(x_1, y_1), f_2(x_2, y_2)]$. We noted as well that the theorem assumes E to be Paretian. Thus, *ceteris paribus*, an increase in f_1 (resp. f_2) increases E. This is precisely why the best-feasible resource allocation under such a moral theory is Pareto-efficient..

Now enlarge the moral theory to include the idea of needs as an independent category. I shall suppose, for simplicity of exposition, that person 1 has a special need for x. We may suppose that x is a particular medicine and that 1 suffers from that kind of ill-health which requires x. Given that 1 needs x, it would be surprising if it was not partially reflected in his felicity function. Nevertheless, it will not necessarily be *wholly* captured. If it were, this commodity need would not have an independent status. This being so, information regarding the two people's felicities is not sufficient in our enlarged, pluralist, moral theory. What is morally relevant is not only the pair of felicities f_1 and f_2, but also x_1, the amount of x that 1 gets to consume. In other words, the goodness of a state of affairs depends upon f_1, f_2 *and* x_1. It follows that the social evaluation function in this enlarged moral theory is defined on f_1, f_2 and x_1. In short, $E = E(f_1, f_2, x_1) = E[f_1(x_1, y_1), f_2(x_2, y_2), x_1]$. Notice how x_1 enters the social evaluation function through two doors: once as an ingredient in person 1's felicity (his felicity matters in arriving at a public judgement), and, second, independently, as an expression of the fact that 1 is in need of x (and needs count as well for arriving at a public judgement). Notice too that efficiency takes on an extended meaning in this enlarged moral theory. It is no longer felicity, or Pareto efficiency, we would be interested in. We have three variables that are morally relevant: f_1, f_2 *and* x_1. Each is a good, a desirable object. We would presumably want to assume that, *ceteris paribus*, an increase in f_1 (resp. f_2 and x_1) increases the value of E. It is then obvious that even then E does *not* subsume the Pareto partial ordering: we can always compensate E for a slight lowering of both f_1 and f_2 by some increase in x_1.[22]

How is the Second Fundamental Theorem modified? In particular, can the best resource allocation in this enlarged moral theory be arrived at by a conjunction of lump-sum transfers and competitive markets? The answer is yes, but with one difference. In addition to imposing the desired lump-sum transfers, the government must as well grant a subsidy to person 1 for each unit of commodity x he purchases in the market. (The government pays for the subsidy from a lump-sum tax it collects from the two.) Therefore, the two persons do not face the same price for good x. (They do for commodity y.) Person 1 pays less for each unit of x he purchases than person 2. The difference is the magnitude of the subsidy. The difference reflects the social evaluation of 1's need for x. But this in turn means that the government must prohibit certain felicity-enhancing trades among the two persons.[23] This is the exchange restriction the government must impose. We conclude that the most desirable resource allocation is not felicity-, or Pareto-efficient. There is no paternalism here, merely an expression of the view that commodity needs are a moral category.

VI   Concluding remarks

If political philosophy is concerned with the kinds of arguments that ought to be involved in any social evaluation of resource allocations, welfare economic theory is much concerned with the design of social institutions which can implement allocations that are judged to be the best in the light of this social evaluation. In this essay I have discussed at some length the two fundamental theorems of welfare economics from this perspective. In sections II and III the social organizations envisaged by the two theorems were described and their achievements were assessed. It was argued in section II that the First Fundamental Theorem provides a highly restricted, but analytically precise, justification of the market mechanism. Of greater interest is the much deeper result, the Second Fundamental Theorem, which provides the framework of a decentralized social organization in a polity that, in its public evaluation, is much concerned with the distribution of individual felicities. It was argued that the theorem manages an interesting balance between the claims of negative freedom, in particular the freedom to make personal decisions, and the claims of distributive justice, when the notion of justice is restricted to allocations of felicities. In section IV the idea of positive freedom was linked with commodity needs. Commodities were seen as inputs in the production not only of felicity but simultaneously of activities and achievements. Both classical and modern concerns with such non-felicity information about social states were noted and an attempt was made to relate them to one another. In section V, the general aim was to study the way in which the Second Fundamental Theorem would be modified if such pluralist moral theories were to guide the polity. By way of analysis a simple example incorporating the idea of commodity need was presented. It was argued that there *is* a modification – specifically, a certain pattern of exchange restriction has to be imposed by the government. The resulting outcome is not Pareto-efficient. It was argued that this is precisely what one might expect. Efficiency depends upon the number of attributes of a state of affairs that enter in its social evaluation. Paretianism – and by this I mean the principle that the social evaluation function should subsume the Pareto partial ordering – is certainly defensible if individual felicities are all that count in arriving at public judgements. It is not an obvious moral imperative if other features of a social state call for attention. Pluralist moral theories, it can be argued, will require certain patterns of trade and exchange restrictions, even under the most favourable circumstances concerning the availability of information on the part of the government. This *is* a curtailment of a certain kind of freedom of control. But it is motivated by considerations of freedom of another kind: freedom to achieve things. Such restrictions would be prompted with a view to enhancing both power and control on the part of members of the polity to shape their lives in the light of their sense of the good.

Notes

For extensive discussions and advice on classical and medieval conceptions of the good polity, I am very much indebted to Dr George Garnett of Magdalene College, Cambridge. Over the years I have gained much from discussions with Kenneth Arrow, Peter Bauer, Jeremy Edwards, Frank

Hahn, Eric Maskin, James Meade, Ugo Pagano, Robert Rowthorn, Amartya Sen, Hugo Sonnenschein, Richard Tuck and John Vickers. This essay was written while I was Visiting Professor at the Woodrow Wilson School of Public and International Affairs, Princeton University.

1   One should distinguish those elements of classical and medieval conceptions which are culturally specific from those that characterize their central thrust. As an instance, one should note that the priestly, the warrior and the judicial are, in Marsilius's view, strictly parts of the state and are called the 'honourable' class (*honorabilitatem*). The remaining four are offices only in the 'broad sense of the term, because they are offices necessary to the state'. Persons belonging to these are referred to collectively as the common mass (*vulgaris*). (See Marsilius, tr. Gewirth, 1956, Discourse I, ch. 5, p. 15.) It may be noted that the honourable class are seen as providing what we should today recognize as *public* goods. The common mass are assumed to provide *private* goods. The former are commodities, such as religious truths, warfare and the law, which can in principle be consumed jointly by all; the latter are commodities, such as food, clothing and implements, which cannot be consumed jointly. I do not know if the higher status bestowed upon the providers of public goods is on *account* of their being in charge of the provision of public goods, or whether it is because such commodities as defence, religious truths and the law are regarded in some sense as higher-order goods.

2   For an economist's evaluation of Nozick's work, see Arrow (1978).

3   Mechanisms based explicitly on bargaining among groups, such as the game theoretic concept of the core are others. Nozick (1974) has an excellent discussion of the core as a resource-allocation mechanism. As it happens, there is an intimate connection between the core and the competitive price mechanism. Specifically, it can be shown that in a wide class of circumstances resource allocations that are in the core – i.e. those which result from the kind of bargaining underlying the core – coincide, roughly speaking, with competitive market equilibrium allocations (see Arrow and Hahn 1971). But this connection is of no great importance to the discussion in the text.

4   I have attempted to do this elsewhere. See Dasgupta (1980, 1982).

5   The treatise which demonstrates the logical independence of free markets and political democracy is Lindblom (1977).

6   The fact that the price mechanism is parsimonious as regards the amount of information individuals need to possess in order to bring about co-ordination in their activities has been much discussed in the economics literature. Sonnenschein (1974) addresses this issue in a precise manner. The role that prices play in aggregating dispersedly held information was the focus of attention in Hayek's classic article (1945). For an elaboration of Hayek's concern, see Grossman (1981).

7   The way the theorem has been stated above is the way it is stated in the economics literature. Below I present the statement which the theorem in fact asserts.

8   The expression was coined by Professor Terence Gorman. See Gorman (1968).

9   'Utility' and 'welfare' are used interchangeably in the literature. This is unfortunate, but it is too late to do anything about it. I follow this usage here.

10 Examples of the use of utilitarian reasoning for problems of intergenerational savings, redistributive taxation and future population size are, respectively, Ramsey (1928), Mirrlees (1971) and Dasgupta (1969).

11 See Sen (1970) for a classic exploration. Roberts (1980) and Blackorby, Donaldson and Weymark (1984) present wide-ranging discussions of this class of issues.

12 I should re-emphasize that this is a weakness of generalized utilitarianism, *not* of the Second Fundamental Theorem, for, as I have argued earlier, the theorem does not assume that people maximize their utilities. Evaluations which guide individual choice in the Second Fundamental Theorem can be much wider than mere utility considerations. What I have been referring to as felicity can be quite different from utility. It may coincide with the person's interests and advantage. In section V, I shall raise the question of how much the Second Fundamental Theorem needs to be modified if public judgements as embodied in the social evaluation function are based upon information greater than that summarized in personal felicities.

13 I am basing these remarks on my understanding of the society I myself have come from, namely India. There is also a large formal literature on these matters. See, for example, Miller (1981).

14 I am thinking here of inanimate commodities, of course. The valuation of commodities such as animal protein pose still deeper problems.

15 An excellent source of such information is the annual *World Development Report* of the World Bank in Washington, DC. The World Bank has been collecting and collating such information for over a decade now.

16 Each year the *World Development Report* of the World Bank ranks countries by their per-capita incomes. Indeed, this is the order in which the countries are listed. The *Report* then presents the levels of the social indicators reached in them in separate columns. Needless to say, rankings based on the various indicators do not coincide.

17 See Marx (1970 edn). Commodities that are required for satisfying basic needs are sometimes called 'natural-rights goods' (see Weitzman 1977) and on occasion 'merit goods' (see Musgrave 1958). I should reiterate that needs are not all or nothing. Nevertheless, it is useful to think of basic needs as a well-defined category. I should also add that commodity needs are person-specific. For example, nutrition requirements vary from person to person. People vary in relation to their phenotypes.

18 The clinical literature on the matter is gigantic. Nevertheless, there is much about the physiology of undernourishment which is ill understood. In collaboration with Debraj Ray, I have tried to evaluate the biological evidence pertaining to the phenomenon and the implication of the evidence on worldwide estimates (see Dasgupta and Ray 1987b). Even by the most conservative estimates, more than 500 million people in the world are judged to suffer from some degree of undernourishment, specifically calorie deficiency. The classic estimate, thought today to be on the high side, of over 800 million people, is in Reutlinger and Alderman (1980).

19 The market mechanism, in other words, is not 'horizontally equitable': similar people can be treated very dissimilarly by the market.

20 It should be noted, however, that there are some technical conditions which must be met for the theorem to be valid, such as that individual felicity functions satisfy some mathematical conditions. I am throughout assuming that they are met, since I want to concentrate solely on matters arising from non-felicity aspects of states of affairs.

21   Throughout this essay I have assumed away uncertainty, in particular incomplete knowledge on the part of the government about individual felicity functions. Incomplete information raises a new class of problems concerning the design of social organizations. I have gone into these issues in Dasgupta (1980, 1982, 1986).

22   Notice that in the example each party is self-regarding. The reason why we would wish to violate Paretianism here is not that there is an inbuilt 'externality' in the felicity functions, allied to an insistence on rights, as in Sen's example of the impossibility of a Paretian liberal (Sen 1970). The reason has to do with the manner in which needs have been built into the moral exercise. Nevertheless, there *is* common reason: if social evaluation is based on more information than mere felicities, why *should* we expect the moral theory guiding social evaluation to subscribe to *felicity* efficiency? There is no paradox here.

23   The reasoning is obvious here. If 1 pays \$1 per unit of x in the market and 2 pays \$1.50 (the subsidy to 1 being \$0.50 per unit of x), 1 and 2 would have an incentive to establish a black market, where 1 buys x from the market at \$1 per unit and sells it to 2 at any price between \$1 and \$1.50 per unit. The government needs to prevent the establishment of such black markets.

Bibliography

Ackerman, B. A. 1980: *Social Justice in the Liberal State*. New Haven, Conn., and London: Yale University Press.
—— 1984: The Storrs Lectures: Discovering the constitution. *Yale Law Journal*, 93: 1013–72.
—— 1986: Discovering the constitution. Unpublished manuscript.
Adelman, I. 1980: *Redistribution before Growth*. Leiden: University of Leiden.
Arblaster, A. 1984: *The Rise and Decline of Western Liberalism*. Oxford: Basil Blackwell.
Aristotle, tr. E. Barker 1946: *Politics*. Oxford: Clarendon Press.
—— tr. J. A. K. Thomson 1976: *The Nicomachean Ethics*. Harmondsworth Penguin.
Arrow, K. J. 1951: *Social Choice and Individual Values*. New York: Wiley.
—— 1967: Values and collective decision-making. In P. Laslett and W. G. Runciman (eds), *Philosophy, Politics and Society*, Oxford: Basil Blackwell, 215–32.
—— 1971: Political and economic estimation of social effects of externalities. In M. Intriligator (ed.), *Frontiers of Quantitative Economics*, Amsterdam: North Holland, vol. I.
—— 1978: Nozick's entitlement theory of justice. *Philosophia*, 7: 265–79.
Arrow, K. J. and Hahn, F. 1971: *General Competitive Analysis*. San Francisco: Holden Day.
Austin, J. L. 1956–7: A plea for excuses. *Proceedings of the Aristotelian Society*, 57: 1–30.
Ayer, A. J. 1946: *Language, Truth and Logic*. London: Gollancz.
Baldwin, T. 1984: MacCallum and the two concepts of freedom. *Ratio*, 26: 125–42.
Barry, B. M. 1965: *Political Argument*. London: Routledge and Kegan Paul.
—— 1970: *Sociologists, Economics and Democracy*. London: Collier-Macmillan.
—— 1973: *The Liberal Theory of Justice*. Oxford: Clarendon Press.
—— 1979: Is democracy special? In P. Laslett and J. Fishkin (eds), *Philosophy, Politics and Society*, 5th ser., New Haven, Conn: Yale University Press, 155–96.
—— forthcoming: *Treatise on Social Justice*, vol. I: *Theories of Justice*. Berkeley and Los Angeles: University of California Press.
Barry, N. 1979: *Hayek's Social and Economic Philosophy*. London: Macmillan.
Bauer, P. T. 1971: *Dissent on Development*. London: Weidenfeld and Nicholson.
—— 1984: *Reality and Rhetoric*. London: Weidenfeld and Nicholson.
Bealer, G. 1982: *Quality and Concept*. Oxford: Oxford University Press.
Benn, S. I. and Peters, R. S. 1959: *Social Principles and the Democratic State*. London: Allen and Unwin.
Bentham, J. 1843: Anarchical fallacies. In J. Bowring (ed.), *The Works of Jeremy Bentham*, Edinburgh, vol. II.

Bergson, A. 1938: A reformulation of certain aspects of welfare economics. *Quarterly Journal of Economics*, 52: 310–34.

Berlin, I. 1969: Two concepts of liberty. In *Four Essays on Liberty*, London: Oxford University Press, 118–72.

Bhagwati, J. 1988: *Protectionism*. Cambridge, Mass: MIT Press.

Blackorby, C., Donaldson, D. and Weymark, J. A. 1984: Social choice with interpersonal utility comparisons: a diagrammatic introduction. *International Economic Review*, 25: 327–56.

Boesche, R. 1987: *The Strange Liberalism of Alexis de Tocqueville*. Ithaca, NY: Cornell University Press.

Brennan, G. and Buchanan, J. M. 1984: Voter choice. *American Behavioral Scientist*, 28, 2: 185–201.

—— 1985: *The Reason of Rules*. Cambridge and New York: Cambridge University Press.

Brennan, G. and Lomasky, L. 1985: The impartial spectator goes to Washington. *Economics and Philosophy*, 1: 189–211.

Brennan, G. and Pincus, J. 1987: Rational actor theory in politics. *Economic Record*, 63, 80: 22–32.

Broome, J. 1986: Comments on 'Irreducibly social goods' by Charles Taylor. Paper presented to the International Seminar on Public Economics, Canberra (December).

Buchanan, J. M. 1975: *The Limits of Liberty*. Chicago: University of Chicago Press.

—— 1984: Politics without romance: a sketch of positive public choice theory and its normative implications. In J. M. Buchanan and R. Tollinson (eds), *The Theory of Public Choice II*, Ann Arbor: University of Michigan Press, 11–22.

—— 1986: *Liberty, Market and the State*. Brighton: Wheatsheaf.

Buchanan, J. M. and Tullock, G. 1965: *The Calculus of Consent*. Ann Arbor: University of Michigan Press.

Burnham, W. D. 1982: *The Current Crisis in American Politics*. Oxford: Oxford University Press.

Cameron, D. R. 1985: Public expenditure and economic performance in international perspective. In R. Klein and M. O'Higgins (eds), *The Future of Welfare*, Oxford: Basil Blackwell, 8–21.

Cohen, G. A. 1978: Robert Nozick and Wilt Chamberlain: how patterns preserve liberty. In J. Arthur and W. H. Shaw (eds), *Justice and Economic Distribution*, Englewood Cliffs, NJ: Prentice-Hall.

Cohen, J. 1986a: Autonomy and democracy: reflections on Rousseau. *Philosophy and Public Affairs*, 15: 275–97.

—— 1986b: An epistemic conception of democracy. *Ethics*, 97: 26–38.

—— 1988: The material basis of deliberative democracy. *Social Philosophy and Policy*.

Cohen, J. and Rogers, J. 1983: *On Democracy*. Harmondsworth: Penguin.

Coleman, J. 1980: Efficiency, utility and wealth maximization. *Hosfra Law Review*, 8: 509–51.

Coleman, J. and Ferejohn, J. 1986: Democracy and social choice. *Ethics*, 97 (October): 6–25.

Cranston, M. 1967: *Freedom: a new analysis*, 3rd edn, London: Longman.

Currie, G. 1984: Individualism and global supervenience. *British Journal for the Philosophy of Science*.

Dahl, R. A. 1956: *A Preface to Democratic Theory*. Chicago: University of Chicago Press.

—— 1970: *After the Revolution?* New Haven, Conn.: Yale University Press.

—— 1982: *Dilemmas of Pluralist Democracy.* New Haven, Conn.: Yale University Press.

Dahl, R. A. and Tufte, E. R. 1973: *Size and Democracy.* Stanford, Calif.: Stanford University Press.

Dasgupta, P. 1969: On the concept of optimum population. *Review of Economic Studies,* 36: 295–318.

—— 1980: Decentralization and rights, *Economica,* 47: 107–24.

—— 1982: Utilitarianism, information and rights. In A. Sen and B. Williams (eds), *Utilitarianism and Beyond,* Cambridge: Cambridge University Press, 199–218.

—— 1986: Positive freedom, markets and the welfare state. *Oxford Review of Economic Policy,* 2: 25–36.

Dasgupta, P. and Ray, D. 1986: Inequality as a determinant of malnutrition and unemployment: theory. *Economic Journal,* 96: 1011–34.

—— 1987a: Inequality as a determinant of malnutrition and unemployment: policy. *Economic Journal,* 97: 177–88.

—— 1987b: Adapting to undernourishment: the clinical evidence and its implications. WIDER working paper, Helsinki; forthcoming in J. Dreze and A. Sen (eds), *Poverty and Hunger: The Poorest Billion,* Oxford: Oxford University Press.

Dasgupta, P., Sen, A. K. and Starrett, J. 1973: Notes on the measurement of inequality. *Journal of Economic Theory,* 6: 180–7.

d'Aspremont, C. and Gevers, L. 1977: Equity and the informational basis of collective choice. *Review of Economic Studies,* 44: 199–209.

Datta-Chaudhury, M. 1979: Industrialization and foreign trade: an analysis based on the development experience of the Republic of Korea and the Philippines. ILO working paper, Asian Employment Programme, WP II-4, Bangkok: International Labour Organization.

Debreu, G. 1959: *Theory of Value.* New York: Wiley.

Downs, A. 1957: *An Economic Thoery of Democracy.* New York: Harper and Row.

Duffie, D. and Sonnenschein, H. 1988: Arrow and general equilibrium theory, *Journal of Economic Literature.*

Dunn, J. 1979: *Western Political Theory in Face of the Future.* Cambridge: Cambridge University Press.

Dworkin, R. 1978: *Taking Rights Seriously.* London: Duckworth.

—— 1981: What is equality? *Philosophy and Public Affairs,* 10: 185–246, 283–345.

—— 1985: *A Matter of Principle.* Cambridge, Mass.: Harvard University Press.

Elster, J. 1979: *Ulysses and the Sirens.* Cambridge: Cambridge University Press.

—— 1982: Sour grapes. In A. Sen and B. Williams (eds), *Utilitarianism and Beyond,* Cambridge: Cambridge University Press, 219–38.

—— 1983: *Sour Grapes.* Cambridge, UK: Cambridge University Press.

—— 1986a: The market and the forum: three varieties of political theory. In J. Elster and A. Hylland (eds), *The Foundations of Social Choice Theory.* Cambridge: Cambridge University Press, 103–32.

—— 1986b: Self-realisation in work and politics: the Marxist conception of the good life. *Social Philosophy and Policy,* 3: 97–126.

—— 1986c: *Rational Choice.* Oxford: Basil Blackwell.

Ely, J. H. 1980: *Democracy and Distrust: a theory of judicial review.* Cambridge, Mass.: Harvard University Press.

Federalist Papers 1961: ed. C. Rossiter. New York: New American Library.

Feinberg, J. 1972: *Social Philosophy.* Englewood Cliffs, NJ: Prentice-Hall.

Fink, Z. 1945: *The Classical Republicans*. Evanston, Ill.: Northwestern University Press.

Fishkin, J. S. 1979: *Tyranny and Legitimacy*. Baltimore: Johns Hopkins University Press.

—— 1982: *The Limits of Obligation*. New Haven, Conn.: Yale University Press.

French, P. A. 1979: The corporation as a moral person. *American Philosophical Quarterly*, 16: 207–15.

—— 1984: *Collective and Corporate Responsibility*. New York: Columbia University Press.

Frey, R. G. 1985: *Utility and Rights*. Oxford: Basil Blackwell.

Friedman, M. 1985: The methodology of positive economics. In *Essays in Positive Economics*, Chicago: University of Chicago Press.

—— 1962: *Capitalism and Freedom*. Chicago: University of Chicago Press.

Fuller, L. L. 1969: *The Morality of Law*. New Haven, Conn.: Yale University Press.

Gauthier, D. 1986: *Morals by Agreement*. Oxford: Oxford University Press.

Geach, P. T. 1972: *Logic Matters*. Berkeley and Los Angeles: University of California Press.

Goldsmith, M. M. 1987: Liberty, luxury and the pursuit of happiness. In A. Pagden (ed.), *The Languages of Political Theory in Early-Modern Europe*. Cambridge: Cambridge University Press, 225–51.

Goodin, R. E. 1976: *The Politics of Rational Man*. London: Wiley.

—— 1982: *Political Theory and Public Policy*. Chicago: University of Chicago Press.

—— 1985: *Protecting the Vulnerable*. Chicago: University of Chicago Press.

—— 1986: Laundering preferences. In J. Elster and A. Hylland (eds), *Foundations of Social Choice Theory*, Cambridge: Cambridge University Press.

—— 1988: What is so special about our fellow countrymen? *Ethics*, 98.

Goodin, R. and Roberts, K. 1975: The ethical voter. *American Political Science Review*, 69: 926–8.

Gorman, W. 1968: The structure of utility functions. *Review of Economic Studies*, 35: 367–90.

Gray, J. 1986a: *Liberalism*. Milton Keynes: Open University Press.

—— 1986b: *Hayek on Liberty*, 2nd edn. Oxford: Basil Blackwell.

Green, T. H. 1889: On the different senses of 'freedom' as applied to will and to the moral progress of man. In R. L. Nettleship (ed.), *Works of T. H. Green*, London: Longman's, Green, vol. II.

Griffin, J. P. 1986: *Well-Being*. Oxford: Clarendon Press.

Grossman, S. 1981: An introduction to the theory of rational expectations under asymmetric information. *Review of Economic Studies*, 48: 541–59.

Habermas, J. 1975: *The Legitimation Crisis of Late Capitalism*, tr. T. McCarthy. Boston, Mass.: Beacon Press; London: Heinemann.

—— 1979: *Communication and the Evolution of Society*, tr. T. McCarthy. Boston, Mass.: Beacon Press.

—— 1984: *The Theory of Communicative Action*, vol. I, tr. T. McCarthy. Boston, Mass.: Beacon Press.

Hamlin, A. P. 1984: Public choice, markets and utilitarianism. In D. Whynes (ed.), *What is Political Economy?*, Oxford: Basil Blackwell.

—— 1986a: *Ethics, Economics and the State*. Brighton: Wheatsheaf; New York: St Martin's Press.

—— 1986b: The normative status of consumer sovereignty. Paper presented to the International Seminar on Public Economics, Canberra (December).

—— forthcoming: Rights, indirect utilitarianism and contractarianism.

Hardin, G. 1968: The tragedy of the commons. *Science*, 162: 1243–8.

Hardin, R. 1982: Exchange theory on strategic bases. *Social Science Information*, 21: 251–72.

—— 1985: Sanction and obligation. *Monist*, 68: 403–18.

—— 1988: *Morality within the Limits of Reason*. Chicago: University of Chicago Press.

Hare, R. 1981: *Moral Thinking: its levels, method and point*. Oxford: Clarendon Press.

Harsanyi, J. C. 1955: Cardinal welfare, individualistic ethics and interpersonal comparisons of utility. *Journal of Political Economy*, 63: 309–21.

—— 1975: Nonlinear social welfare functions. *Theory and Decisions*, 6: 311–23.

—— 1976: *Essays in Ethics, Social Behaviour and Scientific Explanation*. Dordrecht: Reidel.

—— 1987: Review of *Morals by Agreement* by D. Gauthier. *Economics and Philosophy*, 3: 339–51.

Hart, H. L. A. 1955: Are there any natural rights? *Philosophical Review*, 64: 175–91.

—— 1961: *The Concept of Law*. London: Oxford University Press.

Hayek, F. A. von 1937: Economics and knowledge. *Economica*, 4: 33–54.

—— 1945: The use of knowledge in society. *American Economic Review*, 35: 519–30.

—— 1960: *The Constitution of Liberty*. London: Routledge and Kegan Paul.

Held, V. 1970: Can random collections of individuals be morally responsible? *Journal of Philosophy*, 67: 471–81.

—— 1972: Moral responsibility and collective action. In P. A. French (ed.), *Individual and Collective Responsibility*, Cambridge, Mass.: Schenkman, 101–18.

Hirschman, A. 1982: *Shifting Involvements*. Princeton, NJ: Princeton University Press.

Hobbes, T. 1651: *Leviathan*. Ed. M. Oakeshott, London: Macmillan, 1962.

Hohfeld, W. 1923: *Fundamental Legal Conceptions*. New Haven, Conn.: Yale University Press.

Horwich, P. 1982: *Probability and Evidence*. Cambridge: Cambridge University Press.

Hume, D. 1739–40: *A Treatise of Human Nature*. Ed. L. A. Selby-Bigge and P. H. Nidditch, 2nd edn, Oxford: Clarendon Press, 1978.

—— 1748: Of the original contract. In *Essays Moral, Political and Literary*, ed. E. F. Miller, Indianapolis: Liberty Press, 1985.

Ignatieff, M. 1984: *The Needs of Strangers*. Harmondsworth: Penguin.

Jackson, F. 1986: Irreducibly social goods: comments. Paper presented to the International Seminar on Public Economics, Canberra (December).

—— 1988: Group morality. In P. Pettit, R. Sylvan and J. Norman (eds), *Metaphysics and Morality*, Oxford: Basil Blackwell.

James, S. 1984: *The Content of Social Explanation*. Cambridge: Cambridge University Press.

Kant, I., tr. T. Humphrey 1983: To perpetual peace: a philosophical sketch. In *Perpetual Peace and other Essays*, Indianapolis: Hackett.

Kleinig, J. 1976: Good Samaritanism, *Philosophy and Public Affairs*, 5: 382–407.

Klosko, G. 1987a: The principle of fairness and political obligation. *Ethics*, 97: 353–62.

—— 1987b: Presumptive benefit, fairness and political obligation, *Philosophy and Public Affairs*, 16: 241–59.

Koopmans, T. C. 1957: *Three Essays on the State of Economic Science*. New York: McGraw-Hill.

Kraus, J. and Coleman, J. 1987: Morality and the theory of rational choice. *Ethics*, 97: 715–49.

Leibenstein, H. 1976: *Beyond Economic Man*. Cambridge, Mass.: Harvard University Press.

Lewis, C. S. 1967: *Studies in Words*. Cambridge: Cambridge University Press.

Lewis, D. 1969: *Convention*. Oxford: Basil Blackwell; Cambridge, Mass.: Harvard University Press.

Lindblom, C. 1977: *Politics and Markets*. New York: Basic Books.

Lindley, R. 1986: *Autonomy*. London: Macmillan.

Locke, J. 1689: *Letter Concerning Toleration*. Modern edn, Indianapolis: Bobbs-Merrill, 1955.

—— 1690: *Two Treatises of Government*. Ed. P. Laslett, Cambridge: Cambridge University Press, 1960.

Lukes, S. 1973: *Individualism*. London: Oxford University Press.

—— 1982: Of gods and demons: Habermas and practical reason. In J. B. Thompson and D. Held (eds), *Habermas: Critical Debates*, London: Macmillan.

—— (ed.) 1986: *Power*. Oxford: Basil Blackwell.

Lyons, D. 1984: Utility and rights. In J. Waldron (ed.), *Theories of Rights*, Oxford: Oxford University Press, 110–36.

MacCallum, G. 1972: Negative and positive freedom. In P. Laslett, W. G. Runciman and Q. Skinner (eds), *Philosophy, Politics and Society*, 4th ser., Oxford: Basil Blackwell.

Macdonald, G. and Pettit, P. 1981: *Semantics and Social Science*. London: Routledge and Kegan Paul.

MacIntyre, A. 1981: *After Virtue*. Notre Dame, Ind.: University of Notre Dame Press.

McCarthy, T. 1978: *The Critical Theory of Jürgen Habermas*. London: Hutchinson.

McKinsey, M. 1981: Obligations to the starving. *Noûs*, 15: 309–23.

Manin, B. 1987: On legitimacy and political deliberation. *Political Theory*, 15: 338–68.

Marshall, T. H. 1965: *Class, Citizenship and Social Development*. Garden City, NY: Anchor.

Marsilius of Padua, tr. A. Gewirth 1956: *The Defender of Peace*. New York: Harper and Row.

Marx, K., tr. 1970: *Capital*. London: Lawrence and Wishart.

Maskin, E. 1978: A theorem on utilitarianism. *Review of Economic Studies*, 45: 93–6.

Meade, J. E. 1976: *The Just Economy*. London: Allen and Unwin.

Meehl, P. 1977: The selfish voter paradox and the thrown-away vote argument. *American Political Science Review*, 71, 1: 11–30.

Meiklejohn, A. 1948: *Free Speech and its Relation of Self-Government*. New York: Harper and Row.

Michelman, F. I. 1986: The Supreme Court, 1985 Term – Foreword: Traces of Self-Government. *Harvard Law Review*, 100: 4–77.

Mill, J. 1820: *Essay on Government*. Modern edn, Indianapolis: Bobbs-Merrill, 1965.

Mill, J. S. 1859: *On Liberty*. Ed. H. B. Acton, London: Dent, 1972.

—— 1861: *On Representative Government.* Ed. H. B. Acton, London: Dent, 1972.

Miller, B. 1981: *The Endangered Sex: neglect of female children in rural north India.* Ithaca, NY: Cornell University Press.

Mirrlees, J. A. 1971: An exploration in the theory of optimal income taxation. *Review of Economic Studies,* 38: 175–208.

Musgrave, R. 1958: *Theory of Public Finance.* New York: McGraw-Hill.

Myrdal, G. 1960: *Beyond the Welfare State.* London: Duckworth.

Nagel, T. 1986: *A View from Nowhere.* Oxford: Oxford University Press.

—— 1987: Moral conflict and political legitimacy, *Philosophy and Public Affairs,* 16: 215–40.

Nozick, R. 1973: Distributive justice. *Philosophy and Public Affairs,* 3: 45–126.

—— 1974: *Anarchy, State and Utopia.* New York: Basic Books; Oxford: Basil Blackwell.

—— 1981: *Philosophical Explanations.* Cambridge, Mass.: Harvard University Press.

Parfit, D. 1984: *Reasons and Persons.* Oxford: Clarendon Press.

Paul, E. F., Miller, F. D. and Paul, J. (eds) 1984: *Human Rights.* Oxford: Basil Blackwell.

Perlman, L. 1987: Parties, democracy and consent. Unpublished.

Pettit, P. 1980: *Judging Justice.* London: Routledge and Kegan Paul.

—— 1982: Habermas on truth and justice. In G. H. R. Parkinson (ed.), Marx and *Marxisms,* Cambridge: Cambridge University Press, 207–28.

—— 1984: Satisficing consequentialism, *Proceedings of the Aristotelian Society,* supp. 58: 165–76.

—— 1986a: Free riding and foul dealing. *Journal of Philosophy,* 83: 361–79; repr. in *The Philosopher's Annual,* 9 (1987).

—— 1986b: Slote on consequentialism. *Philosophical Quarterly,* 36: 399–412.

—— 1987a: Rights, constraints and trumps. *Analysis,* 46: 8–14.

—— 1987b: Towards a social democratic theory of the state. *Political Studies,* 35: 537–51.

—— 1987c: Liberalism and republicanism. *Bulletin of the Australian Society of Legal Philosophy,* 11.

—— 1988: The consequentialist can recognise rights. *Philosophical Quarterly,* 38.

—— forthcoming a: Social holism without collectivism. In E. Ullmann-Margalit (ed.), *The Israel Colloquium in the History, Philosophy and Sociology of Science,* Dordrecht: Reidel, vol. V.

—— forthcoming b: A definition of negative liberty.

Pettit, P. and Brennan, G. 1986: Restrictive consequentialism. *Australasian Journal of Philosophy,* 64: 438–55.

Pettit, P. and Goodin, R. E. 1986: The possibility of special duties. *Canadian Journal of Philosophy,* 16: 651–76.

Pettit, P. and McDowell, J. (eds) 1986: *Subject, Thought and Context.* Oxford: Oxford University Press.

Pocock, J. G. A. 1975: *The Machiavellian Moment: Florentine political thought and the Atlantic republican tradition.* Princeton, NJ: Princeton University Press.

Quiggin, J. 1987: Egoistic rationality and public choice: a critical review of theory and evidence. *Economic Record,* 63, 180: 10–21.

Raab, F. 1964: *The English Face of Machiavelli.* London: Routledge and Kegan Paul.

Ramsey, F. 1928: A mathematical theory of savings. *Economic Journal*, 38: 543–59.

Rawls, J. 1955: Two concepts of rules, *Philosophical Review*, 64: 3–32.

—— 1971: *A Theory of Justice*. Cambridge, Mass.: Harvard University Press; also Oxford: Clarendon Press (1972).

—— 1982: The basic liberties and their priority. *Tanner Lectures on Human Values*, Salt Lake City: University of Utah Press, vol. III.

—— 1985: Justice as fairness: political not metaphysical. *Philosophy and Public Affairs*, 14: 223–51.

—— 1987: The idea of an overlapping consensus. *Oxford Journal of Legal Studies*, 7: 1–25.

Raz, J. 1986: *The Morality of Freedom*. Oxford: Oxford University Press.

Reiman, J. H. 1981: The fallacy of libertarian capitalism. *Ethics*, 92: 85–95.

Reutlinger, S. and Alderman, H. 1980: The prevalence of calorie deficient diets in developing countries. *World Development*, 8.

Riker, W. 1982: *Liberalism against Populism: a confrontation between the theory of democracy and the theory of social choice*. San Francisco: W. H. Freeman.

Rimlinger, G. V. 1983: Capitalism and human rights. *Daedalus*, 112: 51–79.

Roberts, K. 1980: Interpersonal comparability and social choice theory. *Review of Economic Studies*, 47: 421–39.

Rousseau, J. J., tr. J. R. Masters 1978: *On the Social Contract*. New York: St Martin's Press.

Ryan, A. 1983: Property, liberty and *On Liberty*. In A. Phillips Griffiths (ed.), *Of Liberty*, Cambridge: Cambridge University Press, 217–31.

Samuelson, P. A. 1947: *Foundations of Economic Analysis*. Cambridge, Mass.: Harvard University Press.

Sandel, M. 1982: *Liberalism and the Limits of Justice*. Cambridge: Cambridge University Press.

—— (ed.) 1984: *Liberalism and its Critics*. Oxford: Basil Blackwell.

Scanlon, T. M. 1977: Liberty, contract and contribution. In G. Dworkin, G. Bermont and P. Brown (eds), *Markets and Morals*. Washington, DC: Hemisphere, 43–67.

—— 1982: Contractualism and utilitarianism. In A. K. Sen and B. Williams (eds), *Utilitarianism and Beyond*, Cambridge: Cambridge University Press, 103–28.

Schelling, T. C. 1960: *The Strategy of Conflict*. Cambridge, Mass.: Harvard University Press.

Schmitt, C. 1985: *The Crisis of Parliamentary Democracy*, tr. E. Kennedy. Cambridge, Mass.: MIT Press.

Schumpeter, J. A. 1954: *Capitalism, Socialism and Democracy*, London: Unwin.

Scitovsky, T. 1976: *The Joyless Economy*. Oxford: Oxford University Press.

Sen, A. K. 1969: Quasi-transitivity, rational choice and collective decisions. *Review of Economic Studies*, 36: 381–93.

—— 1970: *Collective Choice and Social Welfare*. San Francisco: Holden Day.

—— 1976: Liberty, unanimity and rights. *Economica*, 43: 217–45.

—— 1977: Social choice theory: a re-examination, *Econometrica* 45: 53–89.

—— 1979a: Personal utilities and public judgements: or what's wrong with welfare economics? *Economic Journal*, 89: 537–58.

—— 1979b: Utilitarianism and welfarism, *Journal of Philosophy*, 76: 463–89.

—— 1981: Rights and agency. *Philosophy and Public Affairs*, 11: 3–39.

—— 1983: Poor, relatively speaking. *Oxford Economic Papers*, 35: 153–69.

—— 1985a: *Commodities and Capabilities*. Amsterdam: North Holland.

—— 1985b: Well-being, agency and freedom. *Journal of Philosophy*, 82: 169–221.

—— 1987: *On Ethics and Economics*. Oxford: Basil Blackwell.

Sharpe, L. J. 1973: American democracy reconsidered. Part II. *British Journal of Political Science*, 3, 2: 129–68.

Shue, H. 1980: *Basic Rights*. Princeton, NJ: Princeton University Press.

Simmons, A. J. 1979: *Moral Principles and Political Obligations*. Princeton, NJ: Princeton University Press.

—— 1987: The anarchist position: a reply to Klosko and Senor. *Philosophy and Public Affairs*, 16: 269–79.

Skinner, Q. 1978: *The Foundation of Modern Political Theory*, vol. I. Cambridge: Cambridge University Press.

—— 1983: Machiavelli on the maintenance of liberty. *Politics*, 18: 3–15.

—— 1984: The idea of negative liberty: philosophical and historical perspectives. In R. Rorty, J. B. Schneewind and Q. Skinner (eds), *Philosophy in History*, Cambridge: Cambridge University Press.

Sonnenschein, H. 1974: An axiomatic characterization of the price mechanism, *Econometrica*, 42: 425–33.

Stone, G. 1987: Content-neutral restrictions. *University of Chicago Law Review*, 54: 46–118.

Streeten, P., with Burki, S., ul Haq, M., Hicks, N. and Stewart, F. 1981: *First Things First: meeting basic needs in developing countries*. Oxford: Oxford University Press.

Sugden, R. 1981: *The Political Economy of Public Choice*. Oxford: Martin Robertson.

—— 1985: Why be consistent? A critical analysis of consistency requirements in choice theory. *Economica*, 52: 167–83.

—— 1986: *The Economics of Rights, Co-operation and Welfare*. Oxford: Basil Blackwell.

Sunstein, C. 1984: Naked preferences and the constitution. *Columbia Law Review*, 84: 1689–1732.

—— 1985: Interest groups in American public law. *Stanford Law Review*, 38: 29–87.

—— 1986: Legal interference with private preferences. *University of Chicago Law Review*, 53: 1129–84.

Taylor, C. 1984: Kant's theory of freedom. In Z. Pelczynski and J. Gray (eds), *Conceptions of Liberty in Political Philosophy*, London: Athlone Press, 100–22.

Taylor, M. and Ward, H. 1982: Whales, chickens and collective action. *Political Studies*, 30: 350–70.

Tobin, J. 1972: On limiting the domains of inequality. In J. S. Phelps (ed.), *Economic Justice*, Harmondsworth: Penguin.

Tribe, L. 1978: *American Constitutional Law*. Mineola NY: Foundation Press.

—— 1985: *Constitutional Choices*. Cambridge, Mass.: Harvard University Press.

Tuck, R. 1979: *Natural Rights Theories*. Cambridge: Cambridge University Press.

Tullock, G. 1971: Charity of the uncharitable. *Western Economic Journal*, 9: 379–92.

Tully, J. 1984: Locke on liberty. In Z. Pelczynski and J. Gray (eds), *Conceptions of Liberty in Political Philosophy*, London: Athlone Press, 57–82.

Unger, R. 1987: *False Necessity*. Cambridge: Cambridge University Press.

Urmson, J. O. 1958: Saints and heroes. In A. I. Melden (ed.), *Essays in Moral Philosophy*, Seattle: University of Washington Press, 198–216.

Waldron, J. 1986: Welfare and the images of charity. *Philosophical Quarterly*, 36:463–82.

Walzer, M. 1970: *Obligations: essays on disobedience, war and citizenship*. Cambridge, Mass.: Harvard University Press.

Wasserstrom, R. 1975: Lawyers as professionals: some moral issues. *Human Rights*, 5: 1–24.

—— 1981: Roles and morality. In D. Luban (ed.), *The Good Lawyer*, Totowa, NJ: Rowman and Allanheld, 25–37.

Weale, A. 1983: *Political Theory and Public Policy*. London: Macmillan.

Weinrib, E. J. 1980: The case for a duty to rescue. *Yale Law Journal*, 90: 247–93.

Weinstein, W. L. 1965: The concept of liberty in nineteenth century English political thought. *Political Studies*, 13: 145–62.

Weitzman, M. L. 1977: Is the price system or rationing more effective in getting a commodity to those who need it most? *Bell Journal of Economics*, 8: 517–24.

Wiggins, D. 1987: Claims of needs. In *Needs, Values, Truth*, Oxford: Basil Blackwell.

Williams, B. 1973: A critique of utilitarianism. In J. Smart and B. Williams, *Utilitarianism: For and Against*. Cambridge: Cambridge University Press.

—— 1985: *Ethics and the Limits of Philosophy*. London: Fontana, Collins; Cambridge, Mass.: Harvard University Press.

Zimmerman, M. J. 1987: Remote obligations. *American Philosophical Quarterly*, 24: 199–206.

Contributors

Geoffrey Brennan is Professor of Economics in the Research School of Social Sciences, Australian National University. He is the author, with Nobel Laureate James Buchanan, of *The Power to Tax* (Cambridge University Press, 1980) and *The Reason of Rules* (Cambridge University Press, 1985), and is currently engaged on a book on electoral preferences with philosopher Loren Lomasky.

Joshua Cohen is Associate Professor of Philosophy and Political Science at the Massachusetts Institute of Technology. He works on democratic theory and on issues at the intersection between ethics and historical sociology. He is the co-author (with Joel Rogers) of *On Democracy* and the author of 'The Economic Basis of Deliberative Democracy' (*Social Philosophy and Policy*, forthcoming), a companion piece to the essay published in this collection.

Partha Dasgupta is Professor of Economics at the University of Cambridge. His research interests include game theory, the economics of technical change, and development economics, as well as issues in political economy. He is the co-author (with Ken Binmore) of *Economics of Bargaining* (Basil Blackwell, 1987), and author of 'Utilitarianism, Information and Rights' (in *Utilitarianism and Beyond*, ed. Amartya Sen and Bernard Williams, Cambridge University Press, 1982).

Robert E. Goodin is a Reader in Government at the University of Essex. His principal research interests are in the intersection of political theory and public policy. He is an associate editor of *Ethics* and the *British Journal of Political Science* and author, most recently, of *Reasons for Welfare* (Princeton University Press, 1988). He is soon to take up an appointment at the Australian National University.

Alan Hamlin is an Economist at the University of Southampton. His research interests include the political economy of social institutions, public choice and the ethical basis of welfare economics. He is the author of *Ethics, Economics and the State* (Wheatsheaf Books and St Martin's Press, 1986) and *Public Choice and Economics: subdiscipline or critique?* (Basil Blackwell, forthcoming).

Russell Hardin is the Mellon Foundation Professor of Political Science, Philosophy and Public Policy Studies at the University of Chicago. He is the editor of *Ethics* and the author of *Collective Action* (Johns Hopkins University Press, 1982) and *Morality within the Limits of Reason* (University of Chicago Press, 1988).

Philip Pettit is Professional Fellow in Social and Political Theory in the Research School of Social Sciences, Australian National University. He works on foundational issues in social and political theory, as well as some more specific questions in the theory of rational choice and collective action. He is the author of *Judging Justice* (Routledge and Kegan Paul, 1980) and, in collaboration with Graham Macdonald, *Semantics and Social Science* (Routledge and Kegan Paul, 1981).

Robert Sugden is Professor of Economics at the University of East Anglia. He works on the analysis of choice under uncertainty and on contractarian approaches to welfare economics. He is the author of *The Political Economy of Public Choice* (Martin Robertson, 1981) and *The Economics of Rights, Co-operation and Welfare* (Basil Blackwell, 1986).

Albert Weale is Professor of Politics at the University of East Anglia. His principal research interests are in the theory of public choice, political theory and social policy, and the politics of environmental concern. He is the author of *Political Theory and Public Policy* (Macmillan, 1983).

Index